Building an Application Development Framework

Empower your engineering teams with custom frameworks

Ivan Padabed

Roman Voronin

‹packt›

Building an Application Development Framework

Copyright © 2025 Packt Publishing

Portfolio Director: Kunal Chaudhari
Relationship Lead: Samriddhi Murarka
Project Manager: Ashwin Dinesh Kharwa
Content Engineer: Deepayan Bhattacharjee
Technical Editor: Irfa Ansari
Copy Editor: Safis Editing
Indexer: Tejal Soni
Proofreader: Deepayan Bhattacharjee
Production Designer: Jyoti Kadam, Nilesh Mohite
Growth Lead: Mansi Shah

First published: September 2025

Production reference: 1240925

Published by Packt Publishing Ltd.
Grosvenor House
11 St Paul's Square
Birmingham
B3 1RB, UK.

ISBN 978-1-83620-857-0
www.packtpub.com

I want to express my gratitude to the welcoming country of Portugal – its people, land, ocean, and sun – which gave me and my family new hope and a new home in a time of uncertainty and despair.

– Ivan Padabed

Contributors

About the authors

Ivan Padabed is a co-founder and CEO at System5Dev, a start-up focused on applying AI to systems architecture; a cloud platform architect at Intapp (a B2B SaaS platform); and an expert at Primary Venture Mastermind Network.

He is an experienced IT professional with over 25 years of experience in the industry, having fostered great teams and built high-end products as a systems architect. He is a community leader, conference speaker, writer, systems engineering discipline evangelist, author, and instructor of multiple engineering courses. He's also an active researcher in systems architecture and AI.

Outside of work, Ivan is a happy father of four, a husband, and the proud owner of a black cat. He loves gym workouts, soccer games, exploring mountains and nature trails, and relaxing with Terry Pratchett and Warhammer 40k novels.

I would like to thank my coworkers who were not afraid to take on my crazy ideas and make them work—you know who you are.

Roman Voronin is the co-founder and CTO of System5Dev, where he shapes AI-ready system designs, and a senior MLOps engineer at Intapp. With more than 20 years of experience in technology, he champions AWS-driven DevOps, shares insights as a long-standing AWS Community Builder, and authors practical articles on cloud architecture. Away from keyboards, Roman unwinds by playing guitar and exploring medieval-style fantasy worlds.

For Maria, Katya, Alexa, and Vitaliy. All of them.

About the reviewer

Sergej Tretjakov is a staff software engineer at PandaDoc with 15+ years of experience in backend development, architecture, and technical leadership. He currently leads the document domain and was previously responsible for the ML subdomain, focusing on MLOps and model integration. At WorkFusion, he developed the core product and led engineering teams. Later, in the delivery engineering department, he worked directly with customers to align product capabilities with business needs—driving enhancements to the internal automation framework, prototyping architectural improvements, and building reusable libraries to extend its functionality and accelerate development.

Table of Contents

Part 2: Building a Framework   85

Chapter 4: Defining Your Tech Stack   87

Exploring languages and libraries 92

  Programming languages • 93

    Core programming languages • 93

    Interface programming languages • 94

    Configuration and management languages • 94

  Storage, transport, and calculations • 95

    Typical storage requirements • 95

    Relational databases • 97

    NoSQL databases • 99

    Columnar databases • 104

    Graph databases • 106

    Storage • 108

    File storage • 108

    Block storage • 108

    Object storage • 109

    Distributed log storage • 109

    Vector databases • 112

    RAG storage engine selection • 114

    Transport and contract definition • 115

    Shared memory • 117

    Networking in distributed systems • 118

    Message brokers • 119

    Pub/sub systems • 120

    GraphQL • 126

    gRPC • 128

Part 3: Evolving a Framework 221

Chapter 8: Evolving a Framework 223

Chapter 9: Unlock Your Book's Exclusive Benefits   **257**

Index   **261**

Other Books You May Enjoy   **275**

Preface

Building an Application Development Framework is a hands-on guide for engineers, architects, and technical leads who are ready to go beyond using frameworks and start creating their own. In today's world of rapidly evolving software architectures, reusable abstractions are more valuable than ever – not just as productivity tools, but as strategic assets that encode architecture, reduce cognitive load, and scale engineering culture. This book introduces a structured and pragmatic approach to building your own ADF, grounded in real-world case studies and seasoned with lessons from open source ecosystems and enterprise platforms alike.

Whether you're developing a framework for internal use, open source contribution, or as a core product strategy, this book gives you the tools to make it modular, evolvable, and developer-friendly from day one.

Who this book is for

This book is written for experienced software engineers, architects, platform engineers, and technical product owners. You should be familiar with core software design principles, modern development practices (such as CI/CD), and one or more programming ecosystems (e.g., Python, JavaScript, or Java). No prior experience in framework development is required—just a desire to make something reusable, powerful, and thoughtfully designed.

What this book covers

Chapter 1, Introduction to Application Development Frameworks, provides a clear definition of what a framework is, how it differs from libraries, SDKs, and platforms, and why building your own framework is both powerful and risky.

Chapter 2, Strategizing ADF for Success, covers the business and organizational rationale for building a framework. It introduces the systems engineering perspective and a framework ROI model.

Chapter 3, Application Development Framework Blueprint, introduces the ADF Canvas and internal structural patterns that help you design your framework with clarity, modularity, and long-term vision.

Chapter 4, Defining Your Tech Stack, helps you choose the right programming languages, data storage, communication patterns, and runtime environment for your framework's context.

Chapter 5, Architecture Design, explains how to architect a framework for extensibility, performance, and composability, with design patterns and trade-offs relevant to modern software systems.

Chapter 6, ADF Development Fundamentals, focuses on the runtime behavior of your ADF, including plugin models, processing pipelines, and interaction patterns between framework components.

Chapter 7, Documenting and Releasing a Framework, covers the often-overlooked side of framework development: documentation, release strategy, API publishing, and collaborative issue tracking.

Chapter 8, Evolving a Framework, explores long-term maintainability, maturity modeling, continuous integration of improvements, and how to structure your framework for evolution. As a bonus, this chapter includes a brief outline of AI-native approaches to developing ADF.

To get the most out of this book

You should be comfortable reading and writing code in at least one general-purpose programming language, and familiar with how software projects are structured. Prior knowledge of frameworks such as Django, React, Spring, or LangChain will help you relate to the examples, but is not required. The book is designed to be technology-agnostic while providing real-world code references throughout. You will need the following:

- **Operating system requirements**: Windows, macOS, or Linux
- **Sample stack usage in examples**:

    - Python 3.10+
    - Docker 24+
    - OpenSearch as a vector database
    - GitHub Pages for documentation hosting

You may use your preferred local IDE or cloud-based development environment. Code samples are designed to run in containerized environments with minimal setup. Instructions are provided throughout relevant chapters.

If you are using the digital version of this book, we advise you to type the code yourself or access the code from the book's GitHub repository (a link is available in the next section). Doing so will help you avoid any potential errors related to the copying and pasting of code.

Download the example code files

You can download the example code files for this book from GitHub at `https://github.com/PacktPublishing/Building-an-Application-Development-Framework`.

If there's an update to the code, it will be updated in the GitHub repository.

We also have other code bundles from our rich catalog of books and videos available at `https://github.com/PacktPublishing/`.

Check them out!

Download the color images

We also provide a PDF file that has color images of the screenshots/diagrams used in this book. You can download it here: `https://packt.link/gbp/9781836208570`

Conventions used

There are a number of text conventions used throughout this book.

`Code in text`: Indicates code words in text, database table names, folder names, filenames, file extensions, pathnames, dummy URLs, user input, and X/Twitter handles. Here is an example: "Mount the downloaded `WebStorm-10*.dmg` disk image file as another disk in your system."

A block of code is set as follows:

```
{
    "name": "John Doe",
    "age": 30,
    "isAdmin": false
}
```

Any command-line input or output is written as follows:

```
uv init --lib
```

Bold: Indicates a new term, an important word, or words that you see onscreen. For instance, words in menus or dialog boxes appear in **bold**. Here is an example: "Select **System info** from the **Administration** panel."

> Warnings or important notes appear like this.

> Tips and tricks appear like this.

Get in touch

Feedback from our readers is always welcome.

General feedback: If you have questions about any aspect of this book or have any general feedback, please email us at customercare@packt.com and mention the book's title in the subject of your message.

Errata: Although we have taken every care to ensure the accuracy of our content, mistakes do happen. If you have found a mistake in this book, we would be grateful if you reported this to us. Please visit http://www.packt.com/submit-errata, click **Submit Errata**, and fill in the form.

Piracy: If you come across any illegal copies of our works in any form on the internet, we would be grateful if you would provide us with the location address or website name. Please contact us at copyright@packt.com with a link to the material.

If you are interested in becoming an author: If there is a topic that you have expertise in and you are interested in either writing or contributing to a book, please visit http://authors.packt.com/.

Share your thoughts

Once you've read *Building an Application Development Framework*, we'd love to hear your thoughts! Scan the QR code below to go straight to the Amazon review page for this book and share your feedback.

https://packt.link/r/183620857X

Your review is important to us and the tech community and will help us make sure we're delivering excellent quality content.

Part 1

Foundations of Application Development Frameworks

Understanding the landscape and building a common language.

This part lays the conceptual foundation necessary to build, adopt, or evolve an **Application Development Framework (ADF)**. Whether you're an individual engineer or a technical leader, these chapters will help you define what an ADF is, distinguish it from other engineering tools such as platforms and SDKs, and grasp the core success factors. By the end of this part, you'll be ready to critically evaluate or initiate ADF-related initiatives with clarity and confidence.

This part has the following chapters:

- *Chapter 1, Introduction to Application Development Frameworks*
- *Chapter 2, Strategizing ADF for Success*
- *Chapter 3, Application Development Framework Blueprint*

1

Introduction to Application Development Frameworks

In this book we will be delving into the different aspects of an **Application Development Framework (ADF)** lifecycle, allowing individual software engineers, development teams, and engineering organizations to benefit from ADF's great potential. The initial chapter of the book is focused on providing a wide context for future chapters, setting a common ground for all ADF stakeholders, and introducing basic classifications and definitions for future use.

The concept of Application Development Framework (ADF) has been well-known for a long time, but we need to set up a crystal-clear context for further reading. This is important because it helps us deal with this complex topic by setting common ground for definitions and classifications that will be used throughout the book. First, we explore the evolution of the idea of ADF. After that, we discover the differences and connections between other SDLC-focused technologies, such as Platforms, Libraries, SDKs, and APIs, to craft a brief but concise definition that helps us keep a big picture while diving deep into implementation topics. Then, we review the place of ADF in the Software Development Lifecycle to identify and prove the advantages of adopting an ADF.

In this chapter we're going to cover the following main topics:

- Introduction and historical references
- Breaking down Application Development Framework
- Exploring ADF and Platforms, Libraries, SDKs, APIs
- Integrating into Software Development Lifecycle (SDLC) and Flow
- Differentiating ADF and other types of Frameworks

Getting the most out of this book — get to know your free benefits

Unlock exclusive free benefits that come with your purchase, thoughtfully crafted to supercharge your learning journey and help you learn without limits.

Here's a quick overview of what you get with this book:

Next-gen reader

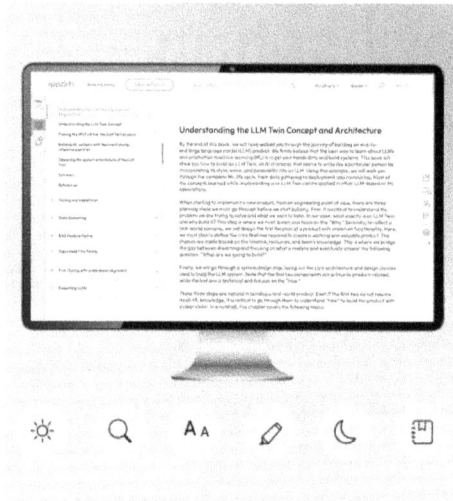

Figure 1.1: Illustration of the next-gen Packt Reader's features

Our web-based reader, designed to help you learn effectively, comes with the following features:

⟲ Multi-device progress sync: Learn from any device with seamless progress sync.

📖 Highlighting and notetaking: Turn your reading into lasting knowledge.

🔖 Bookmarking: Revisit your most important learnings anytime.

☀ Dark mode: Focus with minimal eye strain by switching to dark or sepia mode.

Interactive AI assistant (beta)

Our interactive AI assistant has been trained on the content of this book, to maximize your learning experience. It comes with the following features:

❖ Summarize it: Summarize key sections or an entire chapter.

❖ AI code explainers: In the next-gen Packt Reader, click the Explain button above each code block for AI-powered code explanations.

Note: The AI assistant is part of next-gen Packt Reader and is still in beta.

Figure 1.2: Illustration of Packt's AI assistant

DRM-free PDF or ePub version

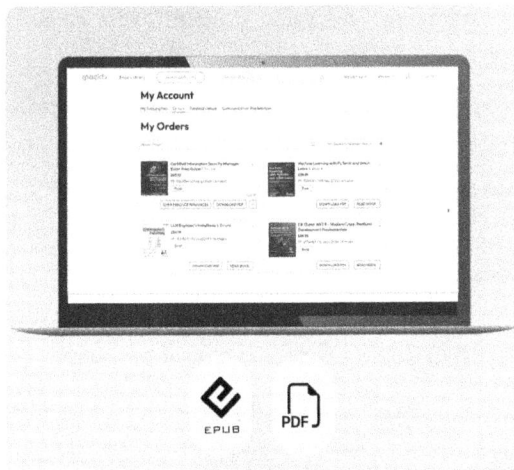

Learn without limits with the following perks included with your purchase:

🖥 Learn from anywhere with a DRM-free PDF copy of this book.

📱 Use your favorite e-reader to learn using a DRM-free ePub version of this book.

Figure 1.3: Free PDF and ePub

Introduction and historical references

Engineers have a long and productive history of creating building blocks for their own convenience. If we do not ignore this historical experience, we can learn many useful lessons for creating our own frameworks.

From the very beginning of the software industry, engineers and scientists have had a tendency to reuse their most successful and efficient ideas. There are quite a few historical practices that share the core objectives of a framework:

- **Architectural Blueprints**: Since ancient times, complex structures like buildings or ships were built based on detailed plans. These plans defined the overall structure, components, and relationships - similar to how frameworks provide a blueprint for software architecture.

- **Modular Design in Engineering**: Even before the computer age, engineers approached complex machines with a modular mindset. Think of early steam engines with interchangeable parts - a principle that carries over to software components within a framework.

- **Mathematical Frameworks**: For centuries, mathematicians have relied on established frameworks like algebra or calculus to solve problems. These frameworks provide a set of rules and structures that guide the approach to solving a specific type of problem.

While these aren't direct equivalents to software frameworks, they all represent historical approaches to structuring complex systems in a way that aligns with the core function of a software development framework—to simplify the lives of its users when dealing with complex problems.

With the advent and adoption of computers, the concept of a framework has gone beyond the art of the elite and has become part of the daily work of many programmers. The idea evolved as computers themselves developed. Here are some contenders for the title of earliest software framework:

- **Early Subroutine Libraries (1940s – 1950s):** In the early days of computing, programmers might develop reusable code blocks for common tasks like mathematical functions or input/output routines. These weren't full-fledged frameworks, but they offered a basic level of reusability and structure.

- **FORTRAN Compilers (1950s):** FORTRAN introduced the concept of high-level languages, allowing programmers to write code that is more human-readable than machine code. While not exactly a framework, it provided a foundational structure for building software.

- **Operating Systems (1960s onwards):** Operating systems like IBM's OS/360 offered a platform for running applications. They provided core functionalities like memory management and device drivers, which later frameworks were built upon.

It's important to remember that the concept of a software development framework as we know it today – offering a comprehensive set of tools, libraries, and design patterns – is a more recent development. However, these earlier practices laid the groundwork for the frameworks we use today. In the modern world, we can only imagine the practical purpose software created on top of one or multiple frameworks.

Note

This book uses both terms "software development framework (SDF)" and "application development framework (ADF)" interchangeably. Usually, "application" is not exactly the same as "software": we have platforms, libraries, SDKs, engineering tools and frameworks as alternative kinds of software. But in the context of the topic ("building frameworks") we can always safely assume that any "software" we are going to develop with our frameworks will serve the same purpose as "application" with a minor exception of "infrastructure management frameworks" which are mentioned explicitly.

While most of the information on the internet about Application Development Frameworks is focused on web and mobile development, we cannot ignore trending frameworks from a non-application software, such as

- Artificial Intelligence and Machine Learning (like PyTorch, TensorFlow, and Apache MXNet),
- Scheduled task management (like Celery, Temporal, and Apache Airflow),
- Infrastructure management (like Terraform, Pulumi, and Crossplane),
- Testing automation (like Selenium, Robot, and webdriverIO),

and many others, including "hybrid" frameworks that provide multiple capabilities at once.

Fortunately, foundational principles of building software frameworks are common between classic ADF and these emerging types of SDF.

There are also vertical ADFs, aiming to cover corresponding business domains. Examples of such frameworks include Gamedev (Flame, Monogame), Data Visualization (Shiny, Seaborn, TensorBoard), Hardware Instrumentation (LabVIEW), etc.

A StackOverflow research in 2023 that involved approximately 90,000 software engineers provided us with data about frameworks they use daily (`https://survey.stackoverflow.co/2023#section-most-loved-dreaded-and-wanted-web-frameworks` - see a Figure 1.4 that summarizes one of the framework-related topics from this survey). In addition to those numbers, we know that many frameworks have their own communities outside of StackOverflow, which means that more than 100k engineers work with software frameworks on a daily basis.

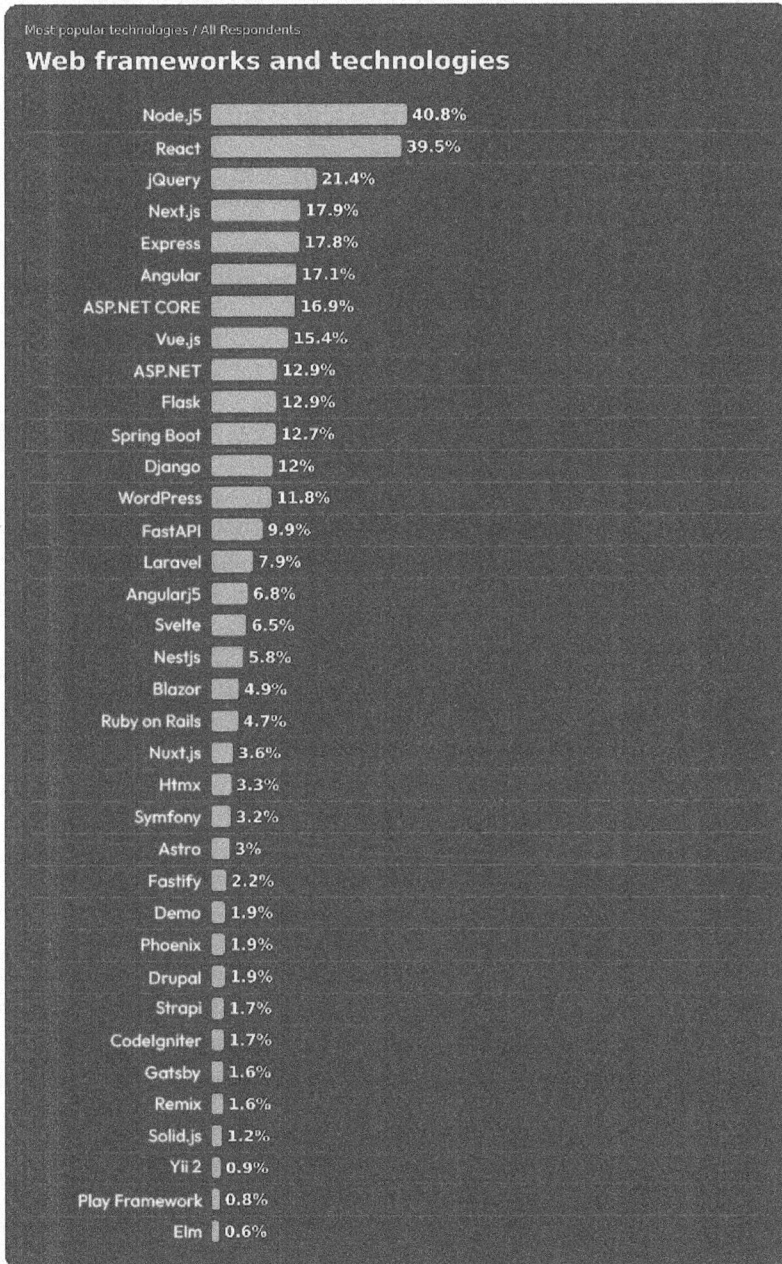

Most popular technologies / All Respondents

Web frameworks and technologies

Technology	Percentage
Node.j5	40.8%
React	39.5%
jQuery	21.4%
Next.js	17.9%
Express	17.8%
Angular	17.1%
ASP.NET CORE	16.9%
Vue.js	15.4%
ASP.NET	12.9%
Flask	12.9%
Spring Boot	12.7%
Django	12%
WordPress	11.8%
FastAPI	9.9%
Laravel	7.9%
Angularj5	6.8%
Svelte	6.5%
Nestjs	5.8%
Blazor	4.9%
Ruby on Rails	4.7%
Nuxt.js	3.6%
Htmx	3.3%
Symfony	3.2%
Astro	3%
Fastify	2.2%
Demo	1.9%
Phoenix	1.9%
Drupal	1.9%
Strapi	1.7%
CodeIgniter	1.7%
Gatsby	1.6%
Remix	1.6%
Solid.js	1.2%
Yii 2	0.9%
Play Framework	0.8%
Elm	0.6%

2024 Developer Survey

Source: survey.stackoverflow.co/2024
Data licensed under Open Database License (ODbL)

Figure 1.4: StackOverflow research summary chart

With all the wide adoption of ADFs, it is confusing to see how many different inconsistent definitions and classifications we have all around the internet. In the following section, we will craft a brief and concise definition based on ADFs unique differentiators in a world of software engineering.

Breaking down Application Development Framework

I often see engineers mixing up libraries, frameworks, and Software Development Kits. They use these words like they mean the same thing. Even more confusion can come if we add APIs, platforms, and DSLs to the conversation. But to make our own framework, we need to understand all these things.

According to Dictionary.com, the formal definition of the term "framework" is *"a basic structure, plan, or system, as of concepts, values, customs, or rules"*.

The collective unconscious of humanity, also known as LLM, suggests the following definition for ADF: *An application development framework is a software library offering a fundamental structure for building applications within a specific environment. It acts as a reusable foundation, supplying pre-defined functionalities and promoting code organization through established conventions. This approach streamlines development by reducing repetitive coding efforts.*

Both definitions are formally correct (except for "library" part of the second one, which I will explain later in this section). But they focus on how the framework is designed but have a lack of explanation about how it works. I am going to fill this gap by adding my own:

> **Definition**
>
> A collection of pre-written code and tools that provide a structured approach to building applications. It simplifies development by enforcing architectural patterns: frameworks always dictate an execution flow, and stipulate specific way to structure your code, promoting maintainability, testability, low coupling, and reusability.

It is a common misunderstanding to confuse frameworks with other engineering concepts aiming towards reusability, like API, software library, SDK, and platform. And there is always a special "tooling" category, which covers a wide range of software from smaller console scripts to powerful configurable logs processing pipelines – they all live their own life as they only used by developers to support their routine tasks, so we keep them out of conversation. Let's set clear boundaries to understand their differences to focus on the most important aspects of our topic.

Application Programming Interface

Starting from **API** (**Application Programming Interface**) as the lowest-level implementation of the development tooling. The traditional understanding of API included any exposed interface available to software developers to perform manipulation with an external subsystem. This external subsystem was treated as a "black box," which means that the developer should not worry about its internal implementation, tech stack, and logic. Thus, API provides a complete set of methods to deal with it. Modern understanding of the API concept drifted towards over-the-network API, like HTTP/gRPC/websocket APIs. Events and message-based communication interfaces are also subsets of APIs – like webhooks.

The best practice of API definition is to use open standards like OpenAPI and AsyncAPI schema languages, or other less popular languages like RAML.org or APIBlueprint.org. However, it is acceptable to use proprietary or vendor-specific tools. API concept can also be visualized with a simple diagram notation (see Figure 1.5 below). Typical representatives of the API are as follows:

- SaaS products' interfaces, e.g. PandaDoc API (`https://developers.pandadoc.com/reference/about`), or OpenAI LLM API (`https://platform.openai.com/docs/api-reference`)

- Cloud management APIs; e.g. AWS (`https://docs.aws.amazon.com/cloudcontrolapi/latest/APIReference/Welcome.html`), or Azure (`https://learn.microsoft.com/en-us/rest/api/azure/`), or (`https://cloud.google.com/service-infrastructure/docs/service-management/reference/rest`)

- Webhooks, like Zapier (`https://zapier.com/blog/what-are-webhooks/`)

- Internal/proprietary messaging-based events and commands schema registries that can be based on Confluent or Redpanda (`https://docs.redpanda.com/current/manage/schema-reg/schema-reg-overview/`)

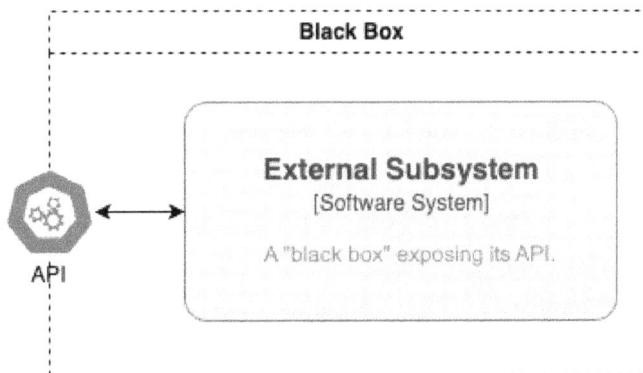

Figure 1.5: Concept-level diagram of API

🔍 Quick tip: Need to see a high-resolution version of this image? Open this book in the next-gen Packt Reader or view it in the PDF/ePub copy.

🔒 The next-gen Packt Reader and a free PDF/ePub copy of this book are included with your purchase. Scan the QR code OR visit packtpub.com/unlock, then use the search bar to find this book by name. Double-check the edition shown to make sure you get the right one.

The diagram helps to see that the API purpose is to provide access to exposed "black box" functions.

Library

The next one to review is a **software library** as a *collection of pre-written code or routines* that developers can use to perform specific tasks or functions within their software applications.

Sometimes developers see any software library as a framework, but the purpose of the library is completely different – it focuses on runtime/operation concerns by implementing a common part of the system, like hardware I/O operations, network protocol, authorization sequence, ranking algorithm, IoT standard, etc. It is also common to have a library to transform a low-level API into a more developer-friendly form by adding enumerables, constants, and conditional logic over a binary code and method signatures of plain API. A Library usually operates as a **gray box,** which means that software developers can see its internal implementation, but it is rarely necessary. In some cases, libraries can come in binary format, which makes them **black boxes**.

Terminology across the industry is not always consistent, we can find other synonyms for the term "software library":

- **Package**; usually means one or multiple software libraries that share the same license and they can be distributed as a single unit.
- **Module**; usually means a built-in software library, distributed with the program.
- **Extension** (aka add-on or plug-in); usually means a software library that follows specific program interface allowing external developers to modify original program behavior without changing any code in the original system.

Another important consideration is **control flow**. For a software library, it is common for developers to have full control over the library functions – so developers are responsible for invoking the library.

Writing software libraries is one of the most common tasks in the industry; many senior developers have experience of creating libs for internal company purposes, or contributing to open-source libs, or at least have them as a part of their pet projects.

Often, a software library evolves into an SDK or a framework after multiple iterations of improvements. And we definitely need to build libraries as part of the ADF development.

To understand the idea of software library better, we can use real examples:

- Algorithm libraries like math (`https://en.wikipedia.org/wiki/List_of_numerical_libraries`), or 3D (`https://en.wikipedia.org/wiki/List_of_3D_graphics_libraries`), or ML (`https://en.wikipedia.org/wiki/Category:Python_(programming_language)_scientific_libraries`)

- Hardware abstraction libraries like HAL (`https://infineon.github.io/psoc6hal/html/index.html`), or device drivers (`https://en.wikipedia.org/wiki/Device_driver`)

- Standard-compliant implementations like OpenAuth (`https://openid.net/developers/certified-openid-connect-implementations/`)

- Programming helpers like Boost (`https://www.boost.org/`) or Requests.py (`https://github.com/psf/requests`) that provide developers with a pre-written code for HTTP requests lifecycle syntaxis helper.

- Any proprietary pluggable reusable code

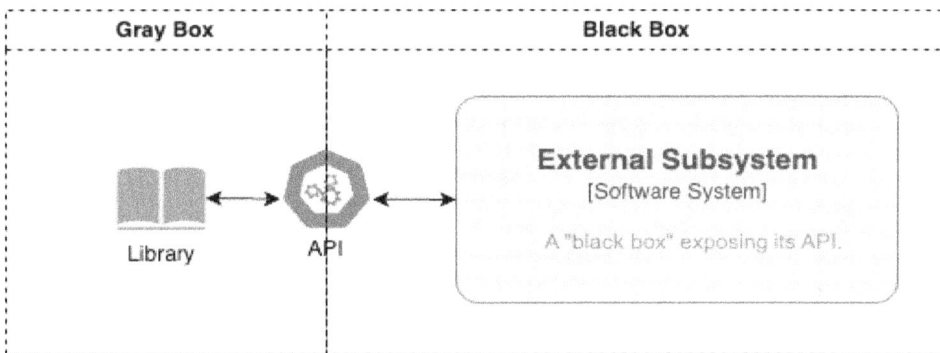

Figure 1.6: Concept-level diagram of API and Library

The diagram suggests that Library can serve as a pre-implemented tool to integrate an API to the application; but basically, it can provide any pre-implemented code for reuse.

Software Development Kit

Similar functions can be also performed by **Software Development Kits (SDKs)** but they usually include much more than just a software Libraries; there is a list of possible SDK internals:

- Libraries.
- Tracing and Debugging tools.
- Documentation.
- Integrated development environments (IDEs)
- Tests.
- Plug-ins.
- Application programming interfaces (APIs)
- Sample code.

SDKs span both design-time (organizational) and runtime/operations (product) concerns but still with focus on a runtime. SDKs are also platform– or vendor-specific, they are developed by API or Platform vendors to improve their products adoption – see Android SDK created by Google (Alphabet) and Windows ASDK developed by Microsoft.

Sometimes bigger SDKs can be designed to include frameworks (like Apple SDK), but we can also see the opposite case, where an SDK is designed as an element of the framework. The following are examples of cases where SDKs are subsystems of ADFs in the list below:

- Operator SDK is part of the Operator Framework: `https://sdk.operatorframework.io/`
- SDKs as a developer-friendly lib wrappers for particular framework, like Treblle provides multiple SDKs including one for a Django framework: `https://github.com/Treblle/treblle-python`
- SDKs have the same control flow as libraries have: the developer is responsible for invoking an SDK, while in the case of frameworks, we usually have the opposite control flow: the framework is responsible for invoking developer's code. There is no exception if the framework is part of an SDK: the framework takes ownership over the control flow.

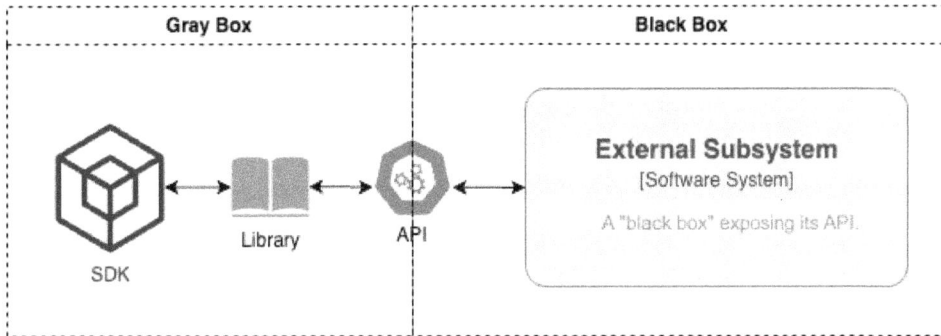

Figure 1.7: Concept diagram of API, Library, and SDK

The diagram above depicts the SDK as a super-entity for a library.

Framework

Let's elaborate on our definition here:

A framework is a collection of pre-written code and tools that provides a structured approach to building applications. It simplifies development by enforcing architectural patterns: frameworks always dictate an execution flow, and stipulate specific way to structure your code, promoting maintainability, testability, low coupling, and reusability.

Of course, frameworks provide more than that, there are some examples below:

- Hide low-level complexity behind a higher-level abstraction;
- Promote faster development by providing pre-built binary/packaged components and functionalities;

But those additional benefits cannot be attributed exclusively to frameworks – libraries or SDKs both have the same value propositions.

The following are the Key aspects of this definition based on usage scenarios and key attributes:

- **"Framework as abstraction"** conceals repetitive code and low-level details by applying software libraries, acting as a higher-level interface. This allows developers to work with core functionalities without getting bogged down in implementation specifics. However, it usually gives an option of direct communication with levels under even if it is unnecessarily for overwhelming majority of scenarios; *in brief, any framework has one or multiple libraries coming as a built-in option or pluggable 3rd-parties.*

- **"Frameworks as tooling"** prioritize simplifying the development process by providing pre-built components, streamlined workflows, and reduced boilerplate code. Their primary focus is on accelerating development, while runtime considerations (like operations, maintenance, portability, performance) are a secondary benefit.
- **"Framework as architectural constraint"** establishes a blueprint for system architecture. It dictates core components, their interactions, and overall structure, influencing key design decisions for developers working within the framework's constraints.

And finally, the relations between a frameworks and APIs, libraries and SDKs are usually follow the common pattern: ADF streamlines the software development flow for the organization, governs the control flow by invoking a custom code made by software developer, having libraries as a proxy to access external subsystem APIs, and allowing to plug in a third-party libraries or SDKs to handle specific integrations.

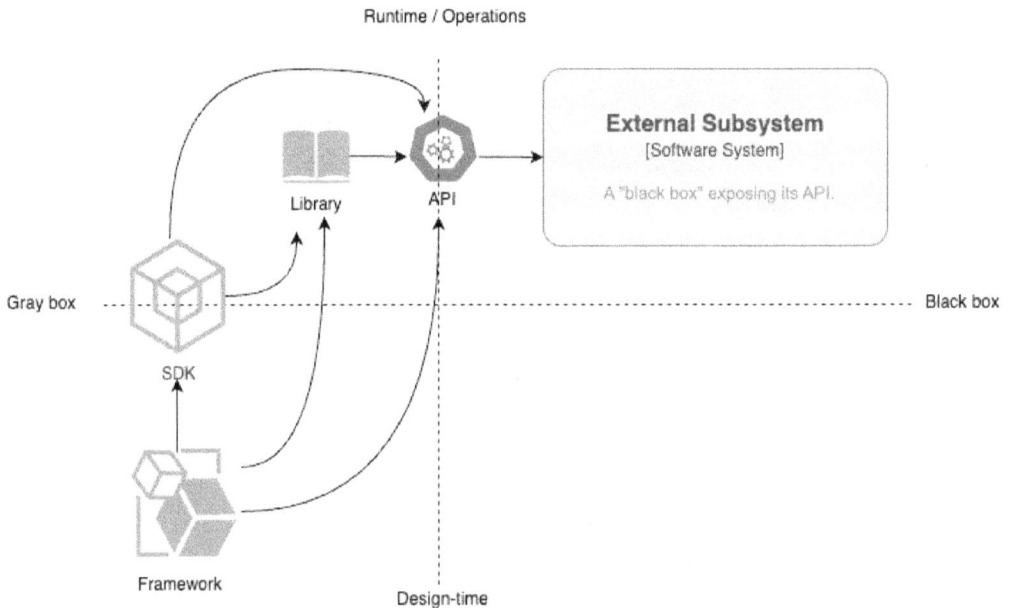

Figure 1.8: Concept diagram of ADF, SDK, Library, and API

There is an extended classification of the Application Development Frameworks:

- Web frameworks like Django, Node.js, Java Play, Ruby-on-Rails, etc
- Enterprise frameworks like Java Spring, Oracle ADF
- Low-code frameworks (https://github.com/topics/low-code-framework) like Flutter, OpenBlocks, Appsmith

- AI/ML frameworks like TensorFlow, Keras, Apache MXNet

- Gamedev frameworks like Unity, UnrealEngine

- Mobile frameworks like React Native, Xamarin, Apache Cordova

- Microservice frameworks like GoMicro, Spring Boot, Molecular

- Test automation frameworks like Selenium, Appium, WebdriverIO

- Desktop OS frameworks like MFC, OS X framework, KDE framework

- Utility frameworks like Python Celery, ActiveTask,

- *Custom frameworks – proprietary ones build for internal use, usually applying ADF format for a domain objects and rules*

- As Frameworks are our focus area, we add more detailed specification for three ADFs to better highlight their commonalities.

The first one to analyze is Django:

- It employs numerous libraries in pluggable way: see `https://djangopackages.org/`

- It focuses on design-time aspects: "encourages rapid development and clean, pragmatic design" (citation from official Django web site: `https://www.djangoproject.com/`)

- It is responsible for a control flow – developers don't need to invoke Django code but to follow a Django project structure to get their code invoked in a right moment;

- It enforces multiple architecture patterns (MVC / MVT as a model-view-template, ORM as object-relational mapping, extendable middleware-based request processing pipeline, class-based views, etc)

- It is vendor- and platform-neutral so it can be used on any cloud platform or a virtual machine that can interpret Python programming language;

- It is a "gray box" software that can be redistributed as a package (see `https://code.djangoproject.com/wiki/Distributions`) but it also has its source code published in a public GitHub repository under the BSD-3 OSS license (see `https://github.com/django/django`)

The second one is Node.js (`https://nodejs.org`), the most popular web full-stack framework based on the JavaScript programming language:

- It has number of standard built-in libraries listed in official documentation (`https://nodejs.org/docs/latest-v12.x/api/`) and hundreds of pluggable external libraries like listed here: `https://github.com/sindresorhus/awesome-nodejs`

- Org design-time focus is clearly emphasized as a key success factor of this framework; see citation of the Node.js creator: "*So for kind of technical reasons, adding a server onto JavaScript worked really well and people who were programming front end websites were able to take those same skills and with just a small amount of additional knowledge were able to program pretty nice web servers that could do long polling or other kinds of real time interactions. And I think there's just a large base of JavaScript users out there, naturally, it being the language of the web, and so there was a lot of people who were able to take their skills and add on Node to that and suddenly become full stack developers.*" (`https://the-stack-overflow-podcast.simplecast.com/episodes/why-the-creator-of-nodejs-created-a-new-javascript-runtime/transcript`)
- It is responsible for the control flow
- It enforces architecture patterns like event-driven, microservices, API-first etc
- It is vendor- and platform-neutral
- It is a "gray box" open-source software

And the final one is React (`https://react.dev/`) is a modern web front-end framework based on JavaScript language:

- Dozens of libraries like here: `https://www.reactlibraries.com/search?qType=libraries&q=*`
- Design-time focus: most of public sources mention developer-oriented benefits as a key advantage of the framework; this list includes declarative syntaxis, reusable components, community support, detailed documentation, etc
- Control flow management based on a virtual DOM concept is the core of the framework
- React's intrinsic architecture patterns include event-driven (hooks), container-based decorators, data repository (provider), etc
- It is vendor- and platform-neutral**
- It is a "gray box" open-source software

As we can see, most ADFs follow the same model which we will explore in more detail in *Chapter 3*.

Platform

And the final concept to review here is a **Platform**. The main differentiator of a Platform, in comparison with all the others: APIs, libraries, SDKs and frameworks, is its hosted server-side execution runtime. But it is important to understand that the runtime concern is a "bonus value" here because the fundamental benefits of Platforms are still organizational design-time toolings.

Platforms usually combine that hosted execution backend with APIs, libraries, and SDKs; and it is common for modern Platforms to provide developers with more advanced tooling like dev portals, resource management console and UI, cloud IDE, infrastructure-as-a-code definitions support and many other org productivity boosters. However, platforms rarely include application development frameworks and vice versa. We still can see frameworks being part of the platform (like AWS Well-Architected Framework is part of AWS platform value proposition, and Microsoft also has the same one: `https://learn.microsoft.com/en-us/azure/well-architected/`), but these are not ADFs but architecture design frameworks (set of values, viewpoints, blueprints and patterns for cloud-native applications).

Typical taxonomy with examples of the Platforms is the following:

- Cloud platforms like AWS, MS Azure or GCP
- Messaging platforms like Confluent Kafka or Redpanda
- Task execution platforms like Temporal.io
- Robotic process automation (RPA) platforms like WorkFusion or UIPath
- Game Platforms like `https://heroiclabs.com/heroic-cloud/`
- Dev platforms like Split.io, Firebase, Launchdarkly

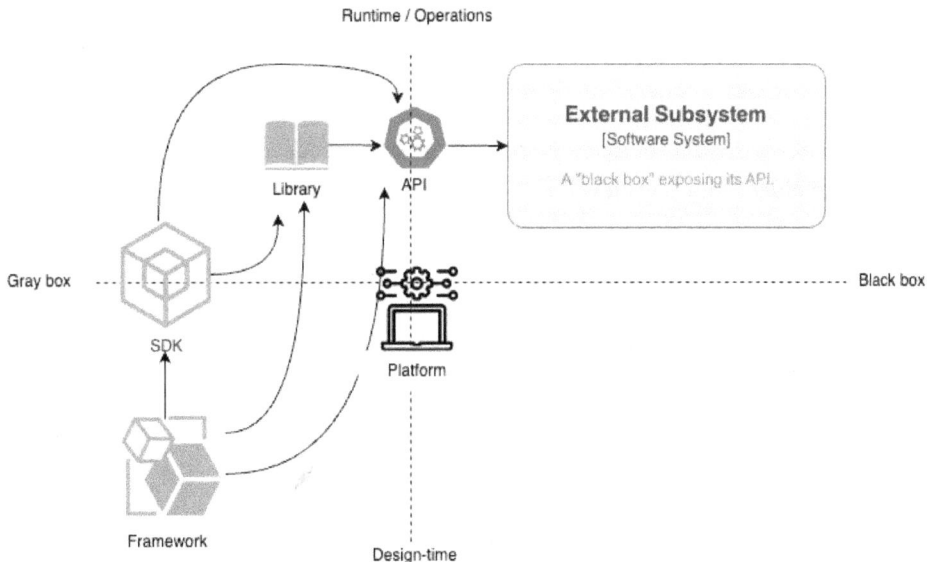

Figure 1.9: Concept diagram of Platform, Framework, SDK, Library, and API

- Platforms are the most complete and mature kind of reusable engineering elements; however, their value comes with a high cost of ownership – this means that only large-scale companies can afford to build and operate an internal software development platform. Please do not confuse internal SDP with commercial PaaS (platform as a service) – we have many examples that successful PaaS can be created and operated with relatively small investment.

Domain Specific Language

Here it is, the bonus addition to the chapter. A **Domain Specific Language** (**DSL**) is a "language" with a higher level of abstraction optimized for a specific class of problems. A DSL uses the concepts and rules from the field or domain.

> **Note**
>
> Please note that DSL is not a programming language but rather a "formal domain description" language. In most cases, DSLs implementations are closer to executable configuration in JSON, YAML, XML or similar formats.

In terms of architecture abstractions, extensibility, and control flow, DSL is very similar to ADF – they both imply certain design patterns, employ libraries for extensibility and portability purposes, and invoke necessary code in the right time, defined by DSL creators.

The difference is the level of freedom for software product developers to code the DSL execution. We may consider DSL a "next level" framework suitable for cases when we want to achieve a high grade of standardization at a high level of abstraction.

Typical simplified taxonomy of the DSLs is the following:

- Workflow/BPMN like Camunda, Oracle BPMS, Nikku
- Rules like Drools
- Infra like Terraform
- Development like Gradle

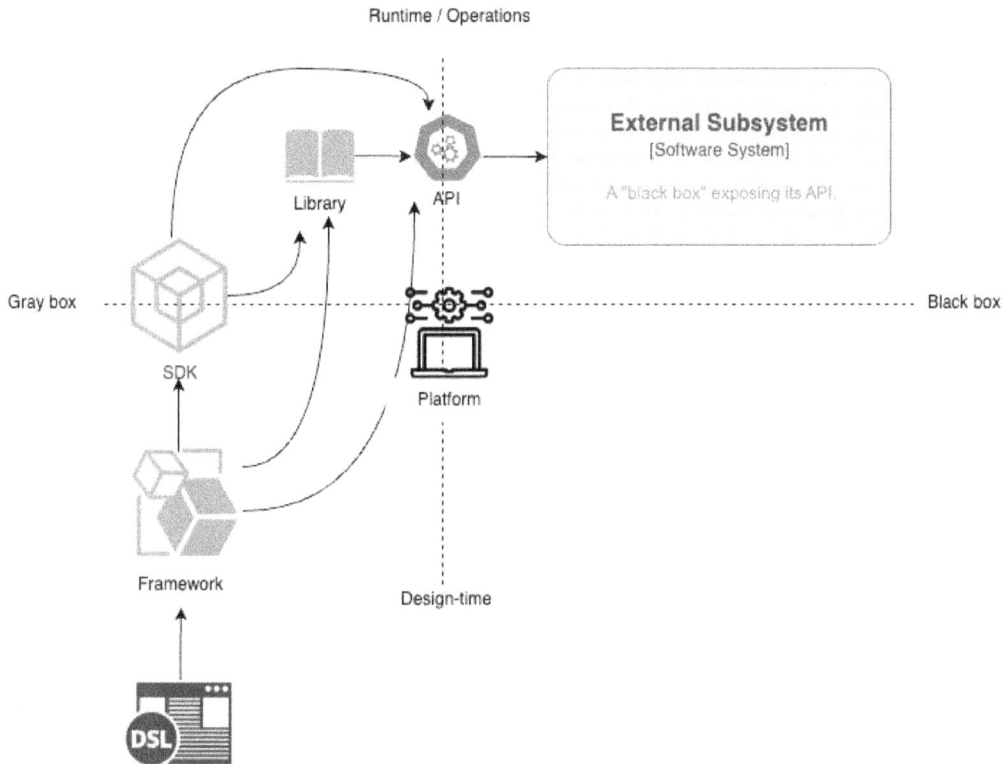

Figure 1.10: Concept diagram with DSL, Platform, Framework, SDK, Library, and API

The diagram demonstrates a DSL primary use case of extending a Framework with limited pre-defined capabilities.

In this section we focused on key differentiators of Frameworks in comparison with other kinds of "engineering building blocks". Now we can concentrate on the most important aspects of Frameworks, including the ones we further discuss in the next chapters.

Differentiating ADF and other Types of Frameworks

There are even more sources of confusion: we have Frameworks that could be used in the process of developing software products, but these Frameworks are not ADFs!

In the realm of software development, **framework** is a broad term encompassing various tools that structure and streamline different aspects of the process. We've established that Application Development Frameworks (ADFs) directly assist with coding. Let's delve deeper into two other crucial categories: **Architecture Frameworks** and **Software Delivery Frameworks**.

One of such kind of Framework is Architecture Frameworks such as "4+1 View", TOGAF, Zachman, SABSA, and DoDAF.

Another kind is Software Delivery Frameworks such as **Scaled Agile Framework (SAFe)**, **Large Scale Scrum (LeSS)**, and **Disciplined Agile Delivery (DAD)**.

Architecture Frameworks

These frameworks provide a structured approach to designing the overall architecture of a software system. Think of them as *organizational architecture design process* blueprints or roadmaps that define the foundation upon which your application will be built.

Here's a breakdown of Architecture Frameworks' types:

Enterprise Architecture Frameworks (EAFs): Focuses on the high-level structure of an entire organization's IT infrastructure, including software applications, data, and hardware. Examples: TOGAF, Zachman Framework.

Software Architecture Frameworks (SAFs): Specializes in designing the internal structure of a single software application. Examples: 4+1 View Model, C4 Model.

The following are some of the benefits of adopting such frameworks:

Consistency: Promotes a standardized approach to design, ensuring all components fit together seamlessly.

Communication: Provide a common language for stakeholders (architects, developers, etc.) to discuss system design.

Reduced Complexity: Break down complex systems into manageable components, simplifying design and development.

The following are some of the popular examples of the architecture frameworks:

- **TOGAF (The Open Group Architecture Framework)**: A widely used EAF known for its comprehensive approach to enterprise architecture.
- **Zachman Framework**: Another EAF, offering a framework for classifying architectural information across different viewpoints (e.g., business, data, application).
- **4+1 View Model**: A SAF focusing on five architectural viewpoints (system, application, deployment, container, and code) for designing software applications.

Architecture Frameworks can be very useful, but they are completely out of scope of this book.

Software Delivery Frameworks

These frameworks focus on streamlining the entire software development and delivery process, particularly for large-scale or complex projects. They don't deal with the specifics of coding or designing the application itself, but rather how to efficiently manage the development lifecycle.

Here's a closer look at **Software Delivery Frameworks**:

Core Principles: Emphasize iterative development, continuous integration and continuous delivery (CI/CD), and agile methodologies.

The following are some of the benefits:

- **Improved Efficiency**: Streamlines workflows and processes to deliver software faster and with fewer errors.

- **Enhanced Communication**: Fosters collaboration between development teams, product managers, and stakeholders.

- Increased Adaptability: Enables teams to respond to changing requirements and market needs more effectively.

The following are some of the popular examples:

- **Scaled Agile Framework (SAFe)**: A popular framework for scaling agile methodologies to large enterprises.

- **Large Scale Scrum (LeSS)**: An adaptation of the Scrum framework designed for large teams working on complex projects.

- **Disciplined Agile Delivery (DAD)**: A framework that integrates various agile practices with other project management methodologies.

These categories provide a glimpse into the diverse landscape of frameworks beyond ADFs. Architecture Frameworks ensure a well-designed foundation for your software system, while Software Delivery Frameworks guide the overall development journey with efficiency and agility. By understanding and leveraging these frameworks, you can build robust and successful software applications.

But as we decided to focus on ADF, we need to pay special attention to a Software Development Lifecycle topic as it covers the key value of using application development frameworks.

Software Development Lifecycle (SDLC) and Flow

To better understand Application Development Frameworks, we need first to understand key scenarios of ADF adoption.

To set up a context, we need to differentiate the design-time and operations (runtime) aspects of the software product development. It is important to note that the **Software Development Lifecycle (SDLC)** can be used as a "blueprint" for software product development iteration. Visual diagram of SDLC can help us better understand this aspect:

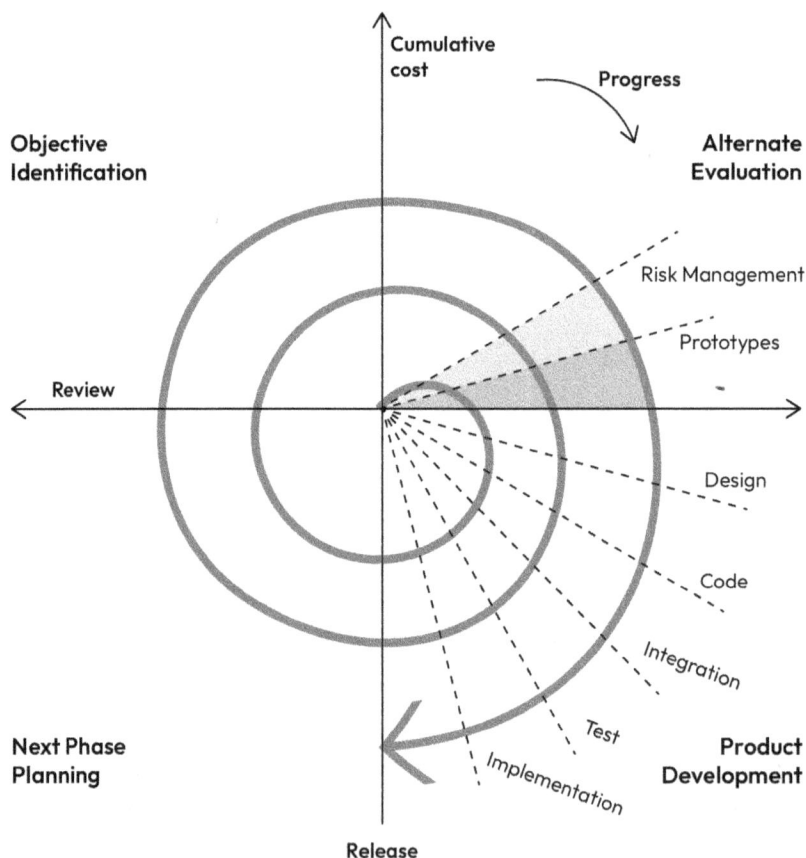

Figure 1.11: Spiral SDLC model is one of the most advanced SDLC models for software development: image credits to https://www.tutorialspoint.com/sdlc/sdlc_spiral_model.htm

We should always assume a repeatable iterative nature of the software product development process not because "agile" is our current state-of-the-art delivery methodology; every lean or efficient delivery approach relies on feedback loops to enable continuous improvement.

While ADF can be defined from both design-time and operations (runtime) perspectives, its primary value is always in design-time and SDLC. We can impact routines as repeatable and re-producible tasks. That's how it is different from software libraries or APIs that can be employed for a one-time task that might never be repeated again (e.g. library that provides integration to specialized hardware or vendor-locked API that can be used in multiple places in source code, but the use of a library is not about repeatable part of SDLC task).

In systems engineering terminology we can declare that SDLC is a "using system" (or a super-system) for ADF, and ADF is a "subsystem" of SDLC. This implies not only the fact that ADF is literally part of SDLC, but also enables the following mental model:

- ADF value, success criteria, and metrics are targeting SDLC improvements
- ADF stakeholders' roles are SDLC participants
- Key ADF architecture viewpoints are defined in SDLC

In addition to SDLC concept, which is focused on engineering and instrumenting the development process, we can apply a "Flow" term to emphasize the systemic aspect of software product development in terms of value throughput and delivery management.

ADF and Flow

All abovementioned means that ADF becomes one of the most influencing ways to optimize a Flow throughput and eliminate bottlenecks related to product and process complexity.

Summary

An Application Development Framework is a software product "skeleton" that offers a fundamental structure for building applications within a specific environment. It acts as a reusable foundation, supplying pre-defined functionalities and promoting code organization through established conventions. This distinguishes it from other ways of reusing code in the form of an SDK, library, or API. It also makes ADF a unique opportunity to streamline development by reducing repetitive coding efforts, decreasing cognitive load, and promoting architecture best practices.

With this knowledge, we can explore the next chapters to find a way to calculate ADF return on investment, meet stakeholders' expectations, and align the ADF roadmap with a common maturity model.

Reference

To know more about the following, please visit the links.

- *Vendor-specific hardware SDKs like Android Studio*: `https://developer.android.com/studio`

- *Samsung TV SDK*: `https://developer.samsung.com/smarttv/develop/getting-started/setting-up-sdk/installing-tv-sdk.html`

- *MS Xbox*: `https://en.wikipedia.org/wiki/Xbox_Development_Kit`

- *Product-specific SDKs like PandaDoc SDK*: `https://developers.pandadoc.com/reference/sdk`

- *Hubspot SDK*: `https://developers.hubspot.com/docs/platform/ui-extensions-sdk`

- *GetStream*: `https://getstream.io/chat/sdk/ios/`

- *Platform SDKs like AWS*: `https://aws.amazon.com/chime/chime-sdk/` & `https://aws.amazon.com/sdk-for-net/`

- *Azure (*`https://github.com/Azure/azure-sdk`*), or GCP*: `https://cloud.google.com/sdk`

Unlock this book's exclusive benefits now

Scan this QR code or go to packtpub.com/unlock, then search for this book by name. Ensure it's the correct edition.

Note: Keep your purchase invoice ready before you start.

2

Strategizing ADF for Success

Every engineer intuitively understands the importance of **Application Development Frameworks (ADFs)**. From the perspective of an ADF builder, we would like to see our framework as part of many popular software products and get positive feedback from experienced engineers. This chapter aims to elaborate on ADF's success through value creation. This chapter is also exciting for the **Technical Product Manager (TPM)** role, as it can help manage stakeholders' expectations for a framework-building initiative.

We review preconditions and opportunities for building our own ADF. To become successful with Application Development Frameworks, we must follow suitable Builder mental models and understand their Consumer mental models. The chapter includes a section on the importance of adopting the Open-Source Software development paradigm even if you build proprietary or commercial ADF. The chapter wraps up with a section on the ADF Maturity Model, allowing readers to align their own organizational context with expected ADF benefits. We will cover the following main topics:

- Introducing Systems Engineering as the Grounding Theory
- Establishing a Context for the Framework
- Defining ADF Success Factors
- Exploring a software development lifecycle model
- Estimating success metrics and ROI
- Shift towards Open-Source Software (OSS) paradigm

So, let's examine why you might be interested in building your own application development framework and why others might be interested in using it.

Introducing Systems Engineering as the grounding theory

In the previous chapter, we emphasized the importance of considering various stakeholders' expectations to succeed in developing an ADF.

This section provides a foundation for this chapter by explaining *success* from the perspective of the Systems Engineering discipline. We use **Systems Engineering** (**SE**) as the grounding theory for this chapter and reference it in many other ones because this discipline was explicitly designed to support a *successful systems* delivery. According to the **Systems Engineering Body of Knowledge** (**SEBoK**, https://sebokwiki.org/), "SE is a transdisciplinary approach and means to enable the realization of **successful systems**. Successful systems must satisfy the needs of their customers, users, and other stakeholders."

While we won't utilize the full-scale SE for framework modeling, we will leverage some core principles of SE to enhance the structure and clarity of our ADF models and descriptions in this book. For more comprehensive information, I recommend referring to the SEBoK and the resources provided by the **International Council on Systems Engineering** (**INCOSE**), which offer comprehensive guidelines and frameworks for addressing the operational environment in systems engineering practices.

This chapter will focus on two concepts derived from systems engineering.

- **Operations environment:** This term refers to the conditions and factors under which a system is anticipated to function. It encompasses both the physical and operational contexts in which the system operates, including environmental conditions, user interactions, and interactions with external systems or processes. Understanding and defining the operations environment is crucial for establishing system requirements and ensuring effective performance under real-world conditions.

  In other words, the *success* conditions of the system come from its operations environment.

- **Lifecycle:** Another vital concept borrowed from systems engineering is the notion of the **lifecycle** (in the software industry, it is called SDLC for **software development lifecycle**). The concept refers to the stages a system undergoes from inception to retirement. According to SEBoK and INCOSE, the system lifecycle encompasses several vital phases: concept definition, development, production, utilization, support, and retirement. As the book is about the framework's creation, we will discuss four initial phases: concept definition, development, production, and utilization.

More importantly, it does not focus on stages but instead on the **lifecycle model**, which operates with *methods of work* that compose the software production flow.

The relation between SDLC and software product is *enabling*: we can say that SDLC *enables* software product.

Let's take what we can get from the first concept: exploring the ADF operations environment.

Establishing a Context for the framework

The first concept from the Systems Engineering that we want to use here is the operations environment. In most cases, applying it to the development process is not valid due to the significant difference between design-time and runtime. However, the framework case is an exception because the most essential part of the framework's value is in design-time. More details will come with the next chapter, but in brief, we have the following decomposition of ADF concerning design-time and runtime focus:

- Runtime (Software Product operations)

    - Libraries, plugins, and extensions

    - Runtime tooling (like logging or performance counters)

- Design-time (SDLC operations)

    - Control flow

    - Architecture guardrails

    - Testing tools

    - SDLC tooling (like scaffolding, deployment, migrations, or linters)

We also mentioned this difference in *Chapter 1* (see *Figure 1.9* as a reference).

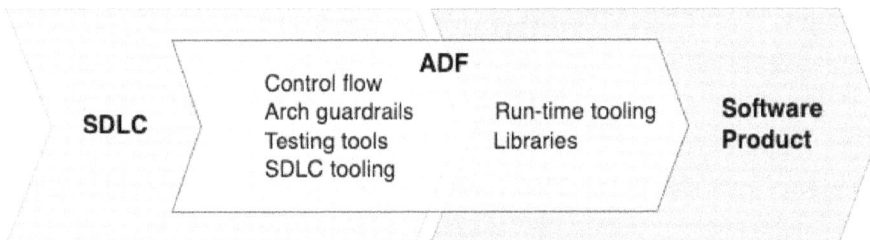

Figure 2.1: SDLC and ADF enable a software product

🔍 Quick tip: Need to see a high-resolution version of this image? Open this book in the next-gen Packt Reader or view it in the PDF/ePub copy.

🔖 The next-gen Packt Reader and a free PDF/ePub copy of this book are included with your purchase. Scan the QR code OR visit `packtpub.com/unlock`, then use the search bar to find this book by name. Double-check the edition shown to make sure you get the right one.

So, for any ADF, we can define its primary operations environment as a production software development project. It means that we literally *operate* (utilize, get value from using it) in the process of working on a production software development project.

We have enough historical evidence that the most natural and evolutionary way to build a framework is to extract it from an ongoing software development project. For reference, two top-tier web frameworks are born from the real-world struggles and demands of building complex software. Let's dive deeper into the two examples using Django and ReactJS to understand how this process works:

Django

- **Problem**: In 2003, developers at the **Lawrence Journal-World newspaper (LJWorld)** faced the challenge of building and maintaining a dynamic news website under tight deadlines. Traditional web development tools often led to repetitive code and difficulties in scaling.

- **Solution**: The developers turned to Python, a language known for its readability and rapid development capabilities. They started extracting reusable components and functionalities from their ongoing website project to meet deadlines and ensure clean, maintainable code. This *code factoring* gradually evolved into a more comprehensive framework – Django.

- **Key Considerations**: Django's design was shaped by the specific needs of a news website: handling content creation, user management (for journalists and editors), and efficient content delivery. These practical constraints drove features like a built-in admin panel, robust content management tools, and a templating system for dynamic page generation – all core functionalities in Django today.

- **Evolution to Open Source**: Though LJWorld itself migrated to WordPress later, Django's open-source release in 2005 allowed other developers to leverage its strengths for various web applications. Today, Django powers complex websites like Pinterest and Instagram, demonstrating its adaptability beyond its original news media purpose.

ReactJS — building a better ads engine

- **Problem**: Between 2011 and 2013, Facebook developers faced challenges in managing the complexity of their search functionality and the upcoming Facebook Ads platform. Traditional DOM manipulation techniques were cumbersome and time-consuming.

- **Solution**: The Facebook engineering team created ReactJS as an internal tool to streamline the development process. React's core principle – a component-based architecture – made building complex **user interfaces** (**UIs**) for features like ad creation and management significantly faster and more efficient.

- **Stakeholder Focus**: The primary beneficiary of ReactJS in its initial stages was the Facebook Ads team. The framework's design catered to their specific needs for building dynamic and interactive ad experiences.

- **Beyond Facebook, Evolution to Open Source**: The open-source release of ReactJS in 2013 allowed developers beyond Facebook to leverage its component-based approach. Today, ReactJS is a dominant force in web development, powering interactive interfaces for countless websites and applications.

These examples showcase how real-world projects can be breeding grounds for powerful frameworks. The challenges faced by the developers (deadlines, complex UIs) translate into core functionalities of the framework (Django's content management, React's component-based structure). These *extracted* frameworks become valuable tools for a broader developer community by addressing specific needs and constraints.

There might be exceptions, but we used to see that real software product development is the best source of ideas, requirements, and decisions for nearly every successful application development framework

We can safely assume that the ADF can be built by the following steps:

1. Build a software product with a particular method of work (see *Table 2.2*).
2. Refactor and extract specific parts of the product to a framework.
3. Reuse the framework to build the following software products based on the same principles in a similar technology area.

The possible alternative to the evolutionary extraction of ADF from the software product is to build the ADF *by specification* as we do any other software product. Unfortunately, this way of building software has all inherited problems of any software built without a fast feedback loop: integration and adoption. Creating ADF upfront is more expensive because achieving an acceptable value outcome from the new framework always requires more than one iteration.

Django framework can be a good example of evolutionary build ADF while React initially was closer to the "by specification" one. In most cases, deriving the ADF from already implemented software is more pragmatic, unless your team has plenty of resources and time for experiments with revolutionary tech. In this book, we recommend the evolutionary way to deliver an ADF by extracting it from a software project.

Defining ADF success factors

Selecting the optimal **application development framework (ADF)** is a critical decision that lays the groundwork for project success. While the technical merits are essential, a successful framework adoption hinges on its ability to satisfy the diverse needs of various stakeholders within the engineering organization. Let's explore these considerations, keeping in mind the possibility of developing your own custom ADF.

Engineering leaders (CTOs, Engineering Directors, Team Leads)

This group of stakeholders is always looking for ways to improve team productivity on different horizons: the team lead role prioritizes short-term improvements, the director-level leader role needs a mid-term improvement strategy, and the VP/CTO-level roles are about long-term vision and drivers. Top-level leaders also care about company brand, intellectual property, and vendor relations.

- **Reduced Complexity and Cognitive Load**: Leaders prioritize frameworks that simplify development. That can be achieved by hiding standardized interactions and dependencies under the unified interfaces, allowing development teams to focus on business features rather than technical scaffolding. **Developing a custom ADF** will enable you to tailor it to your specific needs, potentially reducing cognitive load for your developers even more in the long run.

- **Business Agility Support**: Consider the trade-off between out-of-the-box functionality and customization. While a feature-rich framework can accelerate development initially, it might introduce complexity and a steeper learning curve. For example, we have had to migrate an extensive SaaS system from a Django web framework to a custom one as part of a monolith decomposition initiative to improve teams' autonomy, and simplify development process.

- **Learning Curve and Team Productivity:** Balance the framework's learning curve with your team's existing skillset. Leverage existing knowledge whenever possible to minimize retraining and maintain developer productivity. Open-source frameworks with large communities and extensive learning resources can be advantageous in this regard. However, a **custom ADF** can be designed to seamlessly integrate with your team's expertise, further boosting productivity.

- **Reduced Reliance on External Vendors:** Developing your own framework frees you from vendor lock-in and the potential constraints of third-party licensing models.

- **Intellectual Property Ownership:** A custom ADF can be considered intellectual property, providing a competitive advantage.

- **Development Relations and Technological Brand:** A successfully adopted ADF could be published as **Open-Source Software** (**OSS**) to improve technical brand visibility and attract talents by offering a contribution opportunity.

Architects

Although an organization may not have a dedicated architect position, this role will, in any case, be of great importance in the development of complex systems. You just need to understand that fulfilling this role will fall on someone from the development team or a technical manager. Therefore, we have a responsibility to consider the concerns of this role in any case.

- **Architectural Alignment and Long-Term Maintainability**: Ensure the framework's architectural patterns align with the organization's established best practices. Consider the long-term implications – will the framework facilitate clean, maintainable code as the project evolves? Developing a custom ADF allows for complete control over the architectural patterns, ensuring optimal alignment with your long-term vision.

- **Technical Stack Integration and Security**: The framework should seamlessly integrate with your existing technology stack (databases, deployment tools) and comply with internal security regulations. While many popular frameworks offer good integration options, a custom ADF can be designed to perfectly fit your unique technical environment and address any specific security concerns.

Developers

Beyond the learning curve, consider the overall developer experience. Look for frameworks that offer clear documentation, intuitive APIs, and strong developer tooling support. This translates to faster development cycles and increased developer satisfaction. A custom ADF, if well-designed with developer experience in mind, can become a powerful tool that streamlines workflows and boosts developer productivity.

Quality Assurance (QA)

The framework should provide strong support for testing methodologies. This includes features like unit testing frameworks, dependency injection, and clear separation of concerns. A custom ADF can be designed with testability as a core principle, allowing for the creation of comprehensive test suites and ensuring a high-quality application.

Product Managers and Business Analysts

These or similar roles are critically important to build connections between the system's end users and the development team to ensure software product success. Again, even if your organization don't have dedicated positions and titles like these, someone should definitely be concerned about the following matters:

- **Business Agility** (Understanding Capabilities and Limitations): These stakeholders need to be aware of the framework's capabilities and limitations to make informed decisions. A custom ADF offers complete control over the feature set, allowing you to tailor it to meet specific business needs. However, business analysts should also consider the ongoing maintenance effort required for a custom solution.

- **Perfect Alignment with Business Needs:** A custom solution can be tailored to address your specific use cases and business requirements, potentially leading to a more efficient and practical application.

In conclusion, we make a brief table of general ADF-related benefits and highlight advantages that are only achievable with custom-built ADF:

Possible Benefits	3rd-party or OSS ADF	Custom ADF	No ADF
	No Benefits		
Insufficient opportunities to reuse (RoI < 1)	✗	✗ ✗	✓
	Common Benefits		
Reduced (hidden) Complexity	✓	✓	✗
Business Agility Support	✓	✓	✗
Learning Curve	✓	✗	✗
Team Productivity	✓	✓	✗
Reduced Cognitive Load	✓	✓	✗
Development Experience	✓	✓	✗
Robust Testing Capabilities	✓✓	✓	✗
Architectural Alignment	✓	✓✓	✗
Technical Stack integration	✓	✓✓	✓
Security	✓	✓✓✓	✗
	Only with Custom ADF		
Technological Brand		✓	
Intellectual Property		✓	
Reduced Reliance on Ext Vendors		✓	
Full Alignment with Business Needs		✓	

Table 2.1: External ADF benefits in comparison with a custom-built ADF; please note that the comparison is made based on authors' personal experience and may not cover all edge cases

Please note that custom-built ADF can achieve better outcomes in areas like architectural alignment, technical stack integration, and especially security because it allows complete control over the ADF structure and dependencies.

However, creating and maintaining a custom ADF requires significant investment in time and resources. It is vital to carefully weigh the benefits against the ongoing development and maintenance costs. Please see the following sections for a detailed explanation of the Return on Investment (RoI) metric, which provides the best way to understand whether it is worth getting involved.

Choosing between a pre-built framework and a custom ADF requires careful consideration of your team's skillset, project requirements, long-term vision, and resource constraints. By understanding the priorities of various stakeholders and the potential advantages and drawbacks of each approach, you can make an informed decision that sets your project up for success.

Exploring Software Development Lifecycle models

Now, we will develop more specific and measurable ADF success criteria by leveraging the second of the abovementioned SE concepts: the lifecycle.

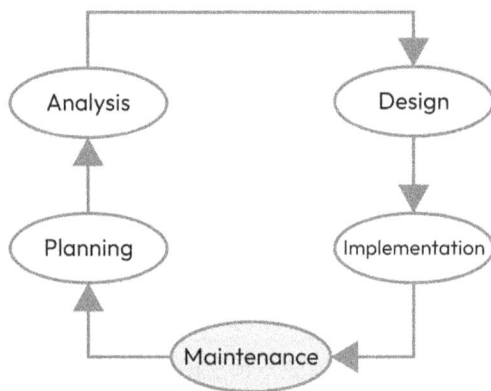

Figure 2.2: Systems development life cycle. (2024, May 19). In Wikipedia. https://en.wikipedia. org/wiki/Systems_development_life_cycle

While the canonical SDLC diagram presented in *Figure 2.1* may not provide significant value for our specific purposes, it is essential to recognize that the *lifecycle model* allows us to zoom in and break down the Implementation stage into more granular levels by introducing *methods of work*. This term is also known as the "ways of working" from the OMG Essence standard (`https://www. omg.org/spec/Essence/2.0/Beta1/PDF`), proposed by Ivar Jacobson. In brief, it means just "the tailored set of practices and tools used by a team to guide and support their work."

This flexibility helps us better understand the system development process. But what work methods do we want to highlight throughout the cycle in our model to extract the maximum possible benefit for the analysis and design of the development framework?

> **Important note**
>
> Application Development Framework always addresses a *method of work* that is repeatable, technologically advanced, and requires significant manual work.

The following are some of the examples:

- ReactJS (FE framework) addresses the work of adding UI components and reusing them in a web application;

- DRF (Django REST Framework) addresses the work of exposing REST API endpoints from a web application;

- LangChain (AI/LLM framework) addresses the work of building AI agents and integrating them into the processing pipeline;

- Django (web framework) is so mature that it addresses multiple types of work at once:

    - adding new web pages to a web application;

    - adding data models;

    - adding middleware processors;

We cannot emphasize more that ADF is a design-time-focused tooling, and its primary value is always in making engineering organization better (more productive, making better quality work), and only secondary effect is about a runtime (software product) itself.

Thus, our first step is to extract the development-centric process with the best potential ROI for extraction as a new ADF. We will use one of the proprietary frameworks we made as a reference; here, we add some context.

As part of the platforming initiative in a B2B SaaS software product, we created the Extensions Framework. We analyzed the flow of adding and managing custom-built micro-front-ends (microFEs), aka Extensions, to our in-application rich content editor.

Regarding the lifecycle model, we addressed the *add and manage microFEs to the host application* method of work. We already had eight extensions built into the host page front-end code, but we anticipated having at least ten more extensions soon. Given our high performance and low-coupling requirements, we knew how difficult it was to add such extensions previously. Overall, our primary drivers were:

- Architecture decoupling of Extension from host to enable proper engineering ownership
- Developers' experience of adding and managing Extensions
- Business agility, as an unblocked opportunity to add 3rd-part or OSS Extensions in the future
- Improved testability for any specific Extension independently

So, after defining a method of work that our ADF will address, we can derive a technical process that needs to be focused on the product side (in runtime).

For example, some well-known frameworks focus on the following technical processes:

- ReactJS (FE framework) focuses on the technical process of injecting and rendering UI components in a web application;
- DRF (Django REST Framework) focuses on the technical process of executing requests to exposed REST API endpoints;
- LangChain (AI/LLM framework) focuses on the technical process of invoking AI agents in the processing pipeline;
- Django (web framework) is so mature that it focuses on multiple technical processes at once:
  - rendering a web page;
  - connecting and performing 2-way sync of data models;
  - invoking a middleware processor; etc.

As you can see, this technical runtime process is a projection of the same entity our lifecycle method addresses. To model any ADF, we need to model both organizational and product parts of ADF together as value factor and cost factor: the first one demonstrates the benefits of using ADF as a difference before and after ADF adoption, and the former one is the cost of implementing ADF scope. In our example, the Extensions ADF value is a decrease in the effort and complexity of adding and managing Extensions. At the same time, ADF cost is the efforts and support of all the components required to operate Extensions in a production environment. Please note that the total value is multiplied by the estimated number of Extension-related features in our product roadmap:

$$ROI_{ADF} = N_{Features} \cdot \frac{\left(E_{Before} - E_{After}\right)}{\left(E_{ADF} + E_{Adopt}\right)}$$

Here:

- $N_{Features}$ is the estimated number of times we can apply our target *method of work* during feature development
- E_{Before} is estimated efforts (could be measured in *worker-hours* for a minor effort, or *team-sprints* for a more significant effort) required to apply our target *method of work* before the ADF adoption
- E_{After} is the estimated efforts required to apply our target *method of work* with the help of the new ADF
- E_{ADF} is estimated efforts required to build the new ADF
- E_{Adopt} is estimated efforts required to onboard engineering teams to the changes in target *method of work*, including migrating existing parts of the software product if necessary

This formula only considers Efforts as a significant input parameter while we have multiple other success factors (see *Table 2.1*). We suggest treating all other ADF benefits as side benefits while using efforts as the only primary ROI-defining factor. This also means that it might be feasible to accept investments in ADF development even with ROI < 1 when side benefits become crucial for engineering strategy, e.g., it helps to decouple a monolithic application to domain microservice.

Estimating success metrics and ROI

Now, we are close to the ability to evaluate the return on investment for creating our framework. A small final step is left: we need to know all input variables of the formula above.

The first one, $N_{Features}$, is probably the simplest variable, but we cannot always know for sure how many times we will need to reuse the framework in the future. If you are lucky enough to have the exact number, it better be more than five: this is an empirical *magic number*, meaning we have never seen successful ADF development initiatives with less than five cases of reuse. The main purpose of this magic number is to give you a ballpark understanding even before you can calculate a RoI forecast. In the case of the UI Extensions framework, we had an estimate of 10+, which means that ten is the pessimistic value.

The second one, E_{Before}, is usually already available for you in cases when you extract ADF from the software project. It is always better to have more than one measurement based on different teams' performance, but its value has the highest confidence anyway. Suppose you build a *framework as a product* without the donor project. In that case, you can try getting the estimate from your potential *customers* – development teams who have experience with similar tasks. However, it is essential not to limit the forecast by implementation efforts only: sometimes, *ownership efforts* of already implemented feature is comparable with the implementation efforts. In the case of UI Extensions Framework, we estimated the cost by the sum of the feature team effort to build the Extension, the domain owners team to guide and review the Extension integration, and the average efforts required to update and troubleshoot the Extension.

The following two, E_{After} and E_{ADF}, are impossible to get empirically because they require your ADF to be already built and integrated into the software delivery flow. We must use predictive modeling techniques to measure these variables, and we put the example of these models in this section below.

And the final one, E_{Adopt}, is the one that is consistently underestimated. Here, we have a migration effort that is usually non-linear due to excessive coupling and technical debt. Here, we have a cost of educating the teams and collecting their feedback with all the necessary adjustments. In total, it might be a *classic* example of the *x3 rule* invented by developers who need to give an estimate for performing a task in an unknown area. Just multiply your estimate by three and be on the safe side.

Getting back to our forecasted variables, **Efforts**$_{AFTER}$ and **Efforts**$_{ADF\,DEV}$. For a more realistic estimate, let's apply the lifecycle modeling techniques to decompose the values into more granular components. For the E_{After}, we break down our "method of work" into smaller operations chunks. For the E_{ADF}, we break down our target technological process related to the method of work. We continue using the same UI Extensions framework as the reference here.

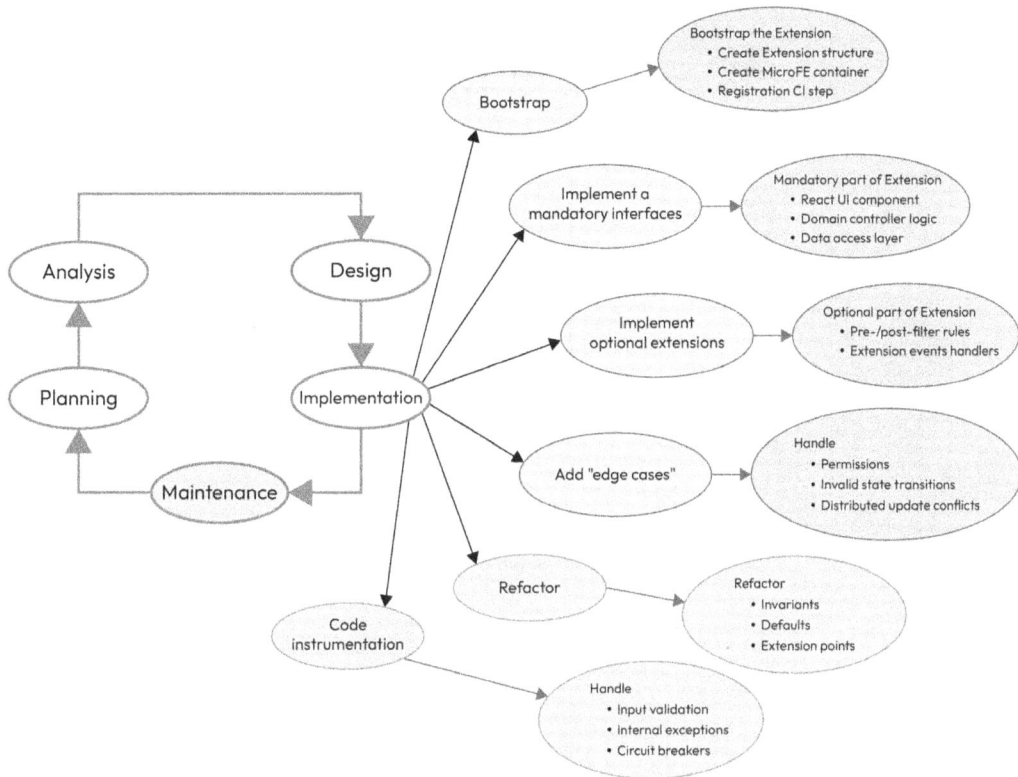

*Figure 2.3: "Method of work" breakdown, based on the original Wikipedia image https://
en.wikipedia.org/wiki/Systems_development_life_cycle*

This diagram describes generalized operations that must be performed to use most ADFs, with
the outer layer containing expanded details about the referred ADF (UI Extensions framework).
Four upper operations are the source of the value of E_{AFTER}. In comparison, we consider two bot-
tom operations unnecessary with the new ADF and can use them to improve the accuracy of the
value of the difference of $E_{Before} - E_{After}$.

The visualization technique used here is not the most convenient way to build the model; in practice, we found a table representation more suitable for this kind of model. It is easier to extend
with additional metadata and can cover a broader part of the lifecycle without losing readability.
You can see the example built for the UI Extensions framework in *Table 2.2* below:

Work Method	Operation	E_{AFTER} for PD Extensions framework (hours)	ADF requirements
Bootstrap	Create Extension structure	4	Documentation (dev guide), Extension manifest template
	Create MicroFE container	2	Documentation (dev guide), MicroFE template
	CI step for the Extension Registration	4	Documentation (dev guide)
Implement mandatory interfaces	React UI component	*? Domain-specific*	n/a
	Domain controller logic	*? Domain-specific*	n/a
	Data access layer	*? Domain-specific*	n/a
Implement optional extensions	Pre-/post-filter rules	4	Documentation (dev guide), Extension Point (host) rendering flow
	Extension events handlers	8	Documentation (dev guide), Extension Point (host) event triggers
Add "edge cases"	Permissions	2	Declarative permissions support in Ext manifest
	Invalid state transitions	4	Extensions state sync with domain service
	Distributed update conflicts	*? Domain-specific*	n/a
Refactoring		0	Extension structure, enumerations, constants
Code instrumentation	Internal/external exceptions	4	Handle internal exceptions, return error codes
	Circuit breakers	4	Remote service calls wrapper

Work Method	Operation	E_{AFTER} for PD Extensions framework (hours)	ADF requirements
Monitoring	Logging	4	Integrated logger
	Collect metrics	0	Default metrics aggregator, default dashboard
TOTAL	...	40	

Table 2.2: The "Method of work" breakdown model is in table format

Table 2.2 provides a reference lifecycle reference model in table format. This first column contains a generic structure suitable for almost any ADF (more details about this structure come in the following chapters). The structure from the first column is too generic for direct use for your ADF as is, but you can adjust your ADF-specific breakdown that we have in the second column. The third column contains estimated efforts related to the target *method of work*. The final fourth column has notes associated with the ADF scope that we need to implement to support our current estimates.

It is evident that the lower the final value of the value of the efforts forecast, the more effective our framework is. Also, you may notice that some estimates have a *"Domain-specific"* value. This is done in those places where the effort estimate depends on the domain in which the logic of expansion is realized. These estimates will not affect the final difference between E_{Before} – and E_{After}.

Exercise

We encourage you to try composing such a table for your framework. Not only will this exercise help you more accurately predict your framework's ROI, but it will also make your value proposition more transparent to everyone.

Please note that this estimate (E_{After}) should always come before the ADF estimate (E_{ADF}) to collect additional, less obvious elements that need to be implemented in the ADF scope. Thus, our next step will be to create a model for assessing the efforts required to develop a framework itself. We will use a similar table format for this model as well. The main difference will be that to evaluate the cost of creating ADF, and we must first produce an architectural design of the framework. This means that the initial section of the table will address a preliminary technical design of the framework. This also means that one of the columns of our table will contain modules of technical architecture. More details on ADF architecture design and modular structure will come in further chapters; here, we use only minimal structure to enable the estimation process. The technical architecture design specific to PD Extensions framework can be seen below in table format:

Lifecycle Phase	Modeling outcome
Architecture Design	Entities and Relations model
	Extension Point (host)
	Extension as a micro-front-end (microFE) app
	App domain
	Information flow model – render all Extensions flow
	Host application load
	Extension Point init
	Extensions query to a back-end (BE) system
	Pre-filter Extensions rules (BE)
	Dynamically load Extensions
	Post-filter Extensions rules on a front-end (FE)
	Delegate Extensions rendering to their respective domains
	Provides common client-side events (re-init, hide, show, etc.)
	Components model (target state)
	Extension Point loader (FE)
	Extensions Catalog service (BE)
	Extension loader (FE)
	Events manager (FE)
	Data persistence model (target state)
	Extension state persistence is in Extension Service (BE, RDB)
	Extension Point persistence is in the host application (config, FS)

Table 2.3: ADF Technical design outline

Now, we are able to build a work breakdown for our reference ADF development; see *Table 2.4* below:

Source of the scope	Scope structure	Efforts estimate (team-sprints)
"Method of work" requirements support	Project structure	
	Extension Point code file	
	Extension Point config	
	Extension Manifest file	
	Extension registration CI step	
	Extensions server repository	1
	Dependencies injection	
	Extension point config	
	Extension registration CI	
	Documentation	
	Development guide	

Source of the scope	Scope structure	Efforts estimate (team-sprints)
Target technological flow implementation (render Extensions)	Input/output data formats Extension manifest JSON serialize/ deserialize/validate Extensions service API OpenAPI definitions (Query, Register) Objects interactions Query extensions Apply pre/post-filter rules Register Extension Load extension Render Extension State transition functions Extension Point init/query/filter/render/re-init Data access layer Register Extension Update Extension state	3
Integrate the ADF with the core product	Internal data sources Entitlement service Identity service External file hosting services and CDN	1
"Add edge case" support	Extension validation microFE validation Circuit breakers	1

Source of the scope	Scope structure	Efforts estimate (team-sprints)
Refactoring	Invariants Extension Points structure Extension manifest structure Extension states enum Defaults (validators, status codes, header values) Extension points Pre/post-filter rules	1
Code instrumentation, Monitoring & Tracing	Extension flow Logging Collect metrics (return code counts, processing time) Errors logging Perform Health checks	1
TOTAL	...	8

Table 2.4: ADF implementation work breakdown for the reference ADF (UI Extensions Framework)

Important note

The work breakdown structure, described in *Table 2.4*, can only be used for estimates. It is not the implementation plan because we need an evolutionary approach for extracting the ADF. To support the evolutionary case, we perform ADF development as part of existing software product refactoring in an agile way with short iterations, taking tasks in a suitable order according to ADF team priorities. At the same time, the work breakdown still provides valid estimates of the total efforts that need to be invested here.

As you can see from the example tables, our formula takes the following values:

- $N_{Features} = 10$ – as we mentioned, we expected at least ten new Extensions coming soon;
- $E_{Before} = 3$ – we know that we needed three team-sprints on average from our previous experience of implementing Extensions without custom ADF;
- $E_{After} = 1$ – from Table 2.2; please note that we converted 40 worker-hours to 1 team-sprint to have consistent measurement units; planning and making estimations are not in scope of this book, but we would suggest to avoid relying solely on expertise of a single engineer but instead apply more advanced techniques like PERT analysis (`https://en.wikipedia.org/wiki/Program_evaluation_and_review_technique`).
- $E_{ADF} = 8$ – from the Table 2.4;
- $E_{Adopt} = 4$ – includes migration of 8 existing Extensions, getting feedback from product teams, conducting learning sessions.

The final calculation of the ROI according to our formula can be found below:

$$ROI_{ADF} = N_{Features} \cdot \frac{(E_{Before} - E_{After})}{(E_{ADF} + E_{Adopt})} = 10 * (3 - 1) / (8 + 4) = \mathbf{1.67}$$

We can also revert the formula and find the minimal number of Extensions we need to add to the product to break even (**ROI**$_{ADF}$ should be equal or greater than 1):

$$N_{Features} = \frac{(E_{ADF} + E_{Adopt})}{(E_{Before} - E_{After})} = (8 + 4) / (3 - 1) = \mathbf{6}$$

To summarize the reference case, we can say that the ROI appeared to have a value higher than one, which means we have economic justification for building our application development framework. In addition to the economic efficiency of the ADF, we achieved multiple non-substantial benefits, like architecture guardrails, improved developers' experience, and better testability.

Shift towards Open Source Software paradigm

We haven't planned to open-source our reference ADF (UI Extensions framework) due to its very specific purpose and tight integrations with internal subsystems like Entitlement management and Identity management services. However, if we continue driving the framework towards its ideal state, we will definitely take a step towards making it Open-Source Software. The motivation behind this intention is not only making someone's life better. Such a decision is also a very pragmatic one due to the following potential benefits that we could achieve with the OSS approach.

Increased innovation and collaboration

By opening up our framework to the broader developer community, we invite a diverse group of talented individuals to contribute. This can lead to new features, bug fixes, and enhancements that we might not have thought of internally. The collaborative nature of OSS often leads to more innovative solutions and rapid development cycles.

Enhanced security

Open-source software benefits from the scrutiny of a global community. With more eyes on the code, potential vulnerabilities can be identified and patched more quickly than in a closed-source environment. This proactive approach to security can significantly reduce the risk of breaches and other security incidents. Please note that you need proper security controls in place and treat a feedback from open-source community as an additional and optional layer of security. However, we wouldn't recommend exposing a business-critical code to the OSS community: you likely won't accept a community contribution here so there are no benefits for you, but at the same time you give away information that can be used against your interests. Fortunately, by its nature, ADF is rarely business-critical but rather productivity-focused.

Cost efficiency

Developing and maintaining software can be expensive. By leveraging the contributions from the open-source community, we can reduce our development costs. This includes savings on development time, resources, and the potential reduction in licensing fees for third-party components if open-source alternatives are adopted.

Improved quality and reliability

Open source projects often undergo rigorous peer review and testing from a wide range of users and developers, employing a wide variety of environments and addressing a broader range of use cases. This collective effort can lead to higher-quality code and more reliable software. It also means that there is a chance that many potential bugs in your ADF can be found without affecting your users.

Technological brand, community, and ecosystem building

Open-sourcing our framework can help build a strong community around it. This community can provide support, create plugins, extensions, and integrations, and advocate for the framework. A vibrant ecosystem can increase the framework's adoption and make it the go-to solution in its niche.

Talent attraction and retention

Contributing to open-source projects can be a significant draw for top talent. Developers often want to work on projects that are visible and impactful. By open-sourcing our framework, we can attract skilled developers who are passionate about contributing to open-source projects and retaining them by providing opportunities to work on innovative solutions.

Market positioning and reputation

Open-sourcing our framework can enhance our company's reputation in the industry. It demonstrates our commitment to transparency, collaboration, and the advancement of technology. This can position us as leaders in our field and build trust with customers, partners, and the developer community. In the case of startups, it also positively affects investor relations.

Please note that there is also a potential risk of damaging your reputation if the framework you open-sourced is below community standards.

Interoperability and standards

Open-source projects often adhere to open standards, making ensuring interoperability with other systems and platforms easier. This can increase the utility and flexibility of our framework, making it more attractive to a broader audience.

Efficient technical problem resolution

When issues arise, the open-source community can be quick to respond with solutions. This collective problem-solving approach can lead to faster resolution times compared to relying solely on an internal team. It doesn't mean the community can assist you in the incident response process or find the root cause of downtime. It is more about finding long-term scalability bottlenecks, resource consumption inefficiency, or other issues with your architecture.

Educational value

Open-source projects serve as valuable learning resources for developers. By making our framework open source, we contribute to the education and skill development of the broader developer community, fostering a culture of continuous learning and improvement. At the same time, your newly hired developers can experience better onboarding by exploring your OSS ADF or even becoming experts in your ADF far before being hired by your company.

Regulatory and compliance benefits

Some industries and regions have regulations that favor or even mandate the use of open-source software for its transparency and flexibility. Open-sourcing our framework can help us comply with these requirements and gain a competitive edge in such markets.

In conclusion, transitioning our reference ADF towards an open-source model aligns with both our altruistic and pragmatic goals. The multitude of benefits, ranging from innovation and security to cost efficiency and community building, make a compelling case for embracing the open-source paradigm. This strategic shift can not only enhance the framework itself but also solidify our standing in the industry as forward-thinking leaders committed to fostering an open, collaborative, and innovative technological landscape.

Summary

By incorporating essential principles of Systems Engineering into our ADF development process, we can significantly enhance our ability to meet stakeholder expectations and deliver successful systems. Systems Engineering provides us with valuable concepts such as the operations environment, system lifecycle, and lifecycle model. These concepts enable us to identify and measure the value that ADF brings to the **Software Development Life Cycle (SDLC)**, addressing key stakeholders' concerns effectively.

This chapter advocates for an evolutionary approach to creating a new ADF, aiming for optimal **Return on Investment (ROI)** and smooth adoption. We explored both the tangible and intangible benefits of building your own ADF, supported by a detailed ROI calculation formula based on a reference case from the authors' previous experience with the UI Extensions framework.

To ensure accuracy in our estimates, we proposed using two fundamental models: the "method of work" and the "technological flow" models presented in table format. We also discussed the "ideal state" for every ADF, which involves embracing the **Open Source Software (OSS)** paradigm.

By aligning with the OSS model, we can reap numerous benefits, including increased innovation and collaboration, enhanced security, cost efficiency, improved quality and reliability, community and ecosystem building, talent attraction and retention, market positioning, and reputation, interoperability and standards, rapid problem resolution, educational value, and regulatory and compliance advantages.

In conclusion, integrating Systems Engineering principles and adopting the OSS paradigm can drive the development of a robust and valuable ADF, ensuring successful outcomes and stakeholder satisfaction.

In the next chapter, we get deeper into ADF structure patterns and maturity model to get more suitable tools to deal with estimates, planning and architecture design work.

Unlock this book's exclusive benefits now

Scan this QR code or go to packtpub.com/unlock, then search for this book by name. Ensure it's the correct edition.

Note: Keep your purchase invoice ready before you start.

3

Application Development Framework Blueprint

Every successful **Application Development Framework (ADF)** follows specific logical patterns. A blueprint is a detailed plan or guide that outlines these patterns, ensuring that developers can build their Frameworks systematically and efficiently.

In the context of ADFs, a blueprint is an essential tool for several reasons. It provides a clear and structured approach to Framework development, reducing the complexity and potential for errors. By following a well-defined blueprint, developers can ensure consistency, maintainability, and scalability in their applications.

This chapter introduces the **ADF blueprint**, a comprehensive guide that leverages the **ADF Canvas** visualization tool. The ADF Canvas allows developers to visualize the Framework's components and their interactions, making it easier to understand and implement the necessary patterns.

We begin by exploring the model's context, giving you a foundational understanding of the Framework's environment and requirements. Next, we introduce a maturity model that can be a valuable supporting tool in defining the path to the ADF target state. The subsequent section presents examples of a completed Canvas, offering a concrete reference to help you grasp the model's structure, functionality, and maturity levels. Finally, we provide a step-by-step guide to the best practices for filling out the Canvas, empowering you to create your own robust and efficient ADF.

By the end of this chapter, you will have a solid understanding of the ADF blueprint and be well equipped to apply these principles to your development projects, leading to more successful and sustainable outcomes.

In this chapter, we're going to cover the following main topics:

- ADF structure patterns
- ADF maturity model
- ADF Canvas guide

ADF structure patterns

This is the final chapter of the book's first part, and it aims to complete the theoretical foundation of Framework building. In software engineering, a blueprint helps us avoid unnecessary efforts in architecture design. It works as a checklist, preventing easy mistakes of unaccounted requirements and missed elements. A blueprint gives a complete, ideal-world structure for any Framework, allowing engineers to cherry-pick necessary elements from it according to their target maturity level and available investments.

We will start by defining the ADF's internal substructures one by one, starting with organizational flow patterns.

From the previous chapter, we know that the primary purpose of the ADF is to improve an engineering organization's productivity and performance by providing a standardized and simplified way to perform one or multiple engineering operations, such as the following:

- Adding a web view to a web application (web Frameworks such as Django or Ruby on Rails)
- Adding a REST API endpoint to a backend (FastAPI)
- Adding an AI agent to an LLM-powered system (LangChain)
- Building a new extension/widget into a host application (such as proprietary UI Extensions Framework that we will use as an example in further chapters)

So, the initial decision that ADF developers need to make is about the decoupling pattern, allowing optimal control over the entity/object life cycle.

Entity/object definition

The flow always has a reference to the primary entity/object (or multiple objects in the case of a complex Framework). In the list of previous examples, we have objects such as *web page*, *REST API endpoint*, *AI agent*, and *extension*.

The ADF expects the application developer to deliver a definition of this entity so that the implemented product flow will perform all the intended steps.

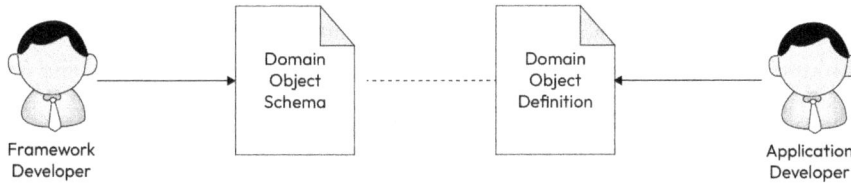

Figure 3.1: Domain object definition structure

As shown in the diagram, both **Framework Developer** and **Application Developer** take care of the same object, but on different levels of abstraction. The Framework cares about a whole class of objects while the application focuses on object instances. This definition can be made in different ways, depending on the complexity of the domain object and Framework maturity. It can be either a simple object defined in the programming language or a complex hierarchical structure defined by a manifesto in the configuration description language, such as YAML or JSON. A more detailed explanation will be covered in *Chapters 5* and *6*.

An application developer could make an entity/object definition by using different methods and techniques, including the following:

- Programmatically via inheritance
- Programmatically via implementing interface
- Declaratively via DSL

Adding a new entity to the system may be accompanied by additional validation and certain actions to change the configuration. To ensure entity/object definition quality, schema-based constraints can be applied by a Framework developer in a way available in a given programming language and technical stack, such as the following:

- Throwing "not implemented" exceptions from the base class
- Declaring mandatory methods
- Declarative schema structure in the XSD or JSON format

After defining this entity/object, we expect the application developer to register it for execution with the ADF control flow.

For more complex entities/objects, ADF developers can introduce a decoupled definition with well-known architecture patterns as a guardrail. The following are the most popular patterns that serve such a purpose.

Model-View-Controller

The **Model-View-Controller** (**MVC**) pattern allows the Framework user to define object data as a Model, object representation as a View, and object behavior as a Controller. This kind of *decoupled object* definition has improved testability, allows the use of layered architecture, and provides a wide range of variations to support all possible use cases. It is primarily used in web and mobile Frameworks; however, Model-View-Presenter can be more suitable in mobile-native projects. You can learn more about MVC and its variations on the internet.

The **Hierarchical Model-View-Controller** (**HMVC**) pattern is an extension of the traditional MVC pattern, designed to handle the complexities of large-scale applications. It introduces a hierarchy of MVC triads, allowing each component to function independently within its own MVC context. This pattern emerged to address the limitations of the traditional MVC architecture when dealing with complex, modular applications. HMVC is supported by Frameworks such as Kohana and CodeIgniter in PHP.

Model-View-Presenter

An alternative name for **Model-View-Presenter** (**MVP**) is **Model-View-ViewModel** (**MVVM**). It is an advanced version of MVC, providing more granular logic and better abstraction between Model and View. The main difference with MVC is a natively supported, bidirectional data binding, provided by a ViewModel in MVVM, allowing to avoid potentially extensive code in a Controller component. That leads to even better testability than in MVC, making it more suitable for larger, enterprise-grade projects. Primarily used in application platforms that support rich client interfaces, such as WPF, Silverlight, Xamarin, and more recently, in web development Frameworks such as Angular, MVVM excels in environments where the **user interface** (**UI**) is data-driven and complex interactions need to be managed without excessive coupling between the UI and its underlying data logic.

There is also MVVM-C, which is a variation of MVVM that adds a Coordinator to the mix. The Coordinator is responsible for handling navigation between different screens or views within the application. This pattern is useful for applications that have multiple screens or views that need to be managed.

Model-View-Template

Model-View-Template (**MVT**) became popular due to the Python Django Framework. It is very close to MVC, but the Controller part is almost entirely handled by the Framework itself, providing an even simpler and more minimalistic way to define the UI for ADF users.

Beyond widely used patterns such as MVC and MVVM, there are several other specialized architectural patterns, such as **Presentation-Abstraction-Control (PAC)**, **View-Interactor-Presenter-Entity-Router (VIPER)**, and **FLUX**. These patterns address specific needs in particular domains, such as PAC for interactive systems, VIPER for iOS application development, and FLUX for managing state in JavaScript applications.

Entity/object registration

This entity must be **registered** somehow in the Framework for subsequent use.

Registration pattern

The **Registration pattern** is a cornerstone of any Framework and, by extension, a platform (as discussed in more detail later in this chapter). The core reason for its significance lies in the fact that a Framework – or platform – governs the control flow of an application. To integrate with this control flow, developers must *register* custom application extensions, such as entities, plugins, or processors. This registration process is essential for extending and customizing the application's functionality within the Framework's predefined structure.

Note the vital difference between a Framework and a platform: the Registration pattern in Frameworks occurs in design time and requires additional steps (compile, build, and deploy) to start bringing value, while in platforms, there is usually a runtime registration API, console interface, or UI that doesn't require any additional coding steps to work. As an example, the provisioning of a message schema to a managed Kafka broker doesn't require a platform to rebuild Kafka and reprovision its instance.

In an ideal scenario, adding a new entity to a Framework should be highly automated and require minimal user effort. The Framework's designers should strive to encapsulate unnecessary complexity within a simple, user-friendly interface. One typical example of such an interface is **inheritance**, frequently used in Framework design across various programming languages. In this approach, a base class manages all necessary actions for entity registration, along with any supplementary operations.

However, inheritance is not the sole method for registering entities within a Framework. Alternatives include directly manipulating configuration files, registering entities via source code, using an annotation/decorator, or placing an entity/object definition file within the appropriate repository structure. This pattern extends the basic definition one.

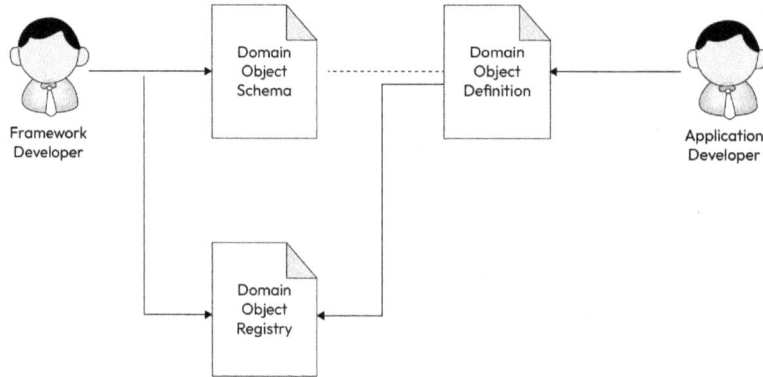

Figure 3.2: Core entity/object registration

🔍 Quick tip: Need to see a high-resolution version of this image? Open this book in the next-gen Packt Reader or view it in the PDF/ePub copy.

🔒 The next-gen Packt Reader and a free PDF/ePub copy of this book are included with your purchase. Scan the QR code OR visit packtpub.com/unlock, then use the search bar to find this book by name. Double-check the edition shown to make sure you get the right one.

The registry is usually a black box to the application developer, so it is visualized in a diagram as the Framework-side concept. Consider examples of implementation of this pattern in some well-known Frameworks:

- **Django** (Python-based web ADF) handles multiple types of core entities:
- Define and register the app entity: Use the "create app" management command
- Define and register the view entity: Write a function in views.py with the HttpRequest object as input and HttpResponse as output; register it by adding a route to urls.py

- Define and register the data model entity: Write a class in `models.py`; register it in the control flow by referring to it in a view method

React.js (web component life cycle):

- Define the component by creating a class or a function that renders your component; register it by importing the JS file with your component from your web application
- Proprietary Framework example: Content personalization Framework (adds web content that should be rendered only for a specific user segment):

Define the content entity/object as an HTML snippet in a file in the repository

Adding and registering a new domain entity/object allows application developers to adapt a Framework to their domain. However, to adjust a generic control flow provided by the Framework to fit application requirements, application developers often need to adjust the control flow by adding or changing Framework processors.

The same is true for a case when ADF developers apply a distributed definition via architectural patterns such as MVC, MVVM/MVP, or MVT. We have separate registration for each aspect, provided by a base class or dependency injection mechanism.

Managing object processors

A domain object that has been added and registered in the Framework will then be used in the control flow by the Framework itself. The Framework executes all necessary operations over the object to achieve essential outcomes designed by the ADF developer; it might be a rendered web application page, an AI agent ready to handle requests, a UI component, and so on. However, any good ADF allows application developers to adjust the processing performed by the Framework without editing the Framework's core implementation. There are two major ways to make such adjustments:

- Core flow modifications allow to change the critical path. Depending on the core flow flexibility and Framework maturity, these kinds of modifications are usually made by applying the Pipeline pattern with pluggable steps.
- As an alternative, the Pre/Post Processing pattern allows the definition of any custom logic before and after the main processing. Some examples of core flow modifiers might be custom serializers, tokenizers, data enrichment, dynamic validators, and so on.

One example of pre/post processing is the .NET MVC Framework, which provides an interface to set custom handlers for pre- and post-events of the core entity life cycle.

The Pre/Post Processing pattern provides a simple interface for core flow adjustments.

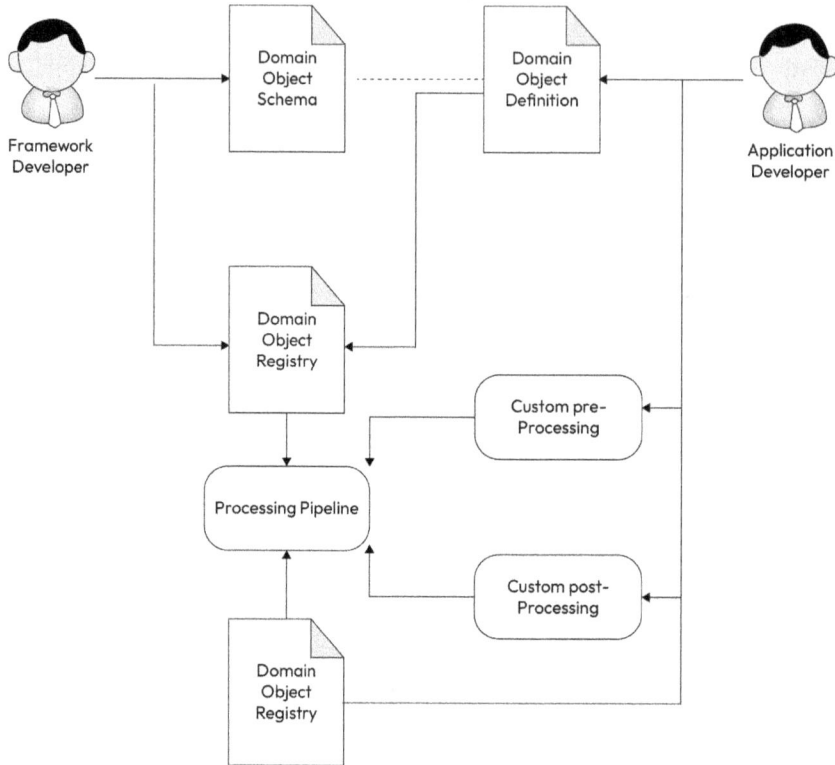

Figure 3.3: Core flow adjustments with the Pre/Post Processing pattern

However, a more mature implementation can be delivered with a Processing Pipeline pattern, allowing more control and granularity over the main flow (see *Figure 3.4*).

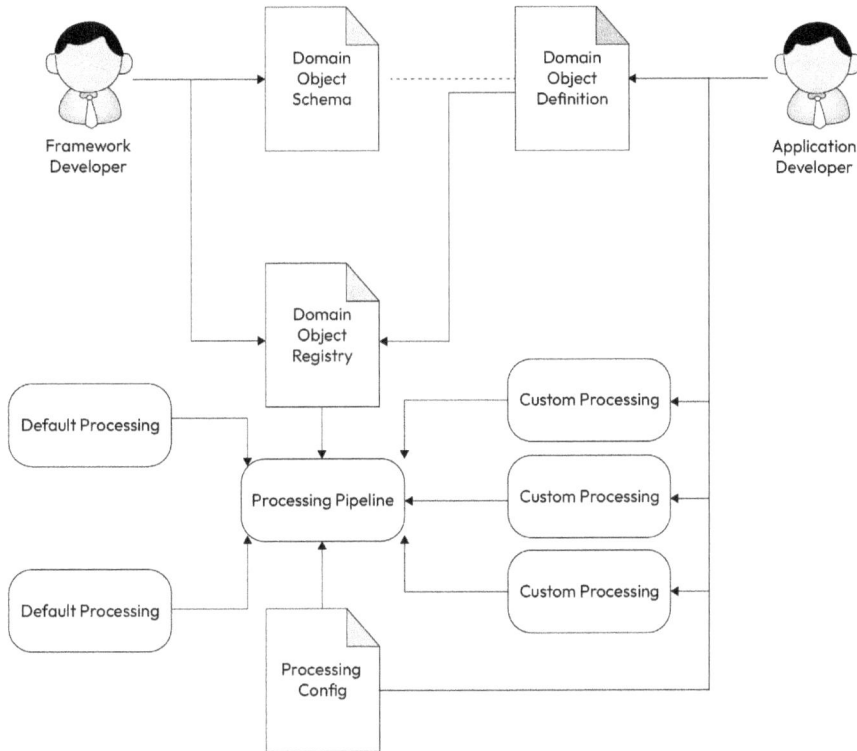

Figure 3.4: Core flow adjustments with a Processing Pipeline pattern

The previous diagram demonstrates a separation of responsibilities between a Framework developer and an application developer. The pipeline itself, its default processors, and the config are on the Framework side, while application-specific processors are on the application side. Here are some examples of an adjustable core flow in existing Frameworks:

Django has middleware to manage the request processing flow:

- Define: Implement required interface methods, or better, use `MiddlewareMixin` as a base class to have a schema of processing steps in your custom code
- Register: Add to a **MIDDLEWARE** setting in the `settings.py` file

Express.js (web Framework based on Node.js) uses a similar way to extend a request processing pipeline:

- Define: Write a function with a predefined signature (req, res, or next)
- Register: Invoke `app.use()` with your middleware function as a parameter

Ruby on Rails:

- Define: Declare a class with a `call` method
- Register: Invoke `config.middleware.insert` with your middleware class as a parameter

Here, we also have the opportunity to apply the **Data-Context-Interaction** (**DCI**) pattern (see `https://www.artima.com/articles/the-dci-architecture-a-new-vision-of-object-oriented-programming` for details). This pattern decouples the system behavior algorithm (the flow) from the domain objects, opposite to the classic **object-oriented programming** (**OOP**) paradigm.

Beyond registration, the Manage Object Processors pattern enables further customization of the Framework's control flow. Developers can modify or extend the core flow using techniques such as the Pre/Post Processing pattern or the Processing Pipeline pattern. Additional adjustments by functional plugins allow for more tailored application behavior, enhancing both **user experience** (**UX**) and **developer experience** (**DevX**) without altering the core Framework implementation.

Extending by functional plugins

These plugins (also known as extensions) structures serve as core flow extensions, aiming to keep the critical path as is but making minor improvements in UX or DevX. Good examples of UX-driven extensions can be the addition of user notifications or progress indicators. DevX extensions could include custom loggers, monitoring modules, domain event triggers, and so on.

Both core flow adjustment patterns can also be used to deliver UX and DevX extensions. Still, it is usually considered an anti-pattern due to the significant difference in processing criticality and SLO between the core flow and plugins; Framework developers should limit possible core flow modification by providing dedicated extension interfaces for UX and DevX purposes only. For example, there might be the following enhancement extension interfaces offered by the ADF developers:

- Notifications
- Event triggers
- Logging
- Monitoring

A good example of applying the Plugin pattern to one of the well-known OSS Frameworks is ASP. NET Core. The ILogger and IHealthCheck interfaces allow custom implementation that should be registered in app settings and `Program.cs` (where applicable).

The following is the visualization of the proposed structure.

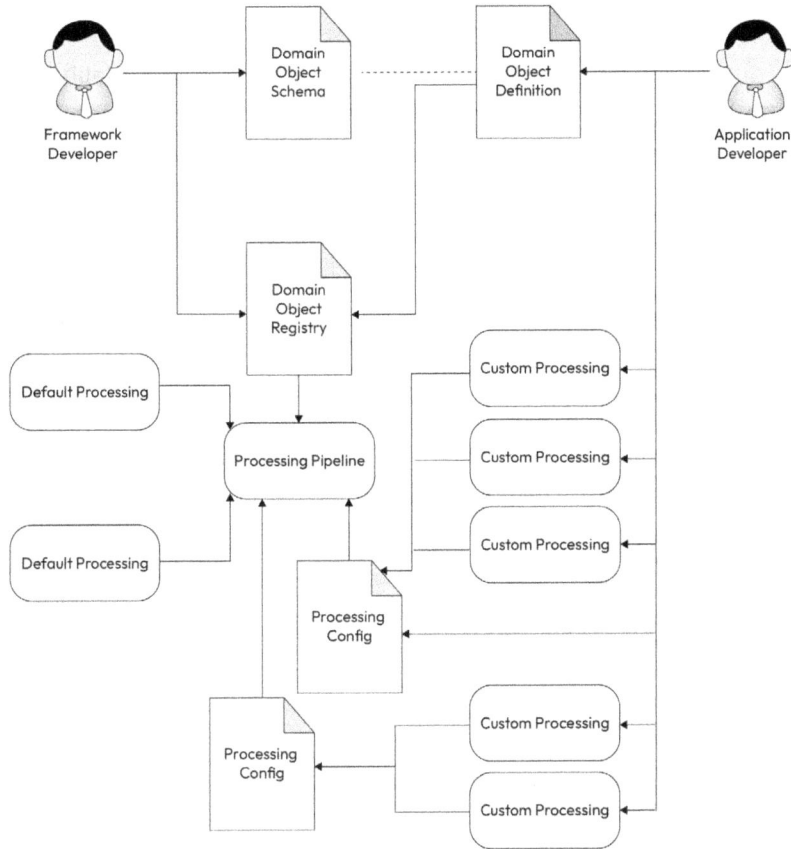

Figure 3.5: Control flow extensions, added by the application developer as plugins

The previous visualization suggests that plugins are integrated with the pipeline, but in a way that differs from the core processing integration. ADF developers can provide additional value with their Framework by building "out-of-the-box" object processors and plugins that can be used without additional effort. It also works in both directions if ADF is exposed as open source software, providing access to community-driven development of an even broader range of object processors and plugins.

Once implemented, these plugins must be registered within the Framework, following a similar registration pattern to what we discussed in the *Entity/object registration* and *Managing object processors* sections. This pattern is essential for integrating custom application extensions, allowing the Framework to manage control flow efficiently. Notably, registration can occur during design time in Frameworks or via platform runtime APIs.

Technical flow pattern

This part of the ADF blueprint is focused on a Framework's runtime execution. The ADF developer should assume a standard project configuration at its baseline, with default entities/objects registered and a default processing pipeline configured. For this setup, the developer must ensure that the system can operate at a production-level quality, covering performance, load tolerance, scalability, traceability, availability, and other critical qualities (often referred to as "-ilities") depending on the developer's goals. This runtime quality is specified by the "glue" code, which is often invisible to end users of the ADF but is crucial to the overall stability and efficiency of the system. Hence, this part of the ADF requires careful attention in the blueprint and involves its own set of architectural patterns.

While these patterns may not directly impact the application developer's experience during the design phase, they are critical to the evaluation of the ADF itself. The quality of the technical flow execution is a significant factor in determining whether the Framework is fit for purpose. These patterns are essential for ADF developers to organize and structure the "hidden" components that perform the runtime jobs, ensuring smooth and efficient operation.

In general, this part of the ADF blueprint aligns with standard principles of software architecture design, such as the following:

- **Separation of concerns**: Ensuring each part of the system has a distinct responsibility
- **Modularity**: Building a system composed of interchangeable and independently functioning modules
- **Standards and best practices**: Adhering to widely accepted coding standards and architectural best practices
- **Runtime quality assurance**: Continuously validating and improving the performance, security, and reliability of the system

The following are some of the key patterns in this context:

- **Configurator**: The Configurator pattern deals with managing the system's runtime configuration, which may include the object registry, the processing setup, and the state of various plugins. Depending on the maturity of your ADF, this configuration can be static (e.g., JSON or YAML files stored in a code repository), dynamic (e.g., coded functions or services that generate configuration at runtime), or a hybrid approach (e.g., a configuration service API that combines static and dynamic aspects).

- **Transformer**: The Transformer pattern is responsible for interpreting user-defined object definitions in a way that the Framework can understand and process. It involves various operations such as serialization and deserialization, type casting, and mapping user object fields to standardized message schemas. As the complexity of the Framework grows, so does the need for sophisticated transformation logic to handle diverse data formats and structures.

- **Data binding**: Data binding refers to the technique of connecting UI elements (such as input fields, text boxes, and dropdowns) directly to the underlying data model, allowing for automatic updates and synchronization. In an ADF, data binding is responsible for managing how data flows from the application's data layer to its presentation layer and vice versa. The primary goal of data binding is to reduce the amount of boilerplate code required for manual data manipulation and event handling, thereby enhancing developer productivity and ensuring a more responsive UI. Let's look into the following variations of this pattern that are available:

  1. **One-way data binding**

     - In this approach, the data flows in a single direction, usually from the data model to the UI components. However, one-way data flow is also possible in the opposite direction, from View to Model (e.g., in the case of sign-up form implementation). Changes in the data model are reflected in the UI, but not the other way around. This is suitable for scenarios where the UI needs to display read-only data or where user input is not required to modify the underlying data.

       Example use case: Displaying a list of products fetched from a server. The UI shows the products, but any changes made to the product data in the backend are not reflected in the list unless it is explicitly re-fetched.

  2. **Two-way data binding**

     - Two-way data binding establishes a bidirectional link between the data model and the UI components. Any change in the data model is automatically reflected in the UI, and vice versa. This type of binding is ideal for interactive applications where user input directly impacts the application's state.

       Example use case: A form where users can edit their profile information. Any change in the input fields is immediately reflected in the data model, and any programmatic change to the model updates the UI.

3. **One-time data binding**

- This is a variant of one-way data binding where the data is bound to the UI components only once, typically at the time of the component's initialization. The UI does not reflect any changes in the data model after the initial binding.

  Example use case: Displaying static data that does not change over the course of the application's lifetime, such as a terms and conditions statement.

There are several mechanisms and techniques for data binding that ADF developers can consider implementing, depending on its criticality, the Framework's maturity, and other possible constraints:

- **Declarative binding**

  - This involves using markup languages (such as HTML or XML) with special attributes or directives to define data bindings directly in the UI templates. This method is common in Frameworks that support declarative syntax, such as Angular or Vue.js.

    Example: `<input type="text" [value]="user.name">` in Angular binds the `user.name` property to the input's value.

- **Imperative binding**

  - This involves using programmatic methods (such as JavaScript functions or APIs) to establish data bindings. This approach offers more flexibility and control, but can lead to more verbose code.

    Example: JavaScript code that manually sets the input field's value based on the data model: `document.getElementById('name').value = user.name;`.

ADF developers should also consider binding context and scope localization to find a balance between technical quality and applicability. Understanding the context in which data binding occurs is crucial for effective implementation. The binding context defines which data model properties are accessible from a given part of the UI. For example, in Frameworks such as React, the binding context is typically the component state or props.

Finally, the following are some advanced techniques for implementing data binding in ADF:

- **Optimize data flow:** Leverage efficient data-binding strategies that minimize unnecessary data updates, such as avoiding two-way binding when not required or using change detection techniques to reduce overhead. Overuse of data binding, especially two-way binding, can lead to performance bottlenecks in large applications due to excessive DOM updates and change detection cycles.

- **Use observables and reactive programming:** Employ observables (e.g., RxJS in Angular) and reactive patterns to handle data flow in a more controlled and predictable manner, especially for complex or asynchronous data sources.

- **Virtual DOM and diffing algorithms:** For Frameworks such as React, data binding is optimized using a virtual DOM. Changes to the data model do not directly alter the real DOM; instead, they update a virtual representation, which is then compared (or "diffed") against the actual DOM to apply the minimal number of changes.

- **Data binding with WebSockets:** Real-time data binding can be achieved using WebSockets to push updates from the server to the client, ensuring the UI reflects the most current state of the data model.

Data binding is a powerful tool within an ADF, reducing the amount of code needed to synchronize the UI and data model while enhancing responsiveness and UX. However, using data binding judiciously is essential, considering the application's performance requirements and complexity. Properly implemented, data binding can significantly streamline application development and maintenance, making it a foundational element of modern software architectures.

Data flow

Data flow refers to the communication components that dictate how data is exchanged within and between applications. These patterns play a crucial role in ensuring that the application's architecture can manage the data flow effectively, which is pivotal for achieving responsiveness, efficiency, and scalability in distributed systems. The following aspects define the data flow:

Protocols and contracts (REST, GraphQL, gRPC/Protobuf, etc.): These define standard ways for components to communicate, ensuring that applications can exchange data reliably and understand each other's data formats. REST excels in defining a data objects's life cycle (e.g., CRUD, state updates). GraphQL is the best tool for complex data hierarchies that allow trusted clients to specify exactly what data they need. gRPC is well suited for imperative communication (e.g., a remote procedure call), combining high performance, schema portability, and manageability by using Protobuf for efficient binary serialization.

Command Query Responsibility Segregation (CQRS): This pattern separates read and write operations for data storage. It allows a system to scale more effectively by optimizing read operations separately from write operations, which can be particularly beneficial in systems where read and write patterns differ significantly.

- **Publish/Subscribe (Pub/Sub)**: This pattern allows messages to be broadcast asynchronously to multiple subscribers. It simplifies the messaging system and decouples the message sender from its receivers, enabling scalable and dynamic communication scenarios.

- **Message queue**: This implements a queue system where messages are stored until they are processed. It is crucial for managing asynchronous communication in systems where operations or data processing are not required to be in real time, but must ensure reliability and consistency of data delivery. It also enables an **event-driven architecture (EDA)** approach to the system design.

- **Batch Processing**: This pattern accumulates data or tasks and processes them collectively: by explicit command, or at scheduled intervals, or once a certain threshold is reached. Batch processing is ideal for efficiently handling large volumes of data where real-time processing isn't required. It enhances system performance by reducing overhead associated with individual item processing, providing predictable resource utilization, and improving throughput for operations such as bulk data imports, exports, report generation, and data transformations.

- **Streaming**: This pattern continuously processes data in real time as it's generated or received. Unlike batch processing, streaming provides immediate processing, enabling timely analytics, monitoring, and rapid responses. It's essential for applications that require real-time data insights, such as event monitoring, fraud detection, real-time analytics, and live data feeds. Streaming architectures typically leverage technologies such as Apache Kafka, Apache Flink, and AWS Kinesis to manage high-throughput, low-latency data flows efficiently. Streaming can also be closely integrated with event sourcing, where changes in application state are captured as a sequence of events, enabling real-time state reconstruction, audit trails, and enhanced system observability.

Error handling and recovery

Another critical aspect of the technical flow pattern is the error handling and recovery subsystem. This pattern focuses on how the Framework deals with unexpected conditions or failures during runtime. An ADF should offer a robust mechanism for error detection, logging, notification, and recovery to maintain high availability and reliability.

Key functions of the error handling and recovery pattern can include the following elements:

- **Error detection and logging**: Identifying errors promptly and logging them with sufficient detail to aid debugging

- **Error propagation**: Deciding whether errors should bubble up through the system or be contained locally

- **Retry strategies**: Implementing configurable strategies for retrying failed operations, such as exponential backoff or immediate retries

- **Fallback mechanisms**: Providing alternative methods or paths when a primary function fails, such as switching to a backup service or using cached data

- **Circuit breaker**: Temporarily halting the execution of failing operations to prevent cascading failures across the system

By incorporating these patterns, the ADF ensures resilience and reliability, allowing applications built on the Framework to handle real-world scenarios gracefully.

Source code structuring

The final implementation of an ADF that correctly integrates all the patterns mentioned earlier may include dozens or even hundreds of code files. It's essential for the ADF developer to keep in mind that their Framework will be integrated into real-world software projects as part of a larger ecosystem. This means all source files of your ADF will coexist in a project repository alongside domain-specific code and potentially even other Frameworks. Therefore, the source code structure of your ADF should be treated as a specialized form of UI; it is a crucial touchpoint for developers who will use, extend, manage, and troubleshoot the project based on your Framework.

The following are the principles of effective source code structuring:

- **Clarity and readability**: Your source code should be organized in a way that is immediately understandable to developers from the targeted domain. This includes using meaningful directory names, clear module separation, and consistent naming conventions. The goal is to minimize the cognitive load on developers when they navigate the project.

  Example: Group files based on functionality (e.g., core, plugins, utils, etc.) and ensure that the directory hierarchy reflects the Framework's logical structure. For instance, placing all serialization functions in a dedicated folder helps developers quickly find and understand auxiliary code.

- **Modularity and encapsulation:** Follow the principles of modularity and encapsulation to ensure that each module or component is responsible for a single concern. This makes the Framework easier to extend, test, and maintain.

  Example: If your ADF includes data transformation and configuration management functionalities, consider placing them in separate modules such as transformers and configurators.

- **Consistency with industry standards:** Align the code structure of your ADF with well-known industry standards and practices, particularly those that are familiar to the target developer audience. Avoid creating a unique or unconventional structure unless there is a clear and documented rationale.

  Example: For frontend Frameworks, follow common directory conventions such as src for source files, components for UI components, services for API integrations, and so on.

Ease of navigation and discoverability

Make it easy for developers to find the files they need to extend or modify. This involves organizing code into clearly defined categories and providing documentation or a guide explaining each folder's purpose and key file.

For example, include a `README.md` file in each central directory, briefly describing its contents and purpose.

Minimal dependencies

Aim to minimize dependencies between different parts of the Framework to reduce coupling and improve maintainability. Ideally, each module or component should be able to function independently or with minimal interaction with others.

For example, avoid tightly coupling your data processing logic with UI components. Instead, use well-defined interfaces or events for communication between disparate parts of the Framework.

Source code availability

As an additional note on ADF adaptability, depending on how your Framework is delivered, the code structure may be partially or fully *squished* by tools such as code minifiers, obfuscators, or package managers – this is especially relevant for frontend web Frameworks such as React and Angular. Despite this, the best practice and development etiquette suggests that a complete source code (even if minified or obfuscated) should be available to users.

For open source Frameworks, provide a clear, easy-to-navigate source code structure that encourages community contributions and fosters collaboration. Use tools such as ESLint and Prettier for consistent coding styles.

Other recommendations and best practices

The following are related suggestions that aren't directly mapped to the Framework architecture, but aim to help in making the Framework development process easier for the Framework developer role:

- **Extract from real-life projects**: The most intuitive source code structures often come from real-life successful projects. Consider using these as a base for your Framework's structure. This will make it easier for developers already familiar with specific patterns to adopt and use your ADF.

  Example: If you are building a Framework for financial applications, examine the code structures of leading financial software projects to identify common patterns and organization strategies.

  > **Note**
  >
  > Please note that here, we discuss a functional structure (one based on a finance subdomain) rather than the technical structure we mentioned in the *Consistency with industry standards* paragraph. Such a functional structure is independent of the technical one, and ADF developers can use any of them as a primary structure. However, for a domain-specific Framework, it is suggested to use a functional structure as the primary one, so each domain-specific folder will have a full set of tech subfolders such as models, components, utils, API, and so on.

- **Document your structure**: Documentation is crucial. Provide detailed guides that describe the organization of your code base, including the purpose of each folder and any dependencies between modules. This will help developers quickly understand how to use and extend the Framework.

  Example: Maintain an up-to-date `architecture.md` file that outlines the Framework's structure, key modules, and their relationships.

- **Enable source code accessibility**: Regardless of whether your Framework follows an open source or proprietary model, ensure the source code is accessible to its users. For internal Frameworks, provide access to the complete source code within the organization to allow for debugging, custom extensions, and internal enhancements.

By adopting these best practices for source code structuring, you create a developer-friendly, maintainable, and scalable environment. The source code structure becomes integral to the Framework's UX, directly influencing how easily developers can adopt, extend, and contribute to your ADF. A well-organized code base reduces friction and increases the overall value and appeal of your Framework in the software development community.

ADF maturity model

A **maturity model for an ADF (ADF MM)** provides a structured path for the evolution of the Framework from its initial concept to a fully mature and robust system. As with any software product, an ADF must grow in capability, quality, and resilience to meet the increasing demands of its users and the broader development community. A maturity model helps Framework developers assess their current state, identify gaps, and plan incremental improvements to achieve a higher level of maturity.

Here are some key reasons why a maturity model is essential for ADFs:

- **Guiding continuous improvement**: A maturity model provides a roadmap for continuous improvement, ensuring that the ADF evolves systematically rather than haphazardly. By defining specific stages of maturity, the model guides Framework developers in enhancing key attributes such as performance, scalability, security, and DevX.
- **Standardizing evaluation criteria**: With a maturity model in place, developers, organizations, and stakeholders can evaluate the quality and readiness of an ADF against standardized criteria. This helps them assess whether the Framework is suitable for production use and whether it can support the needs of complex and large-scale projects.
- **Aligning with organizational goals**: Organizations using or building a proprietary ADF can align the Framework's capabilities with their strategic goals. A maturity model helps ensure that the Framework evolves in a way that supports the organization's specific needs, such as compliance with industry standards to support growth or integration with existing systems.
- **Facilitating stakeholder communication**: A maturity model provides a clear, common language for discussing the Framework's capabilities and future direction for internal and external stakeholders. This shared understanding helps set realistic expectations, secure buy-in, and ensure that all parties are aligned in their vision for the Framework.

- **Keeping it pragmatic**: A maturity model also helps avoid over-investment in capabilities that may not be necessary or valuable to the Framework's stakeholders. By defining and focusing on the maturity levels most relevant to the current needs and strategic goals, Framework developers can prioritize investments in areas that provide the greatest benefit rather than expending resources on features or enhancements beyond the stakeholders' immediate requirements or interests. This ensures that Framework development remains cost-effective and aligned with user expectations.

- **Encouraging contribution and community engagement**: For open source ADFs, a maturity model can serve as a reference for the community to understand how their contributions can help elevate the Framework to the next level. It provides a structured way for contributors to know where they can have the most impact, whether through documentation, new features, bug fixes, or performance improvements.

There are several well-known maturity models in the software and process improvement domains that provide valuable insights into structuring an ADF maturity model. These models have proven successful in guiding organizations and software products toward higher levels of capability and quality:

- **Capability Maturity Model Integration (CMMI)**: CMMI is a process-level improvement training and appraisal program. Initially developed by the **Software Engineering Institute (SEI)** at Carnegie Mellon University, it is widely used for assessing and improving software development processes. CMMI defines five maturity levels (initial, managed, defined, quantitatively managed, and optimizing) that represent a progression from ad hoc, chaotic processes to highly structured and continuously improving processes. The CMMI Framework is particularly useful for organizations seeking to improve their process maturity to deliver software more predictably and efficiently.

- **Agile Maturity Model (AMM)**: The AMM is designed for organizations and teams adopting Agile methodologies. This model focuses on evaluating and enhancing Agile practices across various dimensions, such as team collaboration, iterative development, continuous integration, and customer feedback. This model helps organizations transition from basic Agile practices (e.g., Daily Standups and Sprint Planning) to advanced levels (e.g., continuous delivery, full test automation, and lean startup methodologies). The AMM is useful for teams aiming to measure their Agile adoption and identify areas for growth.

- **DevOps Maturity Model**: The DevOps Maturity Model evaluates the adoption of DevOps practices within an organization. It focuses on aspects such as automation, **continuous integration/continuous deployment (CI/CD)**, monitoring, and collaboration between development and operations teams. The model defines maturity levels that range from "Initial" (where DevOps practices are minimal or non-existent) to "Optimizing" (where DevOps is fully integrated into the organization's culture and processes). For ADFs, considering DevOps maturity is essential for Frameworks supporting smooth deployment, monitoring, and scaling in production environments.

- **Open Source Maturity Model (OSMM)**: The OSMM evaluates the maturity of open source projects based on criteria such as community activity, code quality, documentation, and governance. It is particularly useful for organizations considering the adoption of an open source ADF or for those developing one. The OSMM provides guidelines for assessing whether an open source Framework is reliable and sustainable in the long term.

By adopting a maturity model tailored to ADFs, developers and organizations can ensure their Frameworks grow in a structured, predictable, and sustainable manner. Learning from well-established maturity models, such as the CMM, AMM, and DevOps Maturity Model, can provide valuable insights and benchmarks in corresponding areas. We hope to achieve this with an ADF MM. Ultimately, an ADF MM helps establish a clear path for continuous improvement, adoption, and alignment with strategic goals, ensuring that the Framework remains relevant and valuable in a rapidly evolving software landscape.

ADF MM levels

Now, let's examine proposed ADF MM levels with a focus on simplicity, investment of effort, usability (ease of integration, extension, and management), and universality (ability to support a wide range of technologies or use cases).

Level 1: Unextracted

The ADF is not yet a standalone Framework. It exists only as part of a specific software project, with its control flow and functionality embedded within the container software system. The Framework is not abstracted or modularized and is tightly coupled to the particular project for which it was created.

Its characteristics are as follows:

- **Investment**: Minimal investment beyond what is necessary for the original project; the ADF is created as a byproduct of solving specific problems within that project
- **Complexity**: The source of complexity is the coupling between a Framework and a domain of the original software product; the Framework itself is simplistic due to very narrow use case support
- **Modularity**: Lacks modularity or separation; the Framework is interwoven with the existing project's code base
- **Configurability**: Minimal or non-existent configuration options; any customization requires deep knowledge of the underlying software project
- **Documentation**: Limited or no standalone documentation; instructions are typically part of the overall project documentation
- **Scope**: Only usable within the context of the existing software project; no consideration for broader applicability
- **Control flow**: Managed directly by the container application, with no distinct life cycle or runtime independence
- **Usability and DevX**: Very low usability; not designed for integration or extension outside the original project

The risks are as follows:

- Highly dependent on the original project's architecture and life cycle
- Difficult to reuse or adapt to other contexts or projects
- No scalability or flexibility beyond the initial scope

Example: An internal data handling library within a specific enterprise application, with all logic and processes tightly integrated into the application's main code base.

Level 2: Minimal viable Framework (MVF)

The ADF is designed to meet the most basic needs with minimal development effort. It is simple, with a narrow focus, and is limited to a specific use case or technology stack.

Its characteristics are as follows:

- **Investment**: Low investment in development and maintenance
- **Complexity**: Simple, lightweight, and easy to understand

- **Modularity**: Limited functionality and modularity; provides only core features
- **Configurability**: Limited configuration options
- **Documentation**: Basic documentation
- **Scope**: Usable for single or very similar applications with minimal customization
- **Control flow**: Externalized as a single monolithic module responsible for a whole technical process
- **Usability and DevX**: Low usability; requires manual steps (e.g., copy-paste sources) for integration or extension outside the original project

The risks are as follows:

- Broad focus or prioritizing future capabilities can bloat the ADF backlog
- The ADF initiative can still easily die at this stage without sponsorship due to relatively low value and narrow use case support

Example: A tiny utility Framework to handle HTTP requests within a specific internal project.

Level 3: Bulletproof Framework

The ADF introduces modular components, making it easier to extend and adapt to different contexts while maintaining a simple structure. It supports a range of use cases and technologies, balancing simplicity and flexibility with a focus on usability and ease of integration.

Its characteristics are as follows:

- **Investment**: Moderate investment in development and maintenance, focused on modularity, configurability, and documentation improvement.
- **Complexity**: Increased complexity due to additional abstraction layers introduced to support better extensibility by custom components (e.g., loggers, serializers, and processors).
- **Modularity**: Clear separation of concerns and robust extension mechanisms.
- **Configurability**: Increased configuration options, enabling limited customization.
- **Documentation**: Well-documented APIs and guidelines, and a growing set of utilities or plugins.
- **Scope**: Usable for diverse applications but still prioritizes simplicity; customizations are possible but not officially supported. It can support more than one technology in its core flow, but still cover a single application domain.

- **Control flow**: Extensible modular implementation with the default recommended implementation provided out of the box.

- **Usability and devexperience**: Designed for ease of integration and management across different projects.

The risks are as follows:

- Focus on technical improvements or features is less important at this stage than adoption. It is better to focus on documentation, packaging, and other DevX areas.

Examples: Nuxt.js (JavaScript), Kafka Connect, Express.js (JavaScript), Flask, FastAPI, and many others.

> **Note**
>
> Most proprietary Frameworks should not evolve above this level due to a decrease in **return on investment** (**ROI**) and a limited number of reuses inside a single organization.

Level 4: Advanced extensible Framework

The ADF is highly flexible, with extensive support for integration, extension, and management. It is suitable for a wide range of use cases and environments.

Its characteristics are as follows:

- **Investment**: Significant investment in development, especially in areas such as modularity, customization, and integration.

- **Complexity**: Even more abstractions introduced to cover multiple technology stacks, standards, and platforms (e.g., cloud, on-premises).

- **Modularity**: Improved testability through more granular modularity. It provides extensive APIs, hooks, and extension points.

- **Configurability**: Includes automated tools for configuration management, testing, deployment, and monitoring.

- **Documentation**: Has a library of sample projects implemented with the Framework, tutorials, community support, and an open directory of utilities, modules, and plugins.

- **Scope**: High universality; capable of supporting various technologies and complex use cases. It can span multiple application domains (e.g., web and mobile or data analysis and visualization).

- **Control flow**: Optimized processors with an advanced test harness for scalability, load tolerance, and performance.
- **Usability and DevX**: Very high usability; suitable for complex, large-scale applications and diverse environments.

The risks are as follows:

- Focus on technical improvements or features is less important at this stage than adoption. It is better to focus on documentation, packaging, and other DevX areas.

Examples: A Framework that can handle both frontend and backend (as a server-side rendering tooling), such as Angular. Multiple other well-known Frameworks are include Spring Boot, TensorFlow, and so on.

Level 5: Comprehensive ecosystem Framework

The ADF has evolved into a complete ecosystem and is capable of efficiently supporting a broad spectrum of use cases, technologies, and environments. It is highly optimized for performance, security, and scalability.

Its characteristics are as follows:

- **Investment**: Continuous investment in all areas, including architecture, automation, security, and UX. Community contribution becomes a significant part of the growth factor.
- **Complexity**: Even more abstractions introduced to cover multiple technology stacks, standards, and platforms (e.g., cloud, on-premises).
- **Modularity**: Highly modular, pluggable, and extensible, focusing on best practices and standards.
- **Configurability**: Full life cycle management, including automated CI/CD pipelines, advanced monitoring, analytics, and governance tools.
- **Documentation**: Engages a vibrant community or organizational backing with regular updates and feedback loops, providing books, tutorials, and articles covering a wide range of relevant scenarios.
- **Scope**: Supports various technologies, platforms, and use cases. This range is continuously extended by external software systems that start adding integration capabilities to support your ADF.

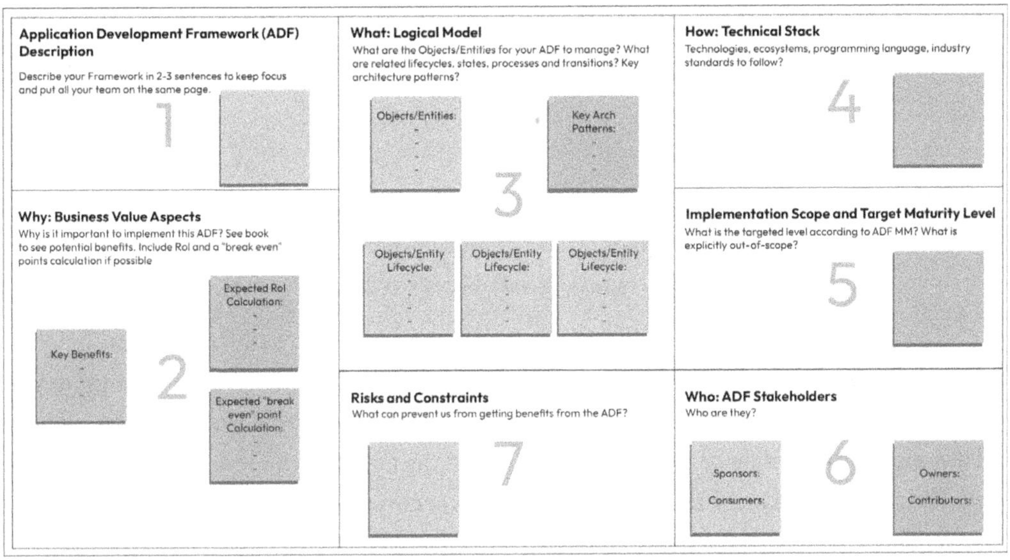

Figure 3.6: Visual Framework development Canvas preview

This Canvas is divided into several key areas, each designed to highlight a critical aspect of the ADF:

1. **Application Development Framework (ADF) Description**: A brief, high-level description of the Framework, ensuring all stakeholders have a unified understanding.

2. **Why: Business Value Aspects:** Outlines the rationale behind implementing the ADF, including key benefits and expected ROI calculations, allowing stakeholders to gauge the financial and operational impact.

3. **What: Logical Model**: Details the core objects, entities, and (optionally) architecture patterns that the ADF will manage, offering a foundational model to guide the design and structure. More information about the technological realms mentioned in this block can be found in Part 3 of the book.

4. **How: Technical Stack:** Lists the technologies, languages, and standards required for implementation, helping teams choose the right tools and ecosystems. There is a dedicated subsection about this part of the Canvas following this one.

5. **Implementation Scope and Target Maturity Level**: Defines the scope of the ADF and the targeted maturity level, offering clear boundaries and goals for the development process.

6. **Who: ADF Stakeholders:** Identifies the key stakeholders, including sponsors, owners, and contributors, ensuring everyone involved understands their roles and responsibilities.

7. **Risks and Constraints**: Highlights potential risks that could impact the success of the ADF, helping teams prepare for challenges and mitigate risks proactively.

> **Note**
>
> Please note that you might not have all the necessary information to fill in all the sections of the initial stage of the ADF implementation initiative. Just keep it updated regularly when more context is available down the road.

By completing each Canvas block, you can create a comprehensive and cohesive strategy for your ADF, ensuring alignment from initial conception to full deployment. You can find all the guidance and descriptions necessary to complete the Canvas in the previous chapters and sections of this book. The only Canvas block that this book has not yet covered is the tech stack block. To fill in this gap, please see the following section.

Defining a tech stack

Before beginning Framework development, it is essential to establish a clear and comprehensive **tech stack**. Usually, this simply involves documenting existing facts, as the technologies and languages are already established. This tech stack will form the backbone of the Framework's architecture, influencing everything from design and functionality to long-term maintenance and scalability.

Please note that *Chapter 4* will give you detailed guidance on the tech stack definition process. The purpose of this section is to outline the topic briefly to allow you to fill in the Canvas before diving into technical details, as suggested by *Chapter 4*. The following are key considerations to make when defining your tech stack.

Technologies

Storages and drivers: This category includes all forms of data storage technologies such as relational databases (MySQL, PostgreSQL), NoSQL databases (MongoDB, Cassandra), and object storage (Amazon S3, Google Cloud Storage). Drivers are essential libraries that enable applications built with the Framework to interact with these storages. They ensure that the Framework can perform data operations such as reading, writing, and managing transactions efficiently across various storage systems.

- **Control flow**: Multiple control flows to support edge cases (such as the Django admin flow that complements the primary web application rendering flow).

- **Usability and DevX**: Extremely high usability; easily integrates with complex enterprise systems and scales effortlessly.

The risks are as follows:

- It might be too expensive to maintain such an ADF without a vibrant community, so at this stage, the focus should be on building a social ecosystem around the Framework.

Examples: A comprehensive Framework such as Kubernetes that supports container orchestration, multi-cloud deployments, and a wide range of development and deployment scenarios. React, Spring, Django, and Node.js are other representatives that can be classified as top maturity ADFs.

> **Note**
>
> These levels allow ADF developers to align their Framework's growth with stakeholder needs and investment strategies. By understanding where the Framework currently stands and where it needs to go, they can avoid over-investing in unnecessary capabilities or complexity. Each level balances simplicity, development effort, usability, and universality in a way that is aligned with the Framework's target audience and use cases. This ensures that the Framework evolves in a controlled, cost-effective manner, providing maximum value to its users without unnecessary complexity.

The following section aims to provide a simple tool for capturing, collaborating on, and presenting a Framework definition that addresses all blueprint elements.

ADF Canvas guide

The ADF Canvas serves as a strategic visualization tool to align stakeholders before the development and implementation of your Framework. By breaking down the ADF into constrained but very specific blocks, the Canvas helps justify the value of your Framework, align your team's focus, and ensure consistency throughout the project life cycle. Please note that the following figure is just a preview; the original-sized Canvas can be found at the link following the figure.

Transport and communication protocols/serialization formats: Protocols and formats such as HTTP, WebSocket, gRPC, and Protobuf are fundamental for defining how data is transmitted between clients and servers. These are crucial for Frameworks that require reliable data exchange mechanisms, supporting features such as **remote procedure calls** (**RPCs**) and real-time data streaming.

Calculations and toolkits: For Frameworks that involve heavy computational tasks, incorporating specialized libraries and toolkits is essential. Examples include OpenCV for image processing tasks, CUDA for accelerating computations using NVIDIA's GPUs, and TensorFlow for machine learning. These toolkits provide optimized functions and operations that enhance the Framework's performance in specific computational domains.

Programming languages

Core programming languages: These are the languages used to write the main components, libraries, and toolkits of the Framework. They determine the Framework's performance, capabilities, and application scope. For example, C++ might be used for developing high-performance game engines, while Python could be favored for Frameworks geared toward rapid development and prototyping in web and data science applications.

- **Interface programming languages**: These are languages used for scripting, templates, and other elements that directly interact with the user or other systems. Examples include JavaScript for client-side scripting, Lua for scripting in game engines, and XML/XSLT for defining and transforming data. These languages facilitate development and provide flexibility in configuring application behaviors.

- **Configuration and management languages**: These languages and formats are used for configuration, describing the runtime environment, and managing the application life cycle. A classic example is Dockerfile, used to create Docker containers specifying the operating system, dependencies, runtime environment, and commands to be executed. These languages are often declarative and specialized for managing infrastructure and resources.

Sometimes, a Framework can directly bring functionality from one programming language to another by utilizing that language. This means that the Framework somehow integrates its control flow with the use of another programming language. Examples include the classic use of JavaScript in web Frameworks such as Django, as well as newer approaches where a Framework such as TensorFlow, which masks the use of C++, and a newer Framework in Python using Rust under the hood, can directly bring the functionality of this language, thus its technological domain to our (see `https://github.com/sparckles/Robyn`).

Development tooling

Code and code structure generators: These tools automatically generate boilerplate code, data models, and even entire project structures based on predefined templates or schemas. They significantly speed up development and ensure consistency across projects by enforcing standard patterns and practices.

Testing engines: These include Frameworks and tools that support unit testing, integration testing, system testing, and sometimes acceptance testing. Popular examples include JUnit for Java, pytest for Python, and Mocha for JavaScript. The effective use of testing engines ensures that the Framework and the applications built with it are reliable and meet quality standards.

Documentation engines: Tools such as Javadoc, Sphinx, and Doxygen automatically generate user-friendly, up-to-date documentation from the code base. Good documentation is crucial for any Framework as it aids developers in understanding and utilizing the Framework correctly, thereby enhancing the DevX and adoption. Tools such as Swagger, for designing and documenting REST APIs, ensure your Framework can interact effectively with other software (such as GitHub pages and wiki-based engines).

By clearly defining these aspects of the tech stack, you can establish a foundation that supports effective development and ensures that the Framework can adapt to future technological changes or enhancements. This preparation not only streamlines the development process but also enhances the Framework's longevity and usability, providing clear guidelines for developers and encouraging consistency across different parts of the Framework.

Summary

This is the final "theoretical" chapter of the book that is focused on better understanding the whole conceptual domain of building Frameworks. Use the information from this chapter to break down your Framework into easy-to-comprehend parts, apply architecture patterns to streamline Framework development and adoption, and make sure you have covered all important aspects. Use the hints provided here to improve your Framework code structure. A maturity model gives you a tool to optimize your investment in the Framework to make it fit its purpose with minimal risk of over-engineering. Finally, use the Canvas to easily capture and communicate significant decisions related to the Framework development.

The following chapters will provide step-by-step guidance for building any complex Framework, referring to the Framework fundamentals covered by the initial three chapters.

Unlock this book's exclusive benefits now

Scan this QR code or go to packtpub.com/unlock, then search for this book by name. Ensure it's the correct edition.

Note: Keep your purchase invoice ready before you start.

Part 2

Building a Framework

Design, architecture, and implementation practices

This part guides you through the architectural and technical practices involved in creating robust and reusable frameworks. From establishing a sound architecture and choosing the right tech stack to managing control flows and release cycles, it will help you transform ideas into working systems. Whether you're bootstrapping a minimal viable framework or evolving a mature one, this section offers actionable insights for engineering execution.

This part has the following chapters:

- *Chapter 4, Defining Your Tech Stack*
- *Chapter 5, Architecture Design*
- *Chapter 6, ADF Development Fundamentals*
- *Chapter 7, Documenting and Releasing a Framework*

4

Defining Your Tech Stack

In the rapidly evolving landscape of software development, understanding and strategically defining your technology stack is paramount. This is especially crucial when viewed through the lens of **Application Development Frameworks (ADFs)**. A technology stack encompasses the intricate ecosystem of programming languages, tools, libraries, and frameworks that collectively power the creation and operation of your applications. Far more than a mere collection of technologies, your stack forms the bedrock of your development and operational infrastructure, profoundly influencing everything from initial project execution to long-term scalability and maintenance.

This chapter delves into the nuanced process of crafting and refining a technology stack tailored for contemporary software frameworks. As organizations increasingly rely on bespoke software solutions to drive innovation and maintain a competitive edge, the significance of a well-architected technology stack cannot be overstated. It not only addresses current operational demands but also ensures the flexibility to adapt to emerging technologies and shifting market dynamics.

We will explore the delicate interplay between domain expertise, user-centric design principles, and strategic technology choices that coalesce to create robust, efficient, and intuitive frameworks. Our discussion will encompass critical components such as data storage solutions, computational tools, and development environments that collectively form the backbone of a successful framework.

We will cover the following topics in this chapter:

- Key concept and alignment with technological realms
- Exploring languages and libraries

Key concept and alignment with technological realms

When developing a technology stack for a new framework, drawing upon deep domain expertise is not just beneficial but often crucial for its success. This expertise ensures that the framework can harness proven methodologies and technologies, reducing the need to reinvent the wheel. In the following diagram, we demonstrate the most common hierarchy of components of a technical stack:

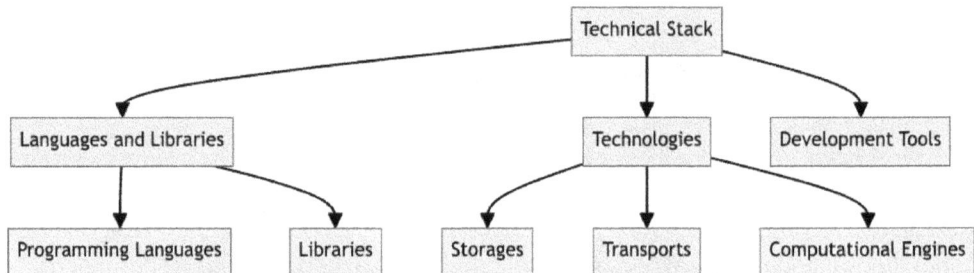

Figure 4.1: Technical stack structure

🔍 Quick tip: Need to see a high-resolution version of this image? Open this book in the next-gen Packt Reader or view it in the PDF/ePub copy.

🔒 The next-gen Packt Reader and a free PDF/ePub copy of this book are included with your purchase. Scan the QR code OR visit packtpub.com/unlock, then use the search bar to find this book by name. Double-check the edition shown to make sure you get the right one.

The following points allow you to find the best match to define a technical stack within your technological realm:

- **Leveraging existing technologies:**
    - Utilize established libraries, frameworks, and tools within the realm
    - Focus on unique features rather than basic functionality

- This accelerates development and improves reliability, especially in complex fields such as AI

- This also enhances performance and scalability without unnecessary detours

- **Aligning with user expectations:**

  - Match the technology stack to end user needs and familiarity

  - Reduce the learning curve and increase adoption rates

  - Ensure compatibility with existing tools and workflows in the domain

  - Facilitate seamless integration into current ecosystems

- **Future-proofing the framework:**

  - Anticipate industry trends and future needs

  - Understand standard technologies, widespread skills, and gaps in current offerings

  - Tailor the framework to address both current and future demands

  - We'll look at the creation of a framework for implementing **Retrieval-Augmented Generation (RAG)** applications based on LLM models as an example and position it at *Level 2 – Validated* in the maturity ladder introduced in *Chapter 3*, so you know which trade-offs (speed over polish, DIY over turnkey, etc.) we are optimizing for.

  - The core idea behind RAG is to enhance the capability of language models by integrating them with a retrieval system. This hybrid approach enables the model to dynamically pull relevant information from a large database or collection of documents during the generation process. This integration allows the model to produce responses that are not only contextually accurate but also enriched by external sources.

Here are some of the key challenges that RAG addresses:

- **Knowledge incorporation:** Traditional language models can struggle with generating responses that require specific knowledge or factual correctness. RAG addresses this by retrieving relevant documents or data entries to enrich the generation process, ensuring that the output is both contextually appropriate and factually accurate.

- **Handling long contexts:** Large language models often find managing long-term dependencies or maintaining context over extended texts challenging. RAG mitigates this issue by pulling in relevant information dynamically as needed, helping to maintain consistency and relevance throughout longer interactions or documents.

- **Reducing training data requirements**: Training a model to generate knowledgeable and accurate text typically requires vast amounts of labeled training data. By leveraging retrieval mechanisms, RAG can generate high-quality output based on less training data because it uses existing databases or document collections to inform its responses.

- **Combatting hallucinations**: One of the common issues with generative models is their tendency to produce "hallucinated" content – fabrications that are not grounded on the input provided. RAG helps reduce these hallucinations by using the retrieved documents as a reality check, ensuring that the generated content aligns closely with verifiable information.

By tackling these challenges, RAG models significantly improve the utility and reliability of language generation systems, and the quickest way to feel this benefit is to run a 20-line PoC.

```python
# --- RAG proof of concept -----------------
from langchain_openai import OpenAIEmbeddings, OpenAI
from langchain_community.vectorstores import FAISS
from langchain.chains import RetrievalQA

docs = ["John bought a new MacBook in Berlin.",
        "Apple's M3 chip was released in 2023.",
        "Berlin's Apple Store is near Ku'damm."]

vectordb = FAISS.from_texts(docs, OpenAIEmbeddings())

rag = RetrievalQA.from_chain_type(
        llm=OpenAI(max_tokens=64),
        chain_type="stuff",
        retriever=vectordb.as_retriever())

print(rag.invoke("Where did John get his laptop?"))
```

💡 Quick tip: Enhance your coding experience with the AI Code Explainer and Quick Copy features. Open this book in the next-gen Packt Reader. Click the Copy button

(1) to quickly copy code into your coding environment, or click the Explain button

(2) to get the AI assistant to explain a block of code to you.

```
                                                    Copy      Explain
    function calculate(a, b) {                       1          2
        return {sum: a + b};
    };
```

🔒 The next-gen Packt Reader and a free PDF/ePub copy of this book are included with your purchase. Scan the QR code OR visit packtpub.com/unlock, then use the search bar to find this book by name. Double-check the edition shown to make sure you get the right one.

Output:

```
(Chapter4) ➜  Chapter4 git:(main) X python rag.py
{'query': 'Where did John get his laptop?', 'result': ' John got his
laptop at the Apple Store near Ku'damm in Berlin.'}
```

This exploration into framework creation is an illustrative guide rather than a definitive model, allowing us to examine design integration and potential complexities.

Let's examine the RAG key components:

- **Retriever**: This is the heart of the RAG system. It processes queries by passing them to the embeddings model, which converts queries into vector representations. These embeddings enable the retriever to interact with the vector search engine in the vector database, retrieve relevant context, and construct prompts. The prompts, context, and original query are then sent to the generative model. This model generates a response from the context, which returns the final answer.

- **Vector database**: This component manages the vector representations of data. It receives embeddings from the retriever, uses vector search to locate relevant document contexts, and returns these contexts to the retriever to aid response generation.

- **Data loader**: This component is responsible for preparing and indexing new data. It processes documents into chunks, computes embeddings through the embeddings model, and indexes these in the vector database to make them searchable for future queries.

With such a definition, we can later define the common logical model of our framework.

Exploring languages and libraries

In many instances, the formation of a tech stack is evolutionary, derived from existing projects within an organization. For example, a typical web application might be built using React for the frontend, Django as the web framework, and PostgreSQL for database management. However, alternative technologies might be integrated based on specific needs or new strategic goals when considering tooling and testing.

The best practice in defining and evolving a tech stack involves meticulously documenting each decision within a common knowledge management system. This documentation can adopt various formats, such as **Architecture Decision Records (ADRs)** or simple tabular representations, ensuring clarity and accessibility for all stakeholders.

For projects starting from scratch or when a new ADF is being extracted from a larger ecosystem, a structured approach is required to define a tech stack that not only meets the current application requirements but is also robust enough to adapt to future challenges and technological shifts. This process typically involves documenting existing facts, as the technologies and languages are already established. This tech stack will form the backbone of the framework's architecture, influencing everything from design and functionality to long-term maintenance and scalability.

There are common considerations that could be considered while defining a tech stack, in the form of a checklist:

- **Define framework-specific features**: The technology needed is dictated by the framework's primary functionality and operational requirements. For instance, a framework designed for real-time data processing might benefit from in-memory databases such as Redis.

- **Check integration with chosen technological realms**: Successful frameworks often must operate within a broader technological ecosystem. Technologies that integrate well reduce complexities and enhance efficiency.

- **Ensure compatibility with the company's existing technological stack**: Compatibility reduces conflicts, minimizes the learning curve for development teams, and leverages existing investments in technology.

- **Consider market coverage of potential storage solutions, community, and a support ecosystem**: A strong community and support ecosystem often leads to quicker problem resolutions, more frequent updates, and a wealth of shared knowledge.

- **Evaluate the cost implications**: Costs can significantly impact a project's budget and overall feasibility, especially for long-term operations.

- **Check license, vendor, and/or community support**: Licensing terms can affect how the technology is used and distributed, especially in commercial applications. Evaluating this factor ensures compliance with legal standards, assesses the level of post-deployment support available, and minimizes risks associated with vendor lock-in, providing flexibility in future technology choices.

According to our taxonomy in *Chapter 3*, we must define at least three important components of the framework's technological stack: programming languages, technologies (including storage, transport, and calculation toolkits), and development tooling specially created for the framework.

Programming languages

Usually, it doesn't make sense to spend a lot of time choosing a programming language, except when the framework under the hood uses a different language from the company's stack to implement some features that are not present in the basic stack.

If different programming languages are used in the framework, we can talk about the presence of a **Core Programming Language** and an **Interface Programming Language**.

Core programming languages

These languages bring the most complexity, computational or cognitive, which, in turn, benefits the applications themselves, isolating the complexity of use at the expense of the framework. This means that the framework somehow integrates its control flow with another programming language. Examples include the classic use of JavaScript in web frameworks such as Django, as well as newer approaches where a framework such as TensorFlow, which masks the use of C++, and a newer framework in Python using Rust under the hood, can directly bring the functionality of this language, thus its technological realm, to our (see https://github.com/sparckles/Robyn).

Interface programming languages

This class of programming languages is oriented to the framework's end users (developers) and allows highly efficient use of its capabilities. In the ideal version, the code of the applications using the framework is described declaratively, and the declaratively described objects are built into the control flow.

Configuration and management languages

These languages and formats are used to configure and describe the runtime environment, and manage the application lifecycle. A classic example is a Dockerfile, which specifies the operating system, dependencies, runtime environment, and commands to be executed when creating Docker containers. These languages are often declarative and specialized for managing infrastructure and resources.

Important Note

There is no doubt that a single language could be of all three types. There are a lot of concerns that make the difference between these types of languages, but frameworks typically use the same programming language for all. An example of this follows.

	Python	Golang	Rust
AI/ML Support	Extensive library ecosystem (LangChain, HayStack) ***	Limited AI/ML libraries*	Less mature AI/ML support*
Integration Capability	Seamless with existing tech stack***	Good but less AI-focused*	Good but complex integration*
Performance	Limited in compute-intensive tasks *	Better performance than Python**	Superior performance***
Development Speed	Rapid development, easy to use*	Go's learning curve is steeper than Python's, yet gentler than Rust's.**	Complex development, slower cycles **
Community Support	Vast, active AI/ML community***	Strong general community*	Growing community*
Scalability	May require optimization for high concurrency*	Excellent***	Excellent***

	Python	Golang	Rust
Learning Curve	Low***	Moderate**	High***
Final Decision	Selected as primary language	Rejected	Rejected

* – evaluation

This table outlines the selection of Python as the primary programming language for the RAG framework, highlighting its suitability due to extensive AI/ML libraries, ease of use, and compatibility with the company's tech stack. It documents the context, considerations, and consequences of this choice, comparing Python to alternatives such as Go and Rust. As the next steps, we need to define the list of technologies for the project, then we will observe the most common ones.

Storage, transport, and calculations

The choice of data storage technology is usually not a significant difficulty, since the data processing process is quite typical for one or another industry.

Expanding on each storage technology with greater depth will involve providing detailed backgrounds, technical specifications, and more comprehensive use cases and market insights.

Typical storage requirements

The **CAP Theorem**, formulated by Eric Brewer, elucidates the intrinsic limitations of any networked data system. It emphasizes that only two of the three pivotal attributes – consistency, availability, and partition tolerance – can be fully achieved simultaneously. This principle is a crucial framework for designing database systems, particularly in distributed environments. Here are the main features to consider:

- **Consistency**: This ensures that all nodes in a database present the same data at any given time. This attribute can manifest in two forms:

    - **Strong consistency – Atomicity, Consistency, Isolation, Durability (ACID)**: These properties are typical of traditional relational databases, prioritizing strict data consistency and integrity across transactions. ACID compliance is essential in scenarios where transaction reliability is critical.

    - **Eventual consistency – Basically Available, Soft-state, Eventually consistent)**: Updates eventually reach all nodes, allowing for temporary disparities but ensuring eventual data uniformity.

- **Availability**: This guarantees responses to requests regardless of the state of any single node, aiming for maximum system uptime and ensuring that the database remains operational across all functional components, even during failures.

- **Partition tolerance**: This is the system's resilience to network failures that might cause communication breaks between nodes. Given the inevitability of network issues, partition tolerance is often deemed essential, dictating that the system must continue to function despite such problems.

The decision to prioritize consistency, availability, or partition tolerance heavily depends on the specific requirements of the application and operational environment.

The criteria for choosing storage technologies are as follows:

- **Data types and structures**:

  - **Relational (SQL) vs non-relational (NoSQL)**: Relational databases are suited for structured data with clear relationships, while NoSQL is preferred for semi-structured or unstructured data, providing greater flexibility.

  - **File versus block storage**: File storage is ideal for systems requiring direct access. Block storage is better for scenarios that demand high performance and low-level data access.

- **Performance and scalability**

  - **Read versus write**: Vertical scalability increases processing power on a single server, while horizontal scalability distributes data across multiple nodes.

- **Data management**

  - **Data consistency**: Choose between strict consistency (ACID) and eventual consistency (BASE).

  - **Retention policies**: Define how long data should be retained and when it should be archived or deleted.

  - **Data deduplication and compression**: Reduce storage costs and enhance data transfer efficiency.

  - **Data lifecycle**: Is the data write-once or read-many? Can it be moved into cool or cold storage?

- **Security and compliance**

    - **Data encryption:** Ensure data security with encryption at rest and in transit.

    - **Access control and authentication:** Implement mechanisms to manage access to data and authenticate users.

- **Availability and resilience**

    - **High availability:** Use mechanisms that ensure data access even during component or node failures.

    - **Replication and backup:** Develop strategies to preserve data and quickly recover from failures.

Relational databases

Relational databases are a type of database system that organizes data into structured tables, where each table consists of rows and columns. The rows represent individual records, while the columns define the attributes or fields of the data. These tables are interconnected through relationships, typically using primary and foreign keys, allowing for efficient data retrieval and complex querying. Relational databases follow the principles of relational algebra and are mainly related tables.

PostgreSQL

PostgreSQL, often called **Postgres,** began as the POSTGRES project at the University of California, Berkeley, in 1986. It was spearheaded by Professor Michael Stonebraker, who aimed to overcome the limitations of the earlier Ingres database by introducing the concept of an object-relational system. It has since evolved to support various features from SQL standards and beyond, including advanced functions, operators, and indexes that allow complex queries, foreign keys, transactions, and extensive data integrity. PostgreSQL is highly respected in industries that require a robust database system with complex querying capabilities. It's particularly popular among tech companies and start-ups due to its open source nature and scalability.

The following are some of its key features:

- **ACID compliance:** Ensures transactional reliability and integrity
- **Advanced indexing:** GIN and GiST indexes support complex queries
- **Extensions and foreign data wrappers:** Allows the database to integrate with other SQL and NoSQL databases
- **License:** PostgreSQL (similar to MIT or BSD)

It is best suited for applications that require reliable data integrity, complex queries, and extensive extensibility. It is ideal for enterprise applications, financial systems, and geographic information systems where advanced data handling is crucial. Also, the rich ecosystem of PostgreSQL includes a whole set of extensions that allow us to use it in many different areas – for instance, a vector database or even an ML platform.

MySQL (MariaDB)

MySQL was created by MySQL AB, a Swedish company founded by David Axmark, Allan Larsson, and Michael Widenius in 1995. Due to its simplicity and speed, it quickly became the database of choice for early web applications. It was acquired by Sun Microsystems in 2008, which was, in turn, bought by Oracle Corporation in 2010. MariaDB was created by the original developers of MySQL, led by Michael "Monty" Widenius, after concerns over MySQL's acquisition by Oracle Corporation in 2010. MariaDB was intended as a drop-in replacement for MySQL, ensuring a continuation of the project under open source terms. The primary goal was to maintain compatibility with MySQL while also adding new features and improvements that are not available in MySQL. Predominantly used by small to medium-sized web applications, it's popular in start-up environments and among independent developers due to its ease of use and integration with web development tools.

The following are some of its key features:

- **ACID compliance**: Ensures transactional reliability and integrity
- **Storage engines**: InnoDB for transactional support, MyISAM for high-speed storage without transactions
- **Replication**: Supports master-slave and master-master configurations
- **License**: dual-licensed (GPL + proprietary) for MySQL, GPLv2 for MariaDB

MySQL is favored for web applications, especially those built using PHP, such as WordPress and other content management systems. It's suitable for applications with relatively simple database access patterns and where cost efficiency is prioritized.

MySQL is often selected over PostgreSQL for simpler applications due to its speed and efficiency with less complex queries. Its widespread use in web development also stems from extensive community support and a vast array of accessible tools and libraries.

Oracle database

Oracle Database, developed by Oracle Corporation, was one of the first commercial relational database management systems. Its development began in 1977, and over the decades, it has been at the forefront of database technologies, often leading innovations that later became industry standards.

Large enterprises predominantly use Oracle Database, requiring high scalability, reliability, and security. It's suitable for critical data management applications in the banking, healthcare, and government sectors. Over the years, Oracle has consistently led innovations in database technologies, including advanced transaction control, support for PL/SQL (an extension of SQL), and enterprise grid computing, which provides high performance and scalability. Oracle leads in industries where database performance and scalability are critical. It has a strong presence in both the private and public sectors and is known for its enterprise solutions.

Compared to other databases such as MySQL, PostgreSQL, or even newer NoSQL databases, Oracle offers unmatched enterprise features but at a higher cost. Its performance, security features, and scalability are top-notch, making it the go-to choice for enterprises that need a dependable, secure, and highly scalable database system.

NoSQL databases

NoSQL databases are non-relational database systems designed to handle large volumes of unstructured, semi-structured, or rapidly changing data. Unlike traditional relational databases, NoSQL databases do not rely on fixed schemas or table-based structures, allowing for more flexible data models such as document, key-value, column-family, or graph formats. This flexibility makes them ideal for applications requiring high scalability, performance, and the ability to store diverse data types, such as big data, real-time web applications, and distributed systems. NoSQL databases are often used when handling large datasets, horizontal scaling, or when the data structure is highly dynamic.

MongoDB

MongoDB was developed by Dwight Merriman, Eliot Horowitz, and Kevin Ryan, who founded the company 10gen (now MongoDB Inc.) in 2007. It was created to address the limitations of traditional relational databases by providing a more flexible schema and scaling horizontally, making it suitable for handling large volumes and varieties of data. MongoDB is popular among start-ups and enterprises that need to manage large sets of unstructured data. It's widely used in the tech industry to develop modern applications requiring a flexible, schema-less data model.

The following are some of its key features:

- **BASE data consistency (multi-document ACID with limitations)**
- **Document-oriented storage**: Stores data in JSON-like documents with dynamic schemas
- **Sharding**: Supports horizontal scaling through sharding
- **Replication**: Provides high availability with built-in replication

It is ideal for applications that require rapid development, frequent iterations, and handling of various data types, such as content management systems, e-commerce applications, and real-time analytics.

MongoDB is often chosen over traditional relational databases such as PostgreSQL and MySQL when applications require schema flexibility, horizontal scalability, and integration with agile software development practices. It handles large volumes of data efficiently, making it suitable for big data applications. MongoDB is a key component of the popular MERN stack, a technology stack used for building full stack web applications. The MERN stack consists of **MongoDB**, **Express.js**, **React**, and **Node.js**, with MongoDB serving as the database layer.

Cassandra

Apache Cassandra was originally developed for inbox search on Facebook in 2008 and then open sourced. It was designed to handle very large amounts of data distributed across many commodity servers while providing high availability without a single point of failure. It's especially favored in industries where large-scale, fault-tolerant, and responsive systems are critical, such as telecommunications, financial services, and internet services.

The following are its key features:

- **Wide-column store**: Uses a table structure that allows the nesting of rows within a row
- **Scalability**: Designed to scale horizontally across many servers seamlessly
- **Fault tolerance**: Offers robust fault tolerance through data replication across multiple nodes

Cassandra is used for applications that require massive scalability and high availability, such as IoT, web analytics, and real-time monitoring systems.

Cassandra stands out when linear scalability and proven fault tolerance on commodity hardware or cloud infrastructure are required. It competes with MongoDB in some use cases but generally handles higher write loads and larger data volumes more effectively.

Redis

Redis, which stands for **Remote Dictionary Server**, was created by Salvatore Sanfilippo in 2009. It started as an open source project to solve scaling issues related to real-time web log analysis. Redis is widely adopted in scenarios where speed and efficiency are crucial, such as gaming, tech, and financial services, where its performance can drive significant user experience improvements. Redis recently transitioned to a more restrictive licensing model, moving away from the open source BSD license to the **Server-Side Public License** (**SSPL**) and the **Redis Source Available License** (**RSAL**). This change has led to several forks of Redis by different communities and companies, aiming to maintain a version of Redis under more permissive licensing terms. For example, the Linux Foundation hosts the Valkey fork, which major tech companies, including Amazon Web Services, Google Cloud, and Oracle, support.

The following are its key features:

- **In-memory data structure store**: Can handle data structures such as strings, hashes, lists, sets, and sorted sets
- **Persistence**: Offers options to dump the dataset to disk and append each command to a log
- **Built-in atomic operations**: Supports atomic operations on these data types

Redis clusters are extensively used for caching to enhance the performance of web applications. They are also used in session management, real-time analytics, and queueing tasks.

> Redis is often selected for its exceptional speed and flexibility to handle various data types, making it ideal for tasks such as caching and real-time analysis in environments where quick data retrieval is critical. It generally complements other databases such as MongoDB or Cassandra by providing a high-performance layer for hot data.

AWS DynamoDB

DynamoDB, launched by **Amazon Web Services** (**AWS**) in 2012, is a fully managed NoSQL database service designed to deliver fast and predictable performance with seamless scalability. It provides a reliable and cost-efficient solution for handling structured and semi-structured data across any application scale. As part of the AWS ecosystem, DynamoDB benefits from high integration with other AWS services, making it a preferred choice for businesses already leveraging AWS for their cloud solutions. It's widely adopted across various industries for critical business functions due to its robust feature set and scalability.

The following are some of the key features:

- **Serverless and fully managed**: AWS manages the hardware provisioning, setup, configuration, and replication, allowing users to focus on the application

- **Single-digit millisecond performance**: It delivers high-performance read and write speeds, ideal for real-time and high-throughput applications

- **Auto scaling**: It automatically adjusts capacities to maintain performance as demand changes, ensuring efficient resource usage

DynamoDB is particularly effective for web, mobile, gaming, ad tech, IoT, and many other applications that require low-latency data access at any scale. It's extensively used in scenarios that demand a robust, highly available, and durable storage system.

DynamoDB often outperforms traditional relational databases in terms of scalability and operational efficiency, especially in environments that handle large volumes of data. Its serverless nature removes the need for database administration tasks, making it a more attractive option for start-ups and enterprises looking to reduce overhead.

Azure Cosmos DB

Azure Cosmos DB is a globally distributed database service from Microsoft Azure, first launched in 2017. It provides multi-model database capabilities and is designed to offer turnkey global distribution, seamless scalability, and guaranteed low latency. Cosmos DB targets large-scale enterprises that need a database solution that can scale globally without compromising on latency and reliability. Its comprehensive multi-model approach allows it to serve various application types and use cases.

The following are some of the key features:

- **Multi-model support**: Supports document, key-value, graph, and column-family data models, all accessible via APIs for SQL, MongoDB, Cassandra, Tables, and Gremlin

- **Global distribution**: Turnkey global distribution allows data to be replicated anywhere in the world with a click of a button, ensuring data is close to users

- **Multi-master replication**: Multi-master replication provides high availability, allowing reads and writes anywhere with latency measured in milliseconds

Cosmos DB is ideal for applications requiring massive scale, global distribution, and multi-model support, such as e-commerce platforms, gaming applications, social networks, and telematics.

Compared to traditional and other NoSQL databases, Cosmos DB offers a unique combination of global distribution, multi-model support, and high availability features. It is often chosen for its robust scalability and flexibility, particularly for applications that operate on a global scale and require real-time access to data across various data models.

Elasticsearch (OpenSearch)

Shay Banon initially created **Elasticsearch** as a scalable search engine. Its development was driven by the need for an accessible, quick, and highly scalable search platform. Over the years, it has evolved to become a comprehensive open source search and analytics engine. Given its versatile nature, it has been embraced by various sectors for diverse applications.

The following are some of the key features:

- **Full-text search**: Built on the Apache Lucene library, it excels in full-text search
- **Real-time processing**: Capable of near real-time search and analytics
- **Scalability**: Efficiently scales horizontally to handle petabytes of structured and unstructured data
- **High availability**: Ensures data availability and robustness through data replication and distributed architecture

Elasticsearch is commonly utilized for application search, website search, enterprise search, logging and log analysis, infrastructure metrics, and container monitoring, among other use cases. It's particularly effective in scenarios requiring rapid search responses and real-time analytics, such as monitoring e-commerce platforms and financial services for fraudulent activity.

Thanks to its powerful search and analytics capabilities, Elasticsearch enjoys widespread adoption across various industries, including technology, finance, retail, and healthcare. Companies value its speed, scalability, and the depth of its search capabilities, which can be integrated into almost any application or system for enhanced data insights.

While Elasticsearch competes directly with other search engines such as Solr (also based on Lucene), it often stands out for its superior scalability and ease of use, particularly in handling real-time data analysis and visualization when paired with Kibana. Compared to traditional databases, it provides faster search capabilities and more efficient handling of complex queries and aggregation.

As an important update, OpenSearch is a community-driven, open source fork of Elasticsearch and Kibana initiated by Amazon. It was started following Elasticsearch's licensing changes, which moved away from the fully open source model to the SSPL. OpenSearch aims to provide users with a fully open source and community-driven alternative, maintaining compatibility with Elasticsearch while evolving independently.

Columnar databases

Columnar databases are a type of database system optimized for reading and writing data by columns rather than rows, making them highly efficient for analytical queries and large-scale data processing. Instead of storing an entire row of data together, columnar databases store data from each column separately. This format enables faster retrieval of specific columns, which is particularly useful for read-heavy workloads such as data warehousing and business intelligence, where only a subset of columns is often queried. By reducing the amount of data that needs to be scanned and leveraging better compression, columnar databases significantly enhance query performance and storage efficiency compared to traditional row-based databases.

ClickHouse

Developed by Yandex, **ClickHouse** is an open source columnar database management system primarily designed for **OnLine Analytical Processing (OLAP)**. It was released as open source in 2016 and is known for its incredible performance with analytical queries. It is preferred in sectors such as advertising technology, finance, and telecommunications, where rapid query performance over large datasets is critical.

The following are some of the key features:

- **Column-oriented DBMS**: Stores data by columns, which allows for faster data retrieval during queries that touch only a subset of columns
- **Vectorized query execution**: Implements vectorized query execution, which significantly improves query performance
- **High performance**: Particularly optimized for running complex queries against large datasets

ClickHouse is primarily used for real-time analytical applications, such as high-frequency data warehousing, large-scale log analysis, and business intelligence applications.

ClickHouse is especially beneficial when query speed is crucial and data is predominantly added and not frequently updated. It competes with traditional data warehousing solutions by providing high throughput and real-time query capabilities. It is a popular choice for businesses that need quick insights from large volumes of data.

Amazon Redshift

Amazon Redshift is a fully managed, petabyte-scale data warehouse service provided by AWS, first released in 2012. It is designed to handle large-scale data warehousing and analytics applications and is popular among businesses that require quick insights from their massive data stores. Due to its scalability, cost-effectiveness, and integration with other AWS services, Amazon Redshift is extensively used by organizations ranging from start-ups to large enterprises. It holds a significant market presence in data warehousing, especially for those already entrenched in the AWS ecosystem.

The following are some of the key features:

- **Column-oriented storage**: Redshift is based on a column-oriented DBMS, which optimizes query speed by effectively storing data in columns and only reading the necessary columns during a query
- **Massively Parallel Processing (MPP)**: It distributes data and the query load across all nodes, enabling high-performance computations on large datasets
- **Redshift Spectrum**: This extends Redshift's capabilities to directly query exabytes of unstructured data in S3 without loading or transforming the data, providing seamless integration with the existing Redshift environment

Redshift is tailored for complex querying and analysis of large datasets. It is used widely in data warehousing, business intelligence, and log analysis, where high query performance is crucial. It serves as the backbone for analytics applications across diverse sectors, including financial services, healthcare, and media. In AWS infrastructure, Amazon Athena can be considered a replacement for Redshift.

Redshift's integration with Redshift Spectrum allows users to perform SQL queries across their data lake stored in Amazon S3, providing a powerful feature that differentiates it from other columnar databases such as ClickHouse. It is preferred for scenarios where the integration of cloud storage and database services can provide enhanced flexibility and scalability, especially in handling varied and extensive data workloads. The capability to handle both structured and semi-structured data without prior transformation makes it a robust choice for enterprises seeking to leverage data for strategic insights.

Redshift offers an appealing solution for companies looking to scale their analytics capabilities rapidly while maintaining cost-efficiency and high performance. Its continuous improvements and updates from AWS ensure that it remains a strong competitor in the fast-evolving data technology landscape.

Graph databases

Graph databases are a type of NoSQL database designed to represent and store data in the form of nodes (entities) and edges (relationships), allowing for efficient modeling and querying of complex, interconnected data. Each node in a graph database represents an object (such as a person, place, or thing), and edges define the relationships or connections between these nodes. This structure makes graph databases ideal for applications where understanding relationships and patterns between data points is critical, such as social networks, recommendation systems, fraud detection, and network topology analysis. Unlike traditional relational databases, graph databases excel at quickly traversing and querying intricate networks of data, offering more natural and intuitive ways to represent and explore relationships.

Neo4j

Neo4j was developed by Neo Technology, founded by Emil Efrem. It was released in 2007 as the first commercially available graph database, using graph structures with nodes, edges, and properties to represent and store data. It is widely adopted in industries such as social networking, e-commerce, and banking, where complex relationships between data points need to be efficiently managed and queried.

The following are some of the key features:

- **Graph data model**: Nodes represent entities, and edges represent relationships between entities, each with associated properties
- **Cypher query language**: It uses a declarative query language specifically designed for handling graphs
- **ACID transactions**: It supports full ACID capabilities for transactional applications

Neo4j is extensively used for recommendations, fraud detection, graph-based search, and network and IT operations.

Neo4j stands out in scenarios requiring the analysis of interconnections within data, such as social networks or recommendation engines. Its graph data model provides significant advantages over relational databases for deeply connected data applications.

Amazon Neptune

Amazon Neptune is a fully managed graph database service offered by AWS, which was launched in 2017. It is designed to store and navigate highly connected data, making it an ideal choice for applications that require complex relationship queries. Neptune supports both **Property Graphs** and **Resource Description Framework (RDF)**, allowing it to handle various graph use cases.

The following are some of the key features:

- **Graph data models**: Supports two graph models: Property Graphs using the open source Apache TinkerPop Gremlin, and RDF using SPARQL—a powerful graph query language
- **Fully managed**: As a managed service, Neptune handles much of the necessary maintenance tasks, such as hardware provisioning, setup, configuration, and backups
- **Highly scalable and durable**: Built to offer high availability, it replicates six copies of data across three Availability Zones and continuously backs up data to Amazon S3, which is also designed for high durability

Amazon Neptune is used in a variety of applications where relationships and connections are crucial. Typical use cases include knowledge graphs, fraud detection, recommendation systems, social networking, and network security. Its ability to quickly process complex queries involving deeply connected data makes it particularly useful in these areas.

Neptune has been increasingly adopted by industries that require efficient processing of connection-heavy data, such as financial services for real-time fraud detection systems and social media platforms for improving user experience through better personalization and recommendations.

Compared to Neo4j, Neptune offers tight integration with the AWS ecosystem, which can be a decisive factor for companies that are already extensively leveraging AWS services. This integration simplifies operations such as data import/export and scaling.

Neptune enhances machine learning workflows by enabling efficient querying of relationships within large datasets, which is essential for features such as real-time recommendation systems and predictive modeling based on social connections or other complex relationship data. Its integration with AWS machine learning services and tools streamlines the ML pipeline, allowing developers to create more intelligent, context-aware applications.

Storage

The main difference between databases and storage systems (such as file, block, and object storage) lies in their functionality and purpose. Databases are designed to manage and query structured or semi-structured data efficiently, offering features such as indexing, transactions, and complex queries. In contrast, storage systems are used for storing raw data without providing advanced querying capabilities. Storage systems are primarily used for unstructured data, while databases focus on organizing and managing data for easy retrieval and manipulation.

File storage

File storage systems such as **Network Attached Storage (NAS)** have been integral to networked data management since the early days of computing, facilitating shared access to files across networks. Solutions such as NAS, Google Cloud Filestore, Azure Files, and Amazon EFS are prevalent in both enterprise and SMB markets, offering cost-effective and efficient solutions for managed file sharing.

The following are some of the key features:

- **Hierarchical structure**: Data is organized in files and folders, mimicking the familiar operating system structure
- **Protocol accessibility**: Commonly accessed through standard protocols such as **Network File System (NFS)** and Server **Message Block (SMB)**
- **Concurrency and locking**: Supports multiple access with mechanisms to lock files during use, preventing conflicts

It is ideal for applications requiring file sharing among multiple users or systems, such as in corporate environments for document storage and collaboration, multimedia content repositories, and environments where data needs to be easily navigable and manageable.

File storage is preferred over block storage when direct file access and shared access are necessary. It offers a more intuitive management system compared to the raw storage provided by block storage. File storage is not as scalable as object storage for web-scale applications but provides better performance for directory-intensive operations.

Block storage

Block storage is foundational to storage architecture. Early computer systems utilized block devices such as hard drives. It is designed to handle structured data storage with high efficiency and performance.

The following are some of the key features:

- **Raw storage blocks**: Data is stored in fixed-sized blocks, which are managed independently, allowing for flexible configurations
- **Low-level access**: Offers low-level control of storage, which can be formatted with the required file system
- **High performance**: Suited for operations that require high I/O throughput and low latency

Block storage is widely used for database hosting, critical applications requiring high performance, and any scenario where data needs to be frequently accessed and modified with high throughput, such as transactional systems. It is prominent in environments where performance and data reliability are critical, such as financial services and high-performance computing applications.

Block storage provides performance advantages over file and object storage in environments that require frequent data manipulation and access at low latencies. It is typically used in conjunction with file storage or as underlying storage for databases and high-performance applications.

Object storage

Object storage technology emerged as a response to the growing need for scalable and cost-effective solutions to manage vast amounts of unstructured data. Services such as Amazon S3, introduced by Amazon in 2006, have set industry standards for object storage, emphasizing accessibility and durability.

Object storage is suitable for multimedia files, backups, big data collections, and data serving applications that require extensive data retrieval capabilities, such as digital media streaming and content distribution networks. Prominent services such as Amazon S3, Google Cloud Storage, and Microsoft Azure Blob Storage dominate the market, offering high durability and availability, which are crucial for enterprises and cloud-native applications.

Object storage offers superior scalability and a simpler data management model than file and block storage, making it ideal for cloud storage solutions where high volumes of unstructured data are common. It is less suited for applications that require low latency and high transaction rates, where block or file storage might be more efficient.

Distributed log storage

Distributed log storage systems such as Apache Kafka and Amazon Kinesis are designed to efficiently handle large volumes of data streams. These platforms are fundamentally built to provide robust, scalable solutions for real-time data processing needs across various applications. Here's an in-depth look at each:

Apache Kafka

Apache Kafka was originally developed by LinkedIn in 2011 and later became part of the Apache Software Foundation. Kafka was designed to address the high-throughput, low-latency needs for handling real-time data feeds at LinkedIn. Its robustness, scalability, and fault tolerance quickly gained popularity. Kafka is a critical component in the tech stacks of many large enterprises, especially in sectors such as finance, retail, telecommunications, and tech start-ups. Its ability to handle high volumes of data makes it indispensable for organizations dealing with large-scale, real-time data needs.

The following are some of the key features:

- **Log-based system:** Stores streams of records in categories known as topics
- **Scalability:** Easily scales horizontally by adding more brokers in the Kafka cluster
- **Fault tolerance:** Uses distributed replication to prevent data loss
- **High throughput:** Can process millions of messages per second
- **Low latency:** Ensures real-time performance in data processing

Kafka is widely used in event-driven architectures, real-time analytics, monitoring systems, and as an intermediary for microservices communications. It excels in scenarios requiring reliable and real-time data exchange, such as financial transactions, IoT data streams, and operational metrics.

Compared to traditional messaging systems, Kafka provides greater durability and scalability, making it more suitable for applications that require robust data handling capabilities. Its distributed nature and partitioning model allow it to outperform many other data throughput and storage systems.

Amazon Kinesis

Amazon Kinesis was launched by AWS in 2013. It was created to make it easier for developers to load and analyze streaming data on AWS, thereby enabling them to build real-time applications quickly and efficiently.

The following are some of the key features:

- **Stream-based data handling:** Allows for collecting, processing, and the analysis of real-time data streams
- **Integration with AWS:** Seamlessly integrates with other AWS services for analytics, storage, and machine learning

- **Scalability**: Automatically scales to match the volume and throughput of data
- **Data sharding**: Data streams are divided into shards, each capable of handling up to 1 MB/sec or 1,000 messages per second

Amazon Kinesis is ideal for real-time applications such as logging and event data collection, analytics, machine learning model inference, and more. It is particularly beneficial for AWS-centric environments that require tight integration with other AWS services.

Kinesis is primarily used by businesses that are already invested in the AWS ecosystem. Its integration with AWS makes it a preferred choice for those leveraging other AWS services such as Lambda, S3, Redshift, and AWS analytics tools.

While both Kafka and Kinesis offer robust solutions for handling real-time data streams, Kinesis provides tighter integration with AWS, which can be a significant advantage for companies operating within the AWS cloud. On the other hand, Kafka offers more flexibility in terms of deployment options and can be used across multiple cloud providers or on-premises environments.

Apache Pulsar

Apache Pulsar is a cloud-native, distributed messaging and streaming platform designed for high-performance, real-time data processing. It supports both message queuing and publish-subscribe models, making it suitable for a wide range of applications, including real-time analytics, log aggregation, and machine learning inference.

Pulsar's architecture separates the serving and storage layers, allowing for seamless scalability and high availability. It offers features such as multi-tenancy, geo-replication, and tiered storage, enabling organizations to build robust, scalable data pipelines.

While Amazon Kinesis is a fully managed service tightly integrated with the AWS ecosystem, Apache Pulsar provides more flexibility in deployment options, including on-premises, cloud, and hybrid environments. This makes Pulsar a compelling choice for organizations seeking an open source, vendor-neutral solution for real-time data streaming.

Feature	Apache Kafka	Amazon Kinesis	Apache Pulsar
Deployment Model	Open source; deployable in on-premises, cloud, or hybrid environments	Fully managed service within the AWS ecosystem	Open source; deployable in on-premises, cloud, or hybrid environments

Feature	Apache Kafka	Amazon Kinesis	Apache Pulsar
Integration	Integrates with various systems such as Apache Flink, Spark, and Hadoop	Seamless integration with AWS services such as Lambda, S3, and Redshift	Integrates with various systems such as Apache Flink, Spark, and Hadoop
Scalability	Horizontally scalable with partitioned topics	Scales by provisioning shards; limited by AWS account shard limits	Horizontally scalable with separate serving and storage layers
Geo-Replication	Requires additional tools or configurations for cross-region replication	Requires additional configuration and services for cross-region replication	Built-in support for geo-replication across data centers
Use Cases	Suitable for diverse environments; ideal for organizations seeking flexibility	Best for AWS-centric applications requiring tight integration with AWS services	Suitable for diverse environments; ideal for organizations seeking flexibility

Vector databases

Vector databases form the retrieval part of modern RAG, recommendation, and similarity analytics pipelines. They differ less in what they store (high-dimensional embeddings) than in how they index, scale, and integrate. The following profiles give a concise but historically grounded view of seven widely used engines – Pinecone, Weaviate, Qdrant, OpenSearch, PostgreSQL and pgvector, and FAISS – highlighting release milestones, architectural choices, typical workloads and a few lesser-known facts that illuminate why each tool thrives in its niche.

Pinecone

Pinecone emerged from stealth in January 2021, launching the first "vector database-as-a-service."

Its serverless architecture, unveiled in public preview in late 2023 and GA in May 2024, splits compute-heavy HNSW/PQ indexes from low-cost object storage, so clusters ("pods") elastically scale from thousands to billions of vectors in seconds.

Use cases span RAG chatbots, real-time personalization, and fraud signal search, and the platform counts Microsoft, Notion, and Plaid among thousands of adopters.

Weaviate

Written in Go/Rust, **Weaviate** couples HNSW with lexical BM25 in a single hybrid query and ships pluggable transformer, reranker, and generative modules out of the box.

A managed, multi-tenant cloud and new **Weaviate Agents SDK** (March 2025) push it toward full stack AI backend status.

Developers reach for Weaviate when they need OSS-friendly licenses, module extensibility, or billions-of-vector scale without relinquishing on-prem control.

Qdrant

Built entirely in Rust, **Qdrant** prioritizes raw throughput and adds payload-level boolean filtering, disk offload, and online PQ compression.

A January 2024 Series A brought $28 million to accelerate enterprise features.

Teams pick Qdrant for high-write IoT streams or multi-facet RAG where attribute filtering is as important as vector similarity.

OpenSearch k-NN

AWS announced the OpenSearch project in April 2021 as an Apache-2.0 fork of Elasticsearch/Kibana and shipped v1.0 GA three months later.

The k-NN plugin integrates HNSW, disk-optimized graph indexes and byte-vector quantization directly into Lucene shards, inheriting all OpenSearch cluster amenities.

Release 2.17 (Sept 2024) added asynchronous batch ingestion and binary quantization for cost-efficient billion-scale search.

Organizations already running the ELK/observability stack adopt k-NN to layer semantic retrieval or hybrid BM25 and vector scoring without new infrastructure.

PostgreSQL and pgvector

The **pgvector** extension debuted on April 20, 2021 and has since added IVF and HNSW ANN indexes, as well as half-precision and sparse vector types.

Version 0.8 (Nov 2024) improved plan-costing, so Postgres chooses exact or ANN indexes dynamically, and major clouds now offer pgvector-enabled Postgres in managed form.

For workloads under ~50 million embeddings, engineers enjoy transactional consistency, rich SQL filtering, and zero new ops surface.

FAISS

Facebook AI Research released FAISS in March 2017, touting 8.5× faster GPU ANN search than the prior state of the art.

It bundles IVF-Flat/PQ, HNSW, and clustering and remains the de facto baseline for offline experimentation or as an embedded engine inside other DBs.

Many SaaS stores (including early Pinecone and Milvus versions) started as FAISS wrappers before adding distributed control planes.

RAG storage engine selection

In our framework, we can highlight three important technological components we can consider **VectorStore** components, which enable vector similarity algorithms.

To design an effective system based on your description of technological needs and challenges, considering various components within the checklist will help ensure the selection of the most appropriate technologies. Your inquiry covers the choice of technology for embeddings and vector storage, which is crucial for implementing search and analytics functions in the proposed system. Here is how you can structure the decision-making process. We deliberately limit our comparison to Open Source Software (OSS) options in order to exclude pricing and vendor lock-in considerations from the evaluation. This ensures a fair, implementation-focused comparison based solely on architectural and technical capabilities.

	OpenSearch	PostgreSQL and pg_vector	FAISS
Scalability	High (distributed architecture)***	Limited (better for smaller deployments)**	Limited (FAISS itself scales to 1 billion plus on GPU/CPU, but you must shard or distribute the index)*
Performance	Fast k-NN searches, high query throughput***	Good for small-scale vector searches**	Highly efficient for NN searches***
Integration	Seamless with existing stack (same DSL, security model, and observability stack as the rest of OpenSearch)***	Native database integration***	Limited distributed capabilities (it is a C++/Python library; no built-in cluster, schema, or ACLs)

	OpenSearch	PostgreSQL and pg_vector	FAISS
Operational Complexity	Higher (you manage shards, replicas, and JVM tuning; serverless reduces that but not to zero)***	Lower (standard DB management)**	Lower for the single system and higher for the clusters *
Use Case Fit	Large-scale vector storage and retrieval***	Small to medium deployments**	Standalone vector search*
Distributed Capabilities	Native sharding, cross-AZ replication, serverless multi-worker	Limited (sharding)	Weak (no out-of-box distribution)
Final Decision	Selected	Rejected	Rejected

By methodically evaluating each aspect according to this structured approach, you can make an informed decision that aligns technological choices with business objectives and operational requirements.

Transport and contract definition

Selecting the right transport technology is critical for ensuring a system's efficiency, scalability, and reliability. The transport layer plays a key role in handling data transmission, minimizing latency, and maintaining secure and consistent communication across diverse network environments. When evaluating transport options, factors such as throughput, fault tolerance, security, and protocol compatibility must be considered to optimize system performance.

The following criteria outline essential aspects to guide the selection of transport technologies:

- **Throughput and scalability:** The transport must handle the current data volumes and scale effectively as demands increase. This ensures that the system can grow without experiencing performance bottlenecks.

- **Latency:** The transport's ability to minimize delay is crucial for applications where timing is critical, such as those requiring real-time interactions. This impacts user experience and operational efficiency.

- **Reliability and fault tolerance:** The chosen transport method must ensure consistent data delivery despite network issues, with robust recovery solutions to maintain service continuity.

- **Support for various network topologies**: Systems that operate globally or across varied network environments need to be adaptable to different network layouts, including dispersed geographical locations.

- **Data transmission security**: Protecting data integrity and confidentiality during transit is essential, particularly for applications handling sensitive or regulatory-bound information.

- **Standards and protocol support**: Compatibility with established protocols ensures the transport can integrate smoothly with existing technologies and infrastructure, facilitating broader system integration.

- **Flow control and congestion management**: Effective mechanisms must be in place to manage data flow, prevent network congestion, and ensure reliable data transmission without loss.

Choosing the right serialization format involves considering how well it handles converting data quickly, its ability to manage changes over time, and how easily it can be integrated into the system for smooth operation and maintenance. Here are the key considerations for selecting serialization formats:

- **Contracts and boundaries**: Design-time (described in the code) or runtime (can be validated in running applications)

- **Serialization/deserialization efficiency**: Formats should facilitate rapid conversion to and from data structures, minimizing latency and processing times, which is critical for maintaining high system performance

- **Data compression**: Efficient compression reduces the volume of data transmitted and stored, conserving bandwidth and storage resources, which is vital for cost-effective scaling

- **Versioning and data migration:** Versioning support is crucial for accommodating changes in the data schema without disrupting existing operations, facilitating smooth transitions and updates

- **Development tool and schema registry integration**: Strong support from commonly used development tools enhances developer productivity and eases maintenance, contributing to more robust and error-free implementations.

> This taxonomy is quite conditional because nothing prevents you from building communication via a database or a storage (so-called shared database), or considering distributed log storage, such as Kafka, as one of the transport options.

Shared memory

Shared memory is a method of **inter-process communication (IPC)** where multiple processes access a common memory space. It's one of the fastest IPC methods because it allows direct data exchange without copying or moving data unnecessarily. This section will outline the specifics of using shared memory as a transport medium, its application scenarios, and considerations for its use in distributed systems. Applicable in monolithic architectures, especially those running on a single machine, shared memory is ideal for high-speed data exchange between components or modules within the same application. Since all components are part of a single application stack, shared memory can be effectively used without the overhead of network communications. Also, it is beneficial for **High-Performance Computing (HPC)** applications, such as simulations and complex calculations that require fast access to large datasets, which can benefit significantly from shared memory. It allows multiple processors to work on different parts of a problem simultaneously while accessing the same data in memory.

The following are some of the benefits:

- **Low latency and high throughput**: Shared memory provides a mechanism for very low-latency communication and high data throughput because it eliminates the need for data to be copied between the sender and receiver.

- **Efficiency**: There are no network protocol stacks to traverse, reducing the CPU overhead required for data transfer.

The following are some of the limitations and challenges:

- **Scalability**: Scalability is limited by the hardware it runs on. Shared memory is generally confined to a single machine, so it doesn't scale well across distributed systems without additional synchronization mechanisms.

- **Concurrency control**: Managing access to shared memory can be complex. Mechanisms such as semaphores, mutexes, or locks are necessary to prevent race conditions and ensure data integrity.

- **Homogeneity requirement**: It works best in environments where all processes are homogeneously designed to interact with the shared memory segment, requiring a consistent approach to memory management across all interacting processes.

- **Dynamic contracts**: In shared memory setups, the interaction contracts—defined as the agreed-upon structure and method for accessing shared data—are inherently flexible. This flexibility allows components to adapt their data exchange methods as the application evolves. However, this can also introduce complexity and potential inconsistencies if not managed correctly. Since the structures and data access patterns are not enforced by rigid protocols (unlike network communications), they can be modified more freely. This is both an advantage and a risk, as it requires rigorous coordination and documentation to ensure all components interact correctly without data corruption.

Networking in distributed systems

Networking is the backbone of communication in distributed systems, enabling different components and applications to exchange data over various physical and virtual channels. This section explores how networking can be effectively used in distributed environments, similar to how shared memory is employed in single-system architectures.

Characteristics and use cases

- **Distributed applications**: Networking is crucial for applications that are spread across multiple physical servers or cloud environments, where components must communicate over a network
- **Service-oriented architecture**: This enables services to communicate through network calls, which can be either synchronous or asynchronous
- **Highly available systems**: Networks enable the replication of data across geographically dispersed data centers, enhancing the availability and resilience of systems.

Benefits

- **Scalability**: Networking allows a system to scale out across multiple machines and locations, handling more requests by adding more resources
- **Flexibility**: Network configurations can be adjusted as requirements change, without the need for significant hardware changes
- **Interoperability**: Different systems and applications, possibly written in different programming languages or running on different platforms, can communicate seamlessly

Limitations and challenges

- **Latency**: Network calls are significantly slower than local calls, and network latency can become a bottleneck in performance-sensitive applications

- **Complexity**: Managing network configurations, handling network failures, and optimizing network performance add complexity to system design and operation
- **Security risks**: Data transmitted over networks can be intercepted, requiring robust encryption and authentication mechanisms to secure communications

Key considerations

- **Network Topology:** The design of the network, including its layout and the protocols used, impacts performance and security.
- **Error Handling:** Mechanisms must be in place to detect, report, and recover from network failures to maintain system reliability.
- **Performance Optimization:** Techniques such as load balancing and traffic shaping are essential to manage the network load effectively.

Message brokers

Message brokers are intermediary platforms that facilitate message exchange between different applications and services. They support various messaging patterns, including queueing, topic-based publish/subscribe, and request/response interactions.

Characteristics and use cases

- **Integration of heterogeneous systems**: This allows different systems, potentially using different technologies, to communicate via a common messaging format and protocol
- **Asynchronous processing**: Messages can be stored in queues and processed asynchronously, which is critical for operations that require decoupling of processing from message reception
- **Load balancing**: This distributes incoming messages across multiple workers or services, balancing the load and improving the throughput of processing

Benefits

- **Reliability**: This provides guaranteed delivery mechanisms, ensuring messages are not lost in transit between sender and receiver
- **Scalability**: This facilitates the scaling of applications by managing communication across multiple instances of services or databases
- **Isolation**: This reduces direct dependencies between communicating components, isolating failures and improving system resilience

Limitations and challenges

- **Complexity of setup and management**: Setting up and maintaining a message broker can be complex and resource-intensive

- **Performance bottlenecks**: High volumes of messages can lead to bottlenecks if the broker is not appropriately scaled or configured

- **Security**: Ensuring secure transmission of sensitive data through brokers requires encryption and secure configuration practices

Key considerations

- **Broker choice**: Selection of the broker technology should be based on the specific requirements of latency, throughput, and feature support

- **System monitoring and maintenance**: Continuous monitoring of the broker's performance and regular updates to its configuration and software to handle evolving system demands

These sections on networking, pub/sub systems, and message brokers outline foundational concepts and considerations that are crucial for designing robust distributed systems and communication strategies.

Pub/sub systems

Publish/subscribe (pub/sub) systems are a type of message-oriented middleware that provides a flexible communication paradigm through asynchronous message passing. This model decouples message producers (publishers) from message consumers (subscribers), enhancing the modularity and scalability of applications.

Characteristics and use cases

- **Event-driven architectures**: Ideal for applications where actions are triggered by events, such as real-time notifications and updates

- **Microservices communication**: Facilitates the communication among loosely coupled microservices by allowing services to publish events without knowing the subscribers

- **Scalability**: Easily scales out to handle large numbers of messages and subscribers by distributing the load across multiple brokers or nodes

Benefits

- **Decoupling**: Publishers and subscribers do not need to know about each other, which simplifies component integration and system maintenance

- **Asynchronicity**: Allows systems to process messages at their own pace, improving responsiveness and overall system efficiency

- **Fault tolerance**: Pub/sub systems can be designed to handle failures gracefully, ensuring that message delivery can resume or be rerouted in the event of a node failure

Limitations and challenges

- **Message overhead**: Managing a large volume of messages can lead to overhead in terms of performance and resource usage

- **Complexity of message management**: Ensuring the correct order and delivery of messages can be challenging, especially in systems with stringent consistency requirements

- **Dependency on brokers**: The reliability of the entire system can depend on the brokers, which introduces a single point of failure unless redundancies are built into the system

Key considerations

- **Broker performance and reliability**: The choice of broker software and its configuration significantly impacts the performance and reliability of the pub/sub system

- **Message durability and retention policies**: Configurations that determine how long messages are stored and how failures in delivery are handled

- **Subscription management**: Efficient management of subscriptions, including adding, removing, and updating subscribers without disrupting the message flow

Serialization formats: defining interaction contracts

Serialization formats play a pivotal role in software development by establishing how data is structured, transported, and reconstructed across various components and systems. By defining clear interaction contracts, these formats ensure consistent data integrity and compatibility across different environments.

JavaScript Object Notation (JSON)

JSON is renowned for its readability and simplicity, which makes it highly favored for manual editing and debugging. JSON is predominantly utilized in web APIs and configuration files, where lightweight data exchange is necessary. It is particularly useful in environments that prioritize developer accessibility, such as settings where quick adjustments to data are common.

Let's look at the following example, where we have configured a user interface setting or transmitted data from a client to a server:

```
{
  "name": "John Doe",
  "age": 30,
  "isAdmin": false
}
```

Protocol Buffers (Protobuf)

Optimized performance: Developed by Google, Protobuf is designed to serialize structured data
efficiently. Its binary format not only minimizes payload size but also enhances processing speed.
Protobuf is extensively used in microservices communication, mobile applications, and perfor-
mance-critical applications such as real-time data streaming, where minimal latency is crucial.

Now, consider a case where we need to define and serialize a simple message in Protobuf:

```
message User {
  required string name = 1;
  required int32 id = 2;
  optional string email = 3;
}
```

Apache Avro

Schema evolution: Avro supports forward and backward compatibility, crucial for systems where
schemas need to evolve over time without disrupting operations. Integrated with big data platforms such as Apache Hadoop and Apache Kafka, Avro is suited for distributed data storage and
messaging systems where schemas are embedded with the data, ensuring proper serialization
and deserialization.

Example: An Avro schema for a user record might look like this:

```
{
  "type": "record",
  "name": "User",
  "fields" : [
    {"name": "name", "type": "string"},
    {"name": "age", "type": "int"}
  ]
}
```

MessagePack

MessagePack is a binary serialization format that acts as a compact, efficient alternative to JSON, reducing CPU and bandwidth usage. It is used in mobile apps and real-time applications that require efficient and compact data exchange, such as gaming and IoT applications.

Example: Encoding a simple dictionary or object with `MessagePack` might look like this when visualized:

```
82 A3 66 6F 6F A3 62 61 72 A3 62 61 7A A3 71 75 78
```

Communication protocols (API styles)

We shall cover the following communication protocols:

- REST
- GraphQL

REST

Representational State Transfer (REST) is a software architectural style that defines constraints for creating web services. Web services that conform to the REST architectural style, termed RESTful web services, provide interoperability between computer systems on the internet. RESTful web services allow requesting systems to access and manipulate textual representations of web resources using a uniform, predefined set of stateless operations. REST is based on several key principles that guide the design and development of the architecture of RESTful systems:

- **Statelessness:** Each request from a client to a server must contain all the information the server needs to understand and process the request. The server cannot store context from one request to another; all context is stored on the client.

- **Client-server architecture**: The client and the server should be independent of each other, allowing both to evolve independently without any dependency on each other.

- **Uniform interface:** To obtain uniformity throughout the application, REST has defined three interface constraints:

  - **Resource identification in requests**: Individual resources are identified in requests using URIs. The resources are conceptually separate from the representations returned to the client.

  - **Resource manipulation through representations**: When a client holds a representation of a resource, including any metadata attached, it has enough information to modify or delete the resource on the server, provided it has permission to do so.

- **Self-descriptive messages**: Each message includes enough information to describe how to process the message.

Use cases

- **Web APIs**: The most common use of REST is in developing web APIs, which expose specific software functions and data to external applications in a secure, reliable, and documented way. These APIs are used extensively in web services and applications.
- **Mobile backends**: REST is used to build backends for mobile applications, providing data and services that mobile applications can consume and manipulate. Given its stateless nature, REST is well-suited to the sporadic connectivity and scalability requirements of mobile applications.
- **Single-page applications (SPAs)**: Many modern web applications are structured around SPAs, where RESTful APIs are utilized to handle data interchange between the server and the web application running in the client's browser.
- **Microservices**: In microservices architectures, REST is used to design lightweight services that interact through clear, well-defined interfaces.

REST's use of standard HTTP methods to manage resources makes it a simple yet powerful system for building APIs that are easy to understand and use. The scalability provided by stateless interactions, combined with the ability to handle data in multiple formats and detailed API documentation through tools such as Swagger or OpenAPI, makes REST a robust choice for public and internal API designs.

Imagine an online bookstore where users can browse books, add them to their cart, and check out. Here's how a RESTful API might be designed to support these operations:

1. List all books: `GET /books`
2. Get details about a specific book: `GET /books/{bookId}`
3. Add a new book: `POST /books`
4. Update existing book details: `PUT /books/{bookId}`
5. Delete a book: `DELETE /books/{bookId}`

Using standard HTTP methods, the client interacts with the bookstore:

The GET request is used to retrieve a resource or a list of resources – for example, to retrieve details for a specific book:

```
GET /books/123
```

This request might return a JSON representation of the book:

```
{
    "bookId": "123",
    "title": "The Great Gatsby",
    "author": "F. Scott Fitzgerald",
    "price": "$15.20"
}
```

The POST request creates a new resource. To add a new book to the catalog, we need to send data like this:

```
POST /books
```

The request body contains the data of the new book:

```
{
    "title": "1984",
    "author": "George Orwell",
    "price": "$18.00"
}
```

The server responds with the URI of the newly created book:

```
HTTP/1.1 201 Created
Location: /books/124
```

The PUT request updates an existing resource fully – for example, changing the price of a book:

```
PUT /books/123
```

The request body contains the updated data:

```
{
    "bookId": "123",
    "title": "The Great Gatsby",
    "author": "F. Scott Fitzgerald",
    "price": "$12.99"
}
```

Finally, the DELETE method removes a resource – for example, deleting a book:

```
DELETE /books/123
```

GraphQL

GraphQL is a query language for APIs and a runtime for executing those queries by using a type system you define for your data. Developed by Facebook in 2012 and released publicly in 2015, GraphQL has emerged as a powerful alternative to REST for designing more efficient and flexible APIs.

Key principles of GraphQL

- **Strongly typed schema**: GraphQL requires defining a schema using a Schema Definition Language (SDL). This schema serves as the contract between the client and the server, ensuring that the data interactions follow a predefined structure.

- **Single endpoint**: Unlike REST, which uses multiple endpoints to access data, GraphQL APIs typically expose a single endpoint through which clients can make all their requests.

- **Client-specified queries**: Clients have the freedom to request exactly what they need – nothing more and nothing less. This reduces the bandwidth and processing power required, as the server only sends the data requested.

- **Hierarchical data structure**: The shape of a GraphQL query closely matches the resulting data, making it easier to predict the outcome of a query.

- **Introspective**: GraphQL supports introspection, allowing clients to query the API for details about the API schema. This feature facilitates building helpful API browsing tools and automating some types of UIs.

Benefits

- **Efficiency**: Reduces the need for multiple round trips between client and server, fetching all required data in a single request.

- **Flexibility**: Clients can tailor requests to their specific needs, fetching data from multiple resources in a single request.

- **Strongly-typed interface**: The schema serves as a contract, which can help prevent run-time errors.

Limitations and challenges

- **Performance concerns**: Complex queries can lead to performance issues if not properly managed, potentially straining the server by requesting deep nested structures.

- **Caching complexity**: Traditional HTTP caching mechanisms are less effective because of the way GraphQL queries are structured, requiring more sophisticated caching strategies on the client or intermediate layers.

- **Rate limiting and complexity analysis**: Protecting the server from resource-intensive queries can be more challenging than REST.

Use cases

- **Complex systems**: Systems that require interacting with multiple data sources in a single query can benefit from GraphQL's ability to aggregate data.

- **Rapid iteration on frontends**: Frontend teams can adjust data requirements on the fly without needing backend adjustments.

- **Mobile applications**: Mobile applications operating in environments with fluctuating network conditions benefit from GraphQL's ability to minimize data loads by allowing clients to specify exactly what data is needed.

Imagine a social media platform where users can post articles, comment, and like posts. Here's how a GraphQL API might support these operations:

```
query {
  getPost(id: "1") {
    title
    author {
      name
      profilePic
    }
    comments {
      text
      author {
        name
      }
    }
  }
}
```

This query fetches the post with ID "1", including the title, author's name, and profile picture, and the text of comments, along with the names of their authors:

```
mutation {
  createPost(title: "New GraphQL Article", content: "Content of the
article", authorId: "2") {
    id
    title
```

```
      content
    }
  }
}
```

This mutation creates a new post, returning the new post's ID, title, and content:

```
subscription {
  postLiked(postId: "1") {
    id
    title
    likes
  }
}
```

In production, you usually supply argument values via GraphQL variables:

```
mutation CreatePost($title:String!,$content:String!,$authorId:ID!){
  createPost(title:$title, content:$content, authorId:$authorId){
    id
    title
    content
  }
}
```

This is invoked with a JSON payload such as {"title":"Hello","content":"...","authorId":"2"} -because a constant query string plus separate variables lets gateways cache by query hash, keeps sensitive data out of logs, cuts payload size, and enables persisted-query workflows, whereas inline literals are fine only for quick, human-readable demos.

gRPC

gRPC is a modern, open source, high-performance Remote Procedure Call (RPC) framework that can run in any environment. It can efficiently connect services in and across data centers with pluggable support for load balancing, tracing, health checking, and authentication. Originally developed by Google, it is now part of the Cloud Native Computing Foundation. gRPC is based on the concept of defining a service, specifying the methods that can be called remotely with their parameters and return types. On the server side, the server implements this interface and runs a gRPC server to handle client calls. On the client side, the client has a stub that provides the same methods as the server.

Key principles of gRPC

- **Interface Definition Language (IDL)**: gRPC uses Protocol Buffers (Protobuf) by default as its interface definition language to define the structure of the data and service.

- **HTTP/2 as transport layer**: gRPC uses HTTP/2 for transport, which enables multiplexed streams over a single connection, allowing multiple requests and responses to be in flight at the same time.

- **Contract-first API development**: Service definitions are decoupled from their implementations.

Benefits

- **Performance**: gRPC uses HTTP/2, which reduces latency and saves bandwidth through header compression and multiplexing. Protocol Buffers, a method of serializing structured data, are smaller, faster, and simpler than JSON.

- **Bidirectional streaming and flow control**: gRPC supports bidirectional streaming and excellent flow control, allowing for advanced scenarios in real-time communication and high throughput.

- **Language agnosticism**: gRPC tools support multiple languages, making it easy to build a multi-language system.

- **Pluggable**: Authentication, load balancing, retries, and monitoring can all be configured globally and per service.

Limitations and challenges

- **Limited browser support**: Native gRPC is not fully supported in browsers due to the lack of HTTP/2 support with the necessary features. gRPC-Web offers a workaround, but with some limitations.

- **Complexity**: Handling gRPC and Protocol Buffers adds a learning curve and complexity in development compared to REST APIs.

- **Error handling**: gRPC error handling is less transparent than HTTP status codes, as it uses its own status codes.

Use cases

- **Microservices**: Ideal for microservices communication due to its low latency and support for multiple languages.

- **Real-time services**: Useful for services needing real-time bidirectional data flow such as live updates and chat services.

- **Network-intensive applications**: Effective for mobile apps that require frequent server communication, which is efficient over gRPC's HTTP/2-based transport.

Example: gRPC service for user management

A gRPC service for a user management system could provide functions to create, retrieve, update, and delete user profiles.

Here's the service definition (Protocol Buffers):

```
syntax = "proto3";
package usermanagement;
// The user service definition.
service UserService {
  // Creates a user
  rpc CreateUser (User) returns (UserResponse);
  // Retrieves a user by ID
  rpc GetUser (UserRequest) returns (UserResponse);
}

// The request message containing the user's data.
message User {
  string id = 1;
  string name = 2;
  string email = 3;
}
// The request message for getting a user.
message UserRequest {
  string id = 1;
}
// The response message containing the user's data.
message UserResponse {
  string id = 1;
  string name = 2;
  string email = 3;
}
```

In the gRPC client and server interaction, client sends a `CreateUser` request to create a new user with the user's data. The server then responds with `UserResponse` containing the created user data.

Imagine an e-commerce marketplace that wants to give shoppers an "AI shopping assistant."

A customer opens the mobile app, taps the chat icon, and types the following:

> *"I'm looking for waterproof hiking boots under $150—what do you recommend, and do you have my size in stock at the San Jose warehouse?"*

Here's the backend RAG pipeline:

1. Understands the query. It embeds the request and retrieves the five most relevant product descriptions, sizing tables, and live-inventory snippets.

2. It generates a tailored reply. It feeds those documents to an LLM that crafts a conversational answer, cites the sources, and suggests three specific SKUs that match price, waterproof rating, and location.

3. It streams the response. As the LLM produces tokens, the app shows the answer in real time, allowing the shopper to interrupt with follow-up questions ("show me women's sizes" or "add the first pair to cart").

Attribute	HTTP/2 + REST	gRPC	Websockets
Performance	High (multiplexing and header compression)**	Very high (binary bidirectional streaming)*	High (full duplex frames)**
Browser Support	Universal***	Limited*	Good**
Setup Complexity	Low***	High*	Moderate**
Use Case Fit	One-shot request/ response***	Service-to-service real-time streaming*	Continuous token stream to client**
Integration Ease	Simple***	Complex*	Moderate**
Tooling/ Ecosystem	Extensive***	Growing**	Good**
Learning Curve	Low***	High*	Moderate
Final Decision	Selected	Rejected	Rejected

Platforms for computation and distributed computing

In modern software development, especially in fields that require intensive computations such as data science, machine learning, and image processing, specialized toolkits provide essential functionalities that can significantly enhance performance and capability. Here, we discuss some of the prominent toolkits, such as CUDA, OpenCL, and others designed for specific computational needs, including distributed computing environments.

Parallelized calculation platforms and APIs

Parallelized calculation toolkits are frameworks that enable the execution of computations across multiple processing cores at the same time, significantly improving the performance of tasks requiring extensive computation, such as data processing, machine learning, or 3D rendering. These toolkits allow developers to distribute complex calculations across a range of processors, from CPUs to GPUs, taking advantage of the hardware's parallel processing capabilities. By breaking down large problems into smaller, independent tasks that can run simultaneously, these toolkits reduce execution time and increase efficiency in handling intensive workloads, especially in fields such as scientific computing and real-time data analysis.

CUDA

Compute Unified Device Architecture (CUDA) is a parallel computing platform and application programming interface (API) model created by NVIDIA. It allows developers to use a CUDA-enabled graphics processing unit (GPU) for general-purpose processing – an approach known as **General-Purpose computing on Graphics Processing Units (GPGPU)**.

Characteristics and use cases

- **High-Performance Computing (HPC)**: CUDA is extensively used in applications that require massive parallel computing, from scientific simulations to deep learning
- **Graphics and video processing**: Enables complex graphics computations to be offloaded to the GPU, speeding up rendering and processing times significantly
- **Machine learning and AI**: Libraries such as cuDNN and TensorFlow leverage CUDA for accelerating neural network computation
- **Benefits**
- **Speed**: Utilizes the parallel nature of GPUs to execute thousands of threads simultaneously, leading to a dramatic increase in computing performance
- **Flexibility**: Supports multiple programming languages, including C, C++, and Python, making it accessible to a broad developer base

- **Ecosystem:** A rich set of libraries and frameworks enhances capabilities in many scientific and analytical computing domains

- **Limitations and challenges**

- **Hardware dependency:** Requires NVIDIA GPUs, which can be a barrier in environments with other hardware

- **Complexity:** Programming for CUDA involves understanding parallel computation and memory management, which can be challenging for newcomers

Open Computing Language (OpenCL)

Open Computing Language (OpenCL) is an open standard for parallel programming of heterogeneous systems. It was developed by the Khronos Group and enables developers to write code that can execute across various platforms, including CPUs, GPUs, FPGAs, and other processors.

Characteristics and use cases

- **HPC:** OpenCL is widely used in scientific simulations, financial modeling, and other applications requiring extensive computational power across diverse hardware.

- **Graphics and video processing:** It facilitates the execution of complex graphics and video processing tasks on GPUs, enhancing rendering speeds and efficiency.

- **Machine learning and AI:** OpenCL supports machine learning frameworks and applications, allowing for accelerated neural network training and inference on various hardware.

Benefits

- **Cross-platform compatibility:** OpenCL can run on a wide range of hardware from different vendors, including AMD, Intel, ARM, and NVIDIA, promoting flexibility and reducing vendor lock.

- **Scalability:** It allows developers to write code that can scale from embedded devices to large supercomputers, utilizing available computational resources efficiently.

- **Portability:** OpenCL code is portable across multiple devices and architectures, ensuring that applications can leverage the best available hardware without significant rewrites.

- **Flexibility:** It supports a range of programming languages, such as C, C++, and Python, enabling developers to choose the best language for their needs.

- **Limitations and challenges**

- **Complexity:** Writing efficient OpenCL code can be complex due to the need to manage memory and concurrency explicitly. This complexity can pose a steep learning curve for developers new to parallel programming.

- **Performance overhead**: Although OpenCL provides portability, it may introduce performance overhead compared to vendor-specific solutions such as CUDA, as it cannot fully optimize for any single hardware architecture.

- **Tooling and ecosystem**: While many vendors support OpenCL, the ecosystem and tooling are not as mature or extensive as those for CUDA, potentially limiting the availability of prebuilt libraries and frameworks.

OpenCL's ability to run across multiple types of processors makes it a versatile choice for applications requiring high-performance computing on diverse hardware, despite the complexities and potential performance trade-offs involved.

Distributed computing engines

Engines such as Apache Hadoop and Apache Spark are crucial for applications that require distributed computing, splitting tasks across multiple computing resources.

Apache Hadoop

When a dataset grows beyond the capacity of a single machine or the response-time budget of disk-bound processing, the conversation inevitably turns to engines that can spread work across a cluster. The two venerable names here are Apache Hadoop and Apache Spark, yet they solve the scaling problem in very different ways and therefore occupy different niches in a modern architecture.

Hadoop appeared first, pairing its distributed file system (HDFS) with the MapReduce programming model. The design goal was durability and throughput, not speed: data blocks are replicated three times across racks, and the computation is "shipped to the data," so a failed node is an inconvenience rather than a disaster.

- **Benefits**: High fault tolerance, scalable storage, and a flexible data processing layer (MapReduce)
- **Challenges**: Complex setup and management, and slower compared to newer systems such as Spark for certain computations

Apache Spark

Spark was created to attack exactly those pain points. It keeps intermediate data in RAM (or at worst on a fast local SSD) by representing each transformation as a node in a directed-acyclic graph and fusing many of those nodes into a single pass. Interactive SQL, iterative machine-learning feature engineering, and micro-batch streams feeding dashboards—these are the domains where Spark routinely delivers in seconds what MapReduce would deliver in tens of minutes.

- **Benefits**: High-level APIs in Java, Scala, Python, and R. Integrates seamlessly with big data tools and supports complex pipelines.

- **Challenges**: Resource management can be intensive, and optimal performance often requires tuning.

In our case, all computational requests will be processed by external models. Who knows, maybe we will need to use a framework that will use a local model application in the future. In this case, we will add such functionality to the framework.

Machine learning models as framework components

Since early 2024, the model landscape has stabilized around two plug-in roles your RAG framework must expose: an embedding block that turns text into vectors for retrieval, and a generator that turns vectors and context back into prose. Everything else – classic boosters and vision backbones – can stay optional.

Here's how to think about the embedding model:

- **Measure what matters**: Public leaderboards such as MTEB report retrieval F1 on 56 tasks; treat them as a filter, then rerun the top five on your corpus. Margins above ±2 pp are rarely significant.

- **Vector size drives storage**: A 1024-dim vector from BGE-large eats three times the RAM of a 384-dim MiniLM vector; that cost multiplies when your index holds billions of documents.

- **Latency versus ops**: Cloud APIs (OpenAI, Cohere) add ~60–100 ms of network overhead but outsource upgrades and scaling; self-host checkpoints need GPUs and paging, yet avoid per-call fees.

- **License and privacy gate**: SaaS may be off-limits for regulated data; Apache-2 models such as BGE or Flag Embedding remove that blocker

- Here's how to choose a generative LLM:

- **Reasoning skill versus context window**: GPT-4o handles 128,000 tokens with state-of-the-art accuracy, while Claude-3 Opus stretches to 200,000+, but at a higher cost and SaaS-only availability.

- **Token price and speed**: GPT-4.1, launched in April 2025, cuts costs by 26% and streams faster than GPT-4o; Mistral Large 2 offers a mid-range price for 128,000 context.

- **Hosting footprint**: Llama 3 70 B runs acceptably on two A100s ($\approx$ 140 GB VRAM); anything over 120 B parameters needs multi-GPU or tensor-parallel clusters.

- **License and fine-tune freedom**: Open checkpoints (Llama 3, Mistral) enable on-prem fine-tuning and sidestep SaaS data-sovereignty concerns; proprietary APIs buy you immediate quality but lock you to vendor deprecations.

Development tooling

Because frameworks not only simplify the creation of applications related to a specific target but also provide guidelines and should support practices for writing code as well, they usually include development tooling to establish such approaches. This tooling can contain the following:

- **Code generators and code structure generators**: These tools automatically generate boilerplate code, data models, or even entire project structures based on predefined templates or schemas. They speed up development and ensure project consistency by enforcing standard patterns and practices.

  This tooling is usually developed together with the framework. In Django, commands such as **startproject** and **startup** are prime examples of code generators. They create directories and files for projects and applications, respectively, setting up a standardized directory structure and essential files such as settings, URLs, and WSGI configurations.

- **Testing engines**: These include frameworks and tools that support unit testing, integration testing, system testing, and sometimes acceptance testing. Popular examples include JUnit for Java, pytest for Python, and Mocha for JavaScript. Using testing engines ensures that the framework and the applications built with it are reliable and meet quality standards. Typically, frameworks build an alternative control flow for testing. In this way, developers can cover with tests only their code because embedding testing scenarios is enabled by the framework itself.

- **Documentation engines and API design libraries**: Tools such as Javadoc, Sphinx, and Doxygen automatically generate documentation from the code base. Good documentation is crucial for any framework, as it aids developers in understanding and utilizing the framework correctly, enhancing the developer experience and adoption. Tools such as Swagger (OpenAPI) for designing and documenting REST APIs ensure your framework can interact effectively with other software.

  By clearly defining these aspects of the tech stack, you establish a foundation that supports effective development and ensures that the framework can adapt to future technological changes or enhancements.

Summary

Throughout this chapter, we emphasized the significance of aligning a framework's technology stack with its intended functionalities and the broader technological ecosystem. From choosing the right programming languages and storage solutions to integrating with existing corporate tech stacks, each decision must be guided by both current requirements and future projections. We also covered the necessity of community support and the economic aspects of technology choices, which can greatly influence a project's long-term viability and success. As we concluded, the careful consideration of these factors not only facilitates smoother development processes but also enhances the framework's ability to adapt to new challenges and opportunities in the evolving tech landscape. This comprehensive approach ensures that the technology stack meets the technical requirements and supports the organization's strategic goals.

In the next chapter, we will observe architectural patterns and solutions that could also be involved in framework design.

Unlock this book's exclusive benefits now

Scan this QR code or go to packtpub.com/unlock, then search for this book by name. Ensure it's the correct edition.

Note: Keep your purchase invoice ready before you start.

5

Architecture Design

This chapter delves into the critical architectural design process within **application development frameworks (ADFs)**. Architectural design plays a pivotal role in laying a foundation for supporting and enhancing application frameworks' functionality and manageability. By establishing a coherent and well-thought-out architecture, developers can ensure that the framework operates efficiently and adapts seamlessly to present and future technological challenges.

The essence of architectural design in framework development revolves around making informed decisions about the structure of system components and their interrelationships. This strategic planning is crucial for aligning project goals, managing scope, accurately estimating efforts, and determining the necessary skills within the development team. Projects may need a robust architectural foundation to handle increased effort, scope creep, and compatibility issues.

Many teams employ software tools to facilitate effective architecture. These tools provide methodologies and tools to create and maintain dynamic and robust architectures. These operations are integral to transforming initial designs into actionable, scalable, and maintainable frameworks.

In this chapter, we're going to cover the following main topics:

- A comprehensive introduction to the principles and practices involved in framework architecture
- Exploring general tasks of framework architecture
- Defining framework architecture components
- Design patterns
- Techniques for designing frameworks that are adaptable and extensible

By the end of this chapter, you will have a thorough understanding of how to approach architectural design for ADFs, enabling you to craft solutions that are both efficient and forward-looking, catering to the evolving demands of the tech industry.

General tasks of framework architecture

Much like software architecture in general, the architecture of a framework is responsible for defining clear boundaries and ensuring effective communication within developer communities. A well-structured framework architecture allows different groups of developers – those building the framework itself, those extending it, and those using it – to work together efficiently.

A framework does not exist in isolation. It operates within a broader ecosystem that consists of four key levels (see *Figure 5.1*), each playing a distinct role in the life cycle of the framework. Understanding these levels is crucial for designing architectures that are both extensible and maintainable.

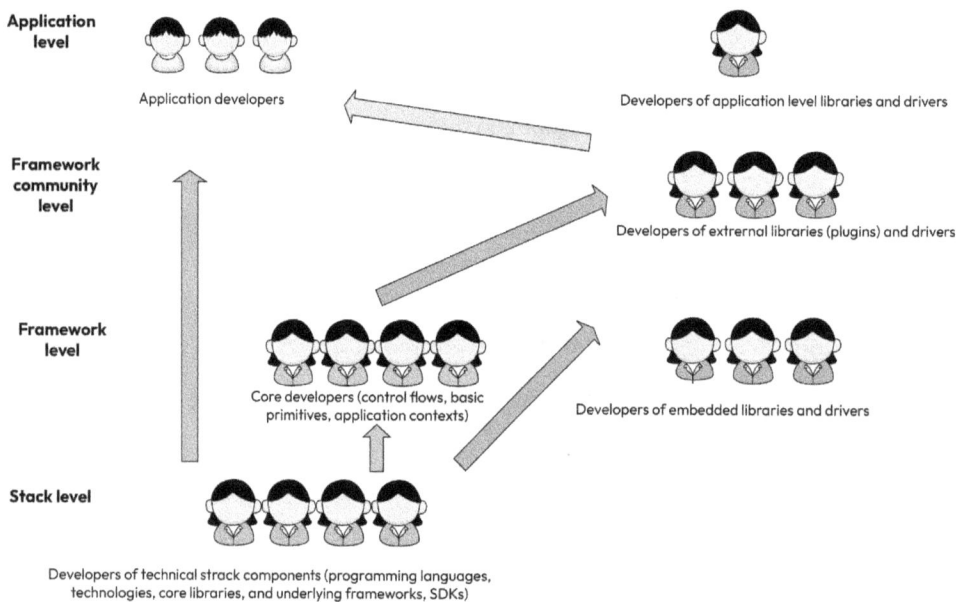

Figure 5.1: Communication architecture around a framework

Core principles are modularity, extensibility, maintainability, and scalability:

- **Modularity**: Design the framework as a collection of independent components or modules with minimal coupling. This separation of concerns allows teams to develop, test, and deploy parts in isolation, reducing complexity and improving maintainability.

- **Extensibility**: Provide clear extension points (such as plugins, hooks, or APIs) so developers can add new functionality without modifying the core. A framework should accommodate new requirements or integrations without necessitating a major rewrite as needs evolve.

- **Maintainability**: Emphasize clean design and code consistency to ease long-term upkeep. Internally, follow consistent conventions and coding standards – the best frameworks are internally consistent and well documented. Documentation is critical – clearly document.

- **Scalability**: Plan the architecture to handle growth in users, features, and data. Scalability means the system can expand without performance degradation. Techniques include designing stateless components that can be load-balanced and using modular services that scale horizontally. For instance, separating concerns (database, logic, and presentation) lets each layer scale as needed. A modular framework can be scaled out by deploying more instances of heavy-use modules or microservices.

Since we have already covered the stack level in detail in the previous chapter, we will now focus directly on the framework itself. This chapter examines the core structure, components, and interaction principles that define how the framework operates and how it supports application development.

Framework level: building the foundation

At the core of any framework is a set of fundamental tools and systems that define how applications are structured and operate. Developers working at this level are responsible for the following:

- Designing and implementing the core architecture of the framework

- Managing state, routing, data handling, and business logic structures that application developers will rely on

- Creating tools, documentation, and APIs that simplify development and ensure consistency across projects

This level is where the biggest architectural decisions happen. It's where developers define control flows, dependency management, and performance optimizations, ensuring that the framework provides a scalable and efficient foundation.

The following are examples:

- Django provides an opinionated **Model-View-Template (MVT)** structure, an ORM, and built-in authentication
- Flask, a micro-framework, offers lightweight routing and request handling but relies on extensions for added functionality
- TensorFlow defines core computation graphs and APIs for machine learning tasks

Without a solid framework level, application developers would struggle with inconsistencies, performance bottlenecks, and a lack of clear guidance on best practices.

Framework community level: extending the ecosystem

Once a framework core is in place, it often grows beyond its original design. No matter how well architected it is, there will always be edge cases, specialized needs, and evolving technology trends. This is where the broader community of developers steps in to enhance the framework's capabilities.

Developers working at this level contribute by doing the following:

- Building plugins, libraries, and tools that extend the functionality of the framework
- Integrating third-party technologies, such as databases, caching systems, or cloud services, into the framework ecosystem

A healthy framework thrives on community contributions. A flexible plugin architecture, an active package ecosystem, and well-documented extension points make it easier for developers to create tools that others can adopt.

The following are examples:

- **Django REST framework (DRF)** extends Django with powerful tools for building REST APIs
- LangChain plugins enable integration with various AI models, expanding the core framework capabilities

This level is what keeps frameworks evolving – it allows them to adapt to industry trends without requiring constant rewrites of their core logic.

Application level: the final layer of implementation

At the outermost level, developers use frameworks to build real-world applications. While they may not contribute directly to the framework's core, their work is crucial: their feedback shapes future improvements, and their use cases drive the need for extensions and refinements.

Developers at this level do the following:

- Use the framework's core features to build full-fledged applications
- Integrate third-party plugins and libraries to extend the framework's capabilities
- Provide real-world feedback that influences future versions of the framework

This level represents the end goal of framework design – making life easier for application developers so they can focus on solving business problems rather than reinventing core functionality.

The following are examples:

- A Django developer building a **content management system (CMS)** for a news website
- A Flask developer creating a REST API for a fintech application
- A machine learning engineer using TensorFlow to deploy a neural network model in production

Understanding these three levels helps framework architects make better design decisions. A well-structured framework isn't just about writing code – it's about designing an ecosystem where developers at all levels can contribute and benefit. By keeping these three levels in mind, architects can ensure that their frameworks remain relevant, extensible, and widely adopted. Now, we will review the basic structure of a typical framework.

Framework architecture components

Let's dig into the framework architecture components that are presented in *Figure 5.2*:

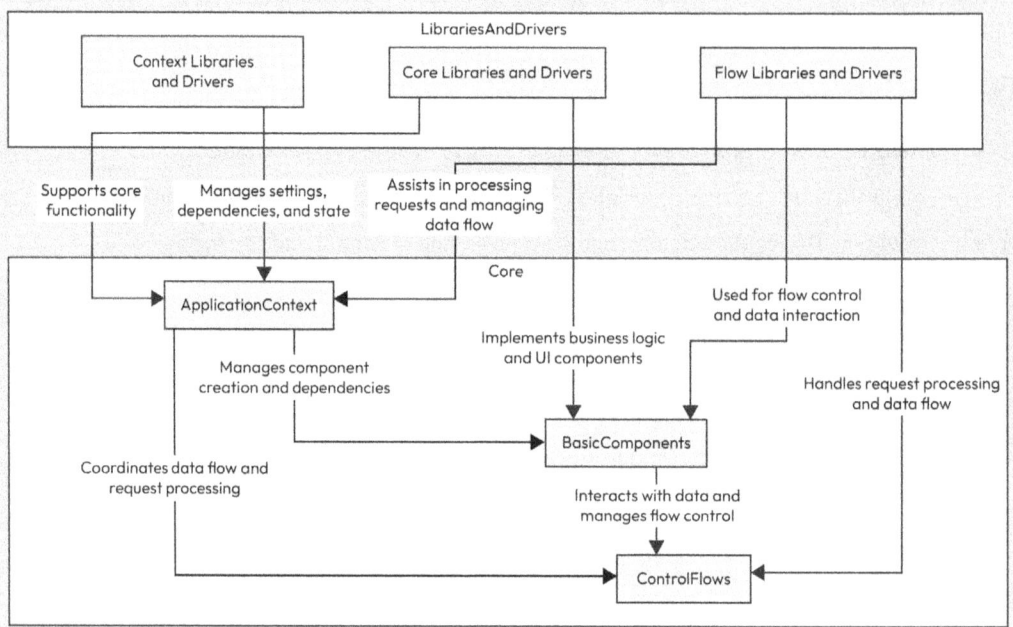

Figure 5.2: Diagram of architecture components

Core

The core is the fundamental structure of a framework, encompassing all critical components required for the application's operation. It provides the foundational infrastructure and manages the application life cycle, configuration, and basic primitives.

The following is the composition of the core:

- **Application context (containers, configuration)**: Manages global dependencies, configurations, and the overall state of the application. For example, in Django, this includes managing configurations through settings.py and handling dependencies via INSTALLED_APPS. Here, INSTALLED_APPS refers to a registry that tracks and manages various framework components, such as routes, middleware, and registered applications. For example, in Django, registries include URLconf for route management and the application registry.

- **Basic components**: Fundamental building blocks used to create objects and implement business logic. For example, in Django, these are represented by model, view, and template components.

- **Control flows**: Logic for managing data-processing workflows and request handling. For example, in Django, this includes processing requests via middleware, routing, and handling views.

Libraries and drivers

Libraries and drivers enable interaction with external technologies such as databases, filesystems, APIs, and other external services:

- **Core libraries and drivers**: Libraries and drivers that perform basic operations with underlying technology stacks, enabling low-level system interactions. For example, in SQLAlchemy, this refers to database-specific drivers used to connect and interact with databases.
- **Context libraries and drivers**: Third-party libraries and plugins added to extend the framework's functionality, typically used to integrate external services or specialized tools, for example, Django plugins, image-processing libraries, or external API integration tools.
- **Application-level libraries and drivers**: Libraries and drivers integrated specifically into applications to handle **user interfaces** (**UIs**), data management, or business logic. For example, in Flutter, this includes widgets and UI libraries; in Django, an example is DRF for building REST APIs.
- **Primitives**: These are basic building blocks within frameworks, forming the foundation for developing complex functionality. The typical workflow involves using primitives to build basic components, which are then registered in registries to be integrated into the control flow. Primitives can be implemented as classes, functions, or templates, often following well-known design patterns.

The following are examples:

- **SQLAlchemy**: Base, engine, and session
- **Flutter**: Widgets, state, and BuildContext
- **LangChain**: Prompts, chains, and agents
- **Jetpack Compose**: Composables and StateFlow

The control flow orchestrates how data and requests move through the framework by invoking registered components in the right order.

The following are examples:

- **SQLAlchemy**: Engine → Session → ORM → SQL query
- **LangChain**: Prompts → Chains → Agents → Results

- **TensorFlow**: Build computation graph → Execute computation graph
- **Flutter**: UI events → State → UI rebuild
- Frameworks often provide mechanisms to extend or alter their default behavior:
- **SQLAlchemy**: Customizing transaction handling or query expressions
- **LangChain**: Creating custom chains and prompts
- **Flutter**: Utilizing inheritance and composition patterns to customize UI behavior

Design patterns

Architectural patterns in a framework shape the way an application is built. The framework's architecture exists not just to connect its own pieces but to help developers use those patterns in their apps. This makes component design easier, improves communication between parts, and lets everything fit smoothly into the framework's control flow.

In this analysis, we will explore two crucial groups of architectural patterns that significantly influence modern software design:

- **Code structure patterns**: These patterns enhance the internal structure of applications by clearly segregating responsibilities, boosting both maintainability and scalability
- **Data management patterns**: Data is typically hosted in different locations and across multiple servers for reasons such as performance, scalability, or availability, and this can present a range of challenges

Code patterns

Code design patterns primarily address two crucial aspects:

- **Separation of concerns**: These patterns delineate clear boundaries within an application, assigning distinct responsibilities to separate components. This approach ensures that changes in one part of the system do not ripple through to others, making it easier to manage and modify.
- **Complexity management**: By organizing code into well-defined modules or layers, these patterns reduce the overall complexity of the system. This modularization helps developers focus on one area at a time and improves the clarity and coherence of the code base.

MVC

The **Model-View-Controller** (**MVC**) pattern was first developed by Trygve Reenskaug during his work at Xerox PARC in 1979. Originally designed for desktop graphical UIs, this pattern has become foundational in web application development. It separates an application into three interconnected components: the model, the view, and the controller, each handling specific development aspects of an application.

MVC is widely used in web development to separate data access, business logic, and the UI, which simplifies management and facilitates scalability. While primarily associated with web applications, MVC is also applicable to the development of desktop and mobile applications.

The pros of using MVC include improved separation of concerns, making applications easier to manage, test, and scale. It enhances reusability across different parts of an application and supports flexible and incremental development. However, MVC can introduce complexity in large applications, making it difficult to maintain as interactions between components become more intertwined. The strict separation can also lead to excessive boilerplate code, increasing development time.

Here's a simplified UML diagram to illustrate the MVC architecture:

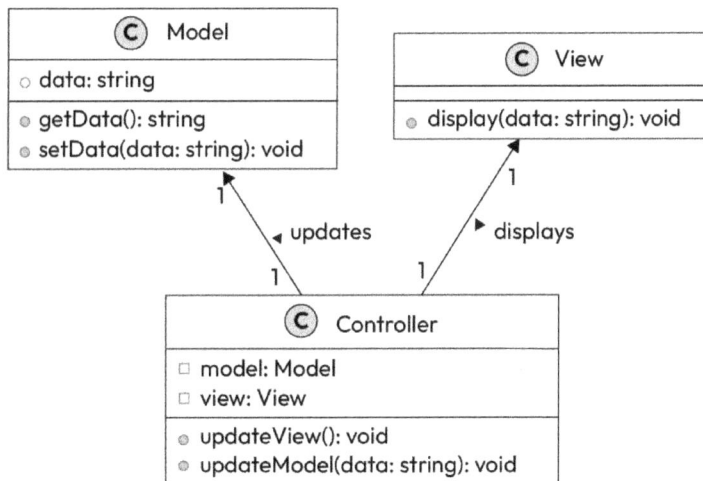

Figure 5.3: MVC pattern

🔍 Quick tip: Need to see a high-resolution version of this image? Open this book in the next-gen Packt Reader or view it in the PDF/ePub copy.

🔒 The next-gen Packt Reader and a free PDF/ePub copy of this book are included with your purchase. Scan the QR code OR visit packtpub.com/unlock, then use the search bar to find this book by name. Double-check the edition shown to make sure you get the right one.

While MVC is supported by numerous frameworks, such as Ruby on Rails and ASP.NET MVC, it's worth noting that Django, often thought to use MVC, actually employs a slightly modified pattern known as **Model-View-Template (MVT)**. In MVT, the controller is handled by the framework itself, and the developer is primarily concerned with models, views, and templates.

HMVC

The **Hierarchical Model-View-Controller (HMVC)** pattern is an extension of the traditional MVC pattern, designed to handle the complexities of large-scale applications. It introduces a hierarchy of MVC triads, allowing each component to function independently within its own MVC context. This pattern emerged to address the limitations of the traditional MVC architecture when dealing with complex, modular applications.

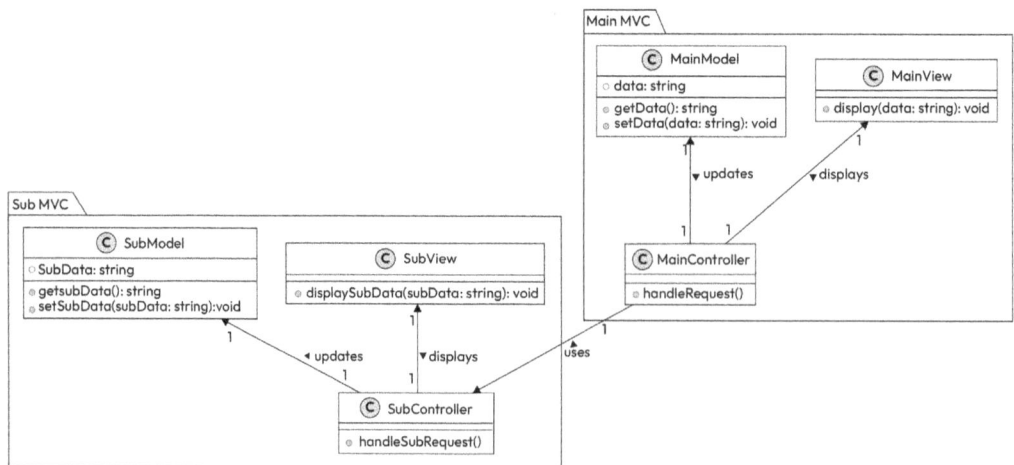

Figure 5.4: HMVC pattern

HMVC is primarily used in large-scale web applications to manage complex UI hierarchies and facilitate modular development. An advantage of HMVC is improved modularity, making it easier to manage and scale large applications by breaking them down into smaller, self-contained modules. This modularity facilitates independent development and testing of different parts of the application. Enhanced reusability is another benefit, as modules can be reused across different parts of the application or even in different projects.

However, HMVC can introduce additional complexity with the nested structure of controllers, views, and models. This can make the application harder to understand and manage, especially for developers unfamiliar with the pattern. The increased number of components and their interactions can also lead to more boilerplate code and potential performance overhead.

HMVC is supported by frameworks such as Kohana and CodeIgniter in PHP.

MVVM

The **Model-View-ViewModel (MVVM)** pattern originated from Microsoft as a specialization of the Presentation Model design pattern. Introduced in the early 2000s to support XAML-based applications, it aimed to simplify the management of complex UI behaviors and data bindings, particularly in **Windows Presentation Foundation (WPF)** and Silverlight. MVVM provides a clear separation between the UI and business logic, making it easier to manage and develop complex UIs.

Primarily used in application platforms that support rich client interfaces, such as WPF, Silverlight, Xamarin, and more recently in web development frameworks such as Angular, MVVM excels in environments where the UI is data-driven and complex interactions need to be managed without excessive coupling between the UI and its underlying data logic.

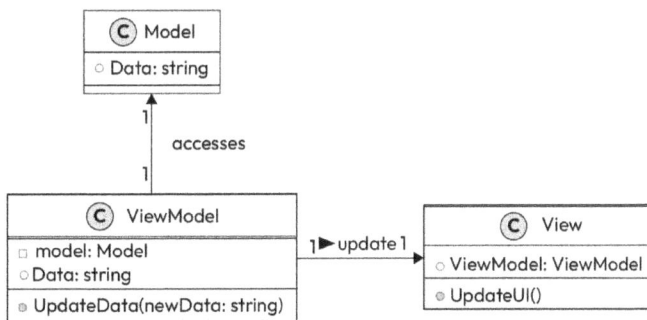

Figure 5.5: MVVM pattern

MVVM offers a strong separation of concerns by decoupling the UI from business logic, facilitating easier maintenance and scalability of UI components. Enhanced testability is another advantage, as the business logic in the ViewModel can be tested without involving the UI. Additionally, ViewModels can be reused across different views if they do not directly reference UI elements. However, the additional layer of ViewModel can introduce complexity, making the system harder to understand and manage, especially for simpler UIs. Data binding mechanisms, central to MVVM, can also introduce performance overhead in scenarios where binding updates are frequent and data-heavy.

MVVM is widely supported by frameworks that prioritize data binding and UI abstraction, such as Microsoft's WPF and Xamarin for mobile applications. Web frameworks such as Angular also utilize concepts similar to MVVM to manage the state and behavior of web components effectively.

MVP

The **Model-View-Presenter** (**MVP**) pattern evolved from the MVC pattern to better address the separation of concerns in complex applications. It was popularized by frameworks such as Apache Flex and .NET Framework for desktop and mobile applications, offering a more structured approach to managing user interactions and business logic.

MVP is commonly used in desktop and mobile applications, as well as web applications. It divides an application into three interconnected components: model, view, and presenter. The model handles the business logic and data retrieval, the view displays the data, and the presenter acts as an intermediary that processes user input and updates the model and the view accordingly.

The advantages of MVP include a clear separation of concerns, making it easier to maintain and test the application. The presenter handles all user interactions, simplifying the view and making it more reusable. Enhanced testability is achieved as the presenter can be tested independently of the UI.

However, MVP can introduce complexity due to the additional layer of the presenter, which may lead to more boilerplate code. This can make the system harder to understand and manage, especially for simpler UIs where the added complexity may not be justified.

MVP is supported by frameworks such as **Google Web Toolkit** (**GWT**) and Android, illustrating its effectiveness in managing user interactions and business logic across different platforms. By clearly separating the responsibilities of the view, model, and presenter, MVP helps developers create applications that are easier to test, maintain, and scale.

Beyond the widely used patterns such as MVC and MVVM, there are several other specialized architectural patterns, such as **Presentation-Abstraction-Control (PAC)**, **View-Interactor-Presenter-Entity-Router (VIPER)**, and Flux. These patterns address specific needs in particular domains, such as PAC for interactive systems, VIPER for iOS application development, and Flux for managing state in JavaScript applications.

Data management patterns

CQRS pattern

Command and Query Responsibility Segregation (CQRS) is an architectural pattern that separates data operations into distinct read and write paths, significantly enhancing application performance, scalability, and maintainability. By segregating these responsibilities, CQRS allows the development of specialized models tailored for efficient data access and command execution.

In traditional CRUD-based systems, a single data model typically handles both data retrieval and updates. While adequate for simple applications, this approach becomes cumbersome as application complexity grows. Queries might demand varied data shapes, resulting in complicated **data transfer object (DTO)** mappings. Similarly, write operations often embed intricate validation logic and business rules, causing the data model to become overly complex.

In contrast, CQRS introduces two distinct models:

- **Commands**: Task-oriented operations (e.g., `BookHotelRoom` instead of `UpdateReservationStatus`) that manage state modifications. Commands frequently employ asynchronous processing queues, improving system responsiveness and reducing bottlenecks.

- **Queries**: Focus solely on data retrieval, returning DTOs without domain logic or side effects. This isolation simplifies query optimizations and enhances read performance.

Additionally, CQRS helps manage complex validation scenarios by enforcing preliminary checks on the client-side UI, which reduces server-side conflicts and improves user experience.

Event Sourcing pattern

Event Sourcing is an architectural approach that captures all state changes as an immutable sequence of domain events, rather than merely storing the current state. This event log serves as the authoritative source of truth, enabling state reconstruction at any time and providing a robust audit trail.

Traditional CRUD approaches often suffer performance degradation and scalability limitations due to direct data store interactions and transactional locks. Concurrent modifications may lead to conflicts, and the historical context of data changes can easily be lost.

Event Sourcing addresses these challenges by doing the following:

- Recording every action or event (e.g., `OrderItemAdded`) in an append-only event store
- Decoupling event production from event consumption, allowing subscribers to asynchronously process events for updating materialized views or external integrations
- Facilitating comprehensive auditing, historical data analysis, and easy state reconstruction by replaying events, greatly simplifying debugging and compliance processes

Events stored in this manner support various use cases, including generating real-time updates for UI views, synchronizing external systems, or creating projections of current entity states.

One of the greatest strengths of Event Sourcing is its ability to preserve a complete, immutable history of everything that happens within the system. But as with any architectural choice, this power comes with trade-offs.

First, the event log grows indefinitely. Since it's an append-only structure, it accumulates all historical activity, which over time can lead to significant storage requirements and increasingly long backup processes.

Second, working directly with raw events makes answering ad hoc questions cumbersome. Business users or developers often need quick access to the current state of the system, but extracting that information from an event stream requires replaying events or building additional infrastructure.

Third, the system naturally operates with eventual consistency. While the event log captures the ground truth immediately, supporting components such as read models or projections typically update asynchronously.

Fourth, evolving the structure of events introduces complexity. As the system grows, event payloads often change, and replaying older events with newer code can cause compatibility issues if not handled properly.

Materialized View pattern

The Materialized View pattern precomputes and stores query-specific data structures optimized for rapid and efficient data retrieval. This pattern is particularly beneficial when the underlying storage format is not suitable for complex or frequent queries, significantly boosting query performance and reducing data access latency.

Typical storage formats, particularly in NoSQL databases, emphasize data integrity, storage efficiency, or scalability at the expense of query efficiency. For example, retrieving partial data (such as order summaries) from aggregated records can require extensive processing, negatively impacting performance.

Materialized views proactively address this by doing the following:

- Precomputing and caching subsets of data specifically tailored to anticipated queries
- Including computed columns, joined data entities, transformations, or aggregated results to directly serve frequent queries without additional processing
- Allowing the cached data to be disposable and easily rebuilt from original sources, enhancing resilience and data integrity

When underlying data changes, materialized views are refreshed through automated triggers, scheduled jobs, or manual initiation, ensuring consistent, up-to-date information availability.

Collectively, these patterns – CQRS, Event Sourcing, and Materialized View – offer robust solutions for effectively managing complex data scenarios, optimizing system responsiveness, scalability, and long-term maintainability in modern distributed systems.

Structuring a framework for extensibility

Designing a software project for extensibility is crucial for maintaining and scaling applications efficiently over time. It involves creating a flexible architecture that allows for future growth, feature additions, and integration with other systems without significant overhauls.

Modular design

A project should be structured into distinct, loosely coupled modules with well-defined interfaces. Each module handles a specific aspect of the application's functionality and can be developed, tested, and updated independently. This approach enhances maintainability, reduces complexity, and increases the ease of adding or updating features. It also supports parallel development across different teams.

Leveraging design patterns

The use of design patterns such as Factory, Strategy, Observer, and Decorator can solve common problems in a reusable and predictable way. These patterns provide proven solutions for frequent architectural issues, promoting adaptability and scalability. Design patterns simplify the development process by providing a tested and understandable approach to recurring design problems, enhancing code readability and reducing errors.

Dependency injection

Dependency injection (DI) is a technique in which objects receive their dependencies from external sources rather than creating them internally. This can be facilitated through frameworks that manage object creation and binding. DI decouples the creation of an object from its usage, making the system easier to extend and modify. It also simplifies unit testing by allowing easy injection of mock dependencies.

API-first design

This design prioritizes the development of APIs before the implementation of services. This approach ensures that the API serves as a contract that guides the development of the application logic. It promotes a clear separation between the frontend and the backend, allowing teams to work independently and making it easier to integrate with external systems and third-party services.

Configuration management

This practice allows the application behavior to be adjusted without code changes, accommodating different environments and scenarios. It enhances flexibility and makes deployment across different environments smoother and more predictable. It also reduces the risk of errors during deployment and configuration changes.

Versioning strategy

This approach for APIs and components ensures backward compatibility and facilitates smooth transitions between different versions of the application. It protects existing clients from breaking changes and provides a clear roadmap for clients and developers about when and how new features and changes are introduced.

Extensible data model

These models can be easily extended to accommodate new features without disrupting existing functionality, which is essential for a scalable system. It reduces the need for database refactoring and simplifies the process of integrating new features, improving the overall robustness of the application.

Event-driven architecture uses events to trigger and communicate between decoupled services in an application. This approach facilitates reactive programming and can scale to handle a high volume of events. It provides a highly scalable and responsive system. It allows adding new event processors or services with minimal impact on existing components.

Summary

This chapter explored architectural design within application frameworks, emphasizing principles that enable robust, scalable, and extensible systems. It addressed the general tasks involved in framework architecture, highlighting key principles such as modularity, extensibility, maintainability, and scalability. The discussion extended to framework architecture components, including core infrastructure, libraries, drivers, primitives, and control flows.

We also covered critical architectural patterns – MVC, HMVC, MVVM, and MVP – detailing their applications, strengths, and limitations. Additionally, essential data management patterns, such as CQRS, Event Sourcing, and Materialized View, were examined for optimizing data handling and performance.

Finally, techniques for designing frameworks for extensibility, including modular design, DI, API-first strategies, configuration management, and event-driven architectures, were introduced. You should now possess the knowledge needed to design future-proof frameworks capable of adapting to evolving technological demands.

The next chapter will detail the essential principles and prototyping methods vital for constructing an ADF. We will explore how to prototype an ADF from scratch. Step by step, we will extract common patterns, define clean abstractions, and structure a lightweight, agent-oriented framework ready for real-world use.

Unlock this book's exclusive benefits now

Scan this QR code or go to packtpub.com/unlock, then search for this book by name. Ensure it's the correct edition.

Note: Keep your purchase invoice ready before you start.

6

ADF Development Fundamentals

This chapter covers the core principles and prototyping techniques crucial for creating an **application development framework (ADF)**. Rather than starting from zero, successful framework development grows out of careful analysis and abstraction of existing application patterns. By spotting the most common control flows, reusable components, and general-purpose features in current applications, developers can build a strong foundation. This approach speeds up the development of future applications in the same domain.

Using real examples, we demonstrate how to prototype a framework by breaking out key components and defining execution flows in stages. As a concrete example, we build a simple agent-oriented framework designed for applications that use **large language models (LLMs)**. This framework abstracts recurring tasks – including user input handling, system prompt generation, model calls, and response parsing – into modular, composable parts.

Starting with a minimal prototype that calls an OpenAI model directly, we gradually add essential abstractions and well-defined control flows. Later iterations include advanced concepts such as role-based agent routing, where different agent "personas" handle specialized tasks. We also cover how to bundle the framework into a reusable Python package, using modern tools and best practices for CI, dependency management, and QA.

Throughout this chapter, you will gain practical insights into the following:

- Exploring prototyping techniques and best practices
- Embracing Agile principles for responsive development

By the end of the chapter, you will be equipped with the skills to prototype and develop frameworks that are scalable, maintainable, and highly adaptable to evolving technological needs.

Prototyping techniques and best practices

When creating a framework, avoid starting from scratch. Instead, review a set of real-world applications and note common control flows, abstractions, and components. These shared elements become a reusable core, speeding up future development within the same domain.

In this section, we provide a practical example of how to prototype a framework by extracting common behaviors from an existing application. In our first iteration, we identify the minimal set of reusable modules and define the essential execution flow.

As our concrete case, we'll show how to build a lightweight agent-oriented framework for LLM-based applications. Our motivation comes from repetitive patterns in existing tools – processing user input, adding context via system prompts, routing to a model backend, and transforming the model's output into usable responses.

We'll demonstrate how these steps translate into core components – messages, models, and routers – and how to incrementally organize them into a composable system. The result of this initial iteration is a functional prototype that encapsulates a clear control flow and abstracts model interaction, forming the conceptual nucleus of a future extensible framework.

You can find this and future examples in the GitHub repository:

`https://github.com/PacktPublishing/Building-an-Application-Development-Framework`.

To run this example, you will need to install the OpenAI Python SDK (**version 1.x+**):

1. **Create an OpenAI account** at `https://platform.openai.com/signup` and obtain your **API key** from the dashboard under **API Keys**.
2. **Set your API key** in the environment so it can be accessed by the script:

```
export OPENAI_API_KEY="sk-****"
```

A minimal agent invocation

Here is the minimal working prototype. It sets up a client using an API key obtained from the environment, sends a simple prompt to the gpt-4o-mini model ("Create a haiku") with the instruction "You are a poet", and prints out the generated haiku returned by the model:

```python
import os
from openai import OpenAI


client = OpenAI(api_key=os.environ.get("OPENAI_API_KEY", ""))



def main():
    user_input = "Create a haiku"
    system_prompt =  "You are a poet"

    response = client.chat.completions.create(
        model="gpt-4o-mini",
        messages=[
            {"role": "system", "content":  system_prompt},
            {"role": "user", "content": user_input}
        ],
        temperature=0.7,
    )
    print(f"User input:{user_input}")
    print("\nAgent answer:\n")
    print(response.choices[0].message.content)
```

Quick tip: Enhance your coding experience with the AI Code Explainer and Quick Copy features. Open this book in the next-gen Packt Reader. Click the Copy button

(1) to quickly copy code into your coding environment, or click the Explain button

(2) to get the AI assistant to explain a block of code to you.

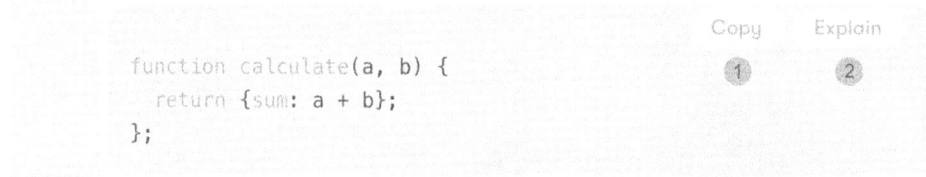

```
                                                        Copy        Explain

function calculate(a, b) {                               1            2
    return {sum: a + b};
};
```

The next-gen Packt Reader and a free PDF/ePub copy of this book are included with your purchase. Scan the QR code OR visit packtpub.com/unlock, then use the search bar to find this book by name. Double-check the edition shown to make sure you get the right one.

If you run this code, your output will look as follows:

```
Output:
User input: Create a haiku

Agent answer:

Whispers in the breeze,
Autumn leaves dance, softly fall,
Time's gentle embrace.
```

Defining core abstractions and control flow

At this stage, we begin extracting a control flow from our minimal working example. We introduce a structured representation of the LLM conversation using explicit message types: SystemMessage, UserMessage, and AssistantMessage. These become the primitives of our agent communication model:

```python
@dataclass(frozen=True)
class Message(abc.ABC):
    """
    Abstract base class for all message types.
    Each message represents a conversational turn.
    """

    content: str

    def __str__(self):
        return self.content


@dataclass(frozen=True)
class UserMessage(Message):
    """
    Represents a message coming from the user.
    """


@dataclass(frozen=True)
class SystemMessage(Message):
    """
    Represents the system prompt that sets up model behavior.
    """


@dataclass(frozen=True)
class AssistantMessage(Message):
    """
```

```
    Represents a message coming from the assistant (model).
    """
```

We also define a single `OpenAIAgent` class responsible for orchestrating this flow: it receives a sequence of messages, formats them according to the OpenAI API, invokes the model, and returns the assistant's reply.

This clean separation of message types and model handling sets the foundation for a composable agent framework:

```
class OpenAIAgent:
    system_prompt: SystemMessage = SystemMessage("You are a poet")
    client: OpenAI
    """
    Encapsulates the control flow for communicating with the OpenAI model.
    Takes a sequence of messages and returns an assistant reply.
    """



    @staticmethod
    def _convert_to_openai_message(msg: Message) -> Any:
        if isinstance(msg, SystemMessage):
            return {"role": "system", "content": msg.content}
        elif isinstance(msg, AssistantMessage):
            return {"role": "assistant", "content": msg.content}
        elif isinstance(msg, UserMessage):
            return {"role": "user", "content": msg.content}
        else:
            raise ValueError(f"Unsupported message: {type(msg)}")

    def generate(self, messages: list[Message]) -> AssistantMessage:
        """
        Accepts a list of Message objects, formats them into OpenAI's
schema,
        calls the model, and returns an AssistantMessage.
        """
```

```
        openai_messages = [self._convert_to_openai_message(self.system_
prompt)]
        for msg in messages:
            if openai_message := self._convert_to_openai_message(msg):
                openai_messages.append(openai_message)

        # Send to OpenAI model
        response = self.client.chat.completions.create(
            model="gpt-4o-mini",
            messages=openai_messages,
            temperature=0.7,
        )

        # Return the model's reply as an AssistantMessage
        return AssistantMessage(content=response.choices[0].message.
content or "")
```

And now our execution flow looks as follows:

```
def main():
    # 1. Create user message (prompt)
    user_message = UserMessage("Create a haiku")

    # 2. Initialize OpenAI API client
    openai = OpenAI(api_key=os.environ.get("OPENAI_API_KEY", ""))

    # 3. Initialize the agent
    agent = OpenAIAgent()
    agent.client = openai

    # 5. Define the conversation so far
    conversation = [user_message]

    # 6. Call the agent to generate a response
    answer = agent.generate(conversation)

    # 7. Display input and output
    print(f"User input:    {user_message}")
```

```
print("\nAgent answer:\n")
print(answer)
```

Introducing roles and agent routing

Previously, we introduced a minimal agent that manages message sequences and returns an assistant response. However, real-world LLM applications often require multiple specialized agents – for example, translators, summarizers, or Q&A bots – each with unique instructions and configurations. Strictly speaking, the previous implementation encodes a minimal linear control flow – a single pass through a prompt-response cycle. While it lacks branches, loops, or error handling, it still centralizes the rules for input transformation and model invocation.

To support such modularity and reuse, we introduce the concept of roles.

A **role** represents a named task or persona that the system can provide. Each role is tied to an agent implementation that receives a list of messages and produces a response. For example, "poet" might use one model setup, while "translator" might use a different one entirely:

```
@dataclass(frozen=True)
class Role:
    """Links a role name to a specific agent."""

    name: str
    agent: Agent
```

RoleRouter acts as a dispatcher. It maintains a registry of roles and is responsible for routing requests (a message list + role name) to the correct agent. This structure mirrors conventional routing logic in web frameworks but is adapted for LLM workflows:

```
class RoleRouter:
    """Routes messages to the correct agent based on the requested role."""

    __registry__: dict[str, Role] = {}

    def register(self, role: Role) -> None:
        """Register a new role in the router."""
        self.__registry__[role.name] = role
```

```
    def navigate(self, role: str, messages: list[Message]) ->
AssistantMessage:
        """Look up the agent for `role` and delegate the messages."""
        if role not in self.__registry__:
            raise RoleIsNotRegisteredError(f"Role '{role}' not
recognized.")

        target_role = self.__registry__[role]
        return target_role.agent.generate(messages)
```

Agent Protocol is a protocol that enforces a single method:

```
class Agent(Protocol):
    """Generic interface for an agent."""
    system_prompt: SystemMessage
    messages: list[Message]

    def generate(self) -> AssistantMessage: ...
```

When calling `router.navigate("poet", messages)`, the system performs the following:

- **Role lookup**: It fetches the `Role` object registered under `"poet"`
- **Agent delegation**: The router invokes the `agent.generate(...)` method using the provided message list
- **Response return**: The agent returns an `AssistantMessage`, which contains the model's response

This pattern not only decouples application logic from model logic but also allows you to register, compose, and dynamically switch between specialized agents without duplicating infrastructure or hardcoding behavior.

First, we need to implement an agent:

```
class GPT4oMiniAgent(Agent):
    system_prompt: SystemMessage = SystemMessage("You are a poet")
    client: OpenAI
    """
    An Agent that calls the 'gpt-4o-mini' model.
    It automatically inserts its default system prompt as the first
message.
    """
```

```python
    @staticmethod
def _convert_to_openai_message(msg: Message) -> Any:
    match msg:
        case SystemMessage():
            return {"role": "system", "content": msg.content}
        case AssistantMessage():
            return {"role": "assistant", "content": msg.content}
        case UserMessage():
            return {"role": "user", "content": msg.content}
        case _:
            raise ValueError(f"Unsupported message type: {type(msg)}")

def generate(self, messages: list[Message]) -> AssistantMessage:
    """
    Prepends the default system prompt, converts all messages
    to OpenAI schema, calls the model, and returns an AssistantMessage.
    """

    openai_messages = [self._convert_to_openai_message(self.system_
prompt)]
    for msg in messages:
        if openai_message := self._convert_to_openai_message(msg):
            openai_messages.append(openai_message)

    # Send to OpenAI
    response = self.client.chat.completions.create(
        model="gpt-4o-mini",
        messages=openai_messages,
        temperature=0.7,
    )


    # Return the model's reply as an AssistantMessage
    return AssistantMessage(content=response.choices[0].message.content or
"")
```

Then, define the execution flow again:

```python
def main():
    # Create an agent and define its role
    openai_api_key = os.environ.get("OPENAI_API_KEY", "")
    openai = OpenAI(api_key=openai_api_key)

    agent = GPT4oMiniAgent()
    agent.client = openai

    poet_role = Role(name="poet", agent=agent)

    # Register the role
    router = RoleRouter()
    router.register(poet_role)

    # Build a conversation (no user system prompt needed; agent adds its
own)
    user_message = UserMessage("Create a haiku")
    conversation = [user_message]

    # Route the conversation
    answer = router.navigate("poet", conversation)

    print(f"User input: {user_message}")
    print("\nAgent answer:\n")
    print(answer)
```

Separating the framework into a package and introducing the application context

At this stage, our code has matured enough to be separated into a proper Python package. This marks the transition from a one-off script to a reusable, extensible framework.

We extract our core abstractions into a dedicated adf/ package. This includes message types, agent protocols, the role router, and the Application class. Meanwhile, the application logic stays cleanly in main.py, importing and using the framework like any other library. As we defined in previous chapters, an application is our container that encapsulates all execution flow logic.

The `Application` class acts as the central container – a simplified `ApplicationContext` holding configuration and registration logic:

```python
from types import SimpleNamespace

from .messages import Message, AssistantMessage
from .routers import RoleRouter, Role


class Application:
    """
    An Application holds:
    - a name (e.g. "poetic")
    - a RoleRouter for dispatching conversations to agents
    - a decorator-based registration mechanism to easily register new
roles/agents
    """

    settings = SimpleNamespace()

    def __init__(self, name: str):
        self.name = name
        self.router = RoleRouter()

    def register(self, role: str):
        """
        A decorator that accepts a role name (e.g. "poet"),
        instantiates the decorated Agent class, and registers it in the
RoleRouter.

        Usage:

            @app.register(role="poet")
            class PoetGPT4oMiniAgent(GPT4oMiniAgent):
                system_prompt = SystemMessage("You are a poet")

        """

        def decorator(agent_cls):
```

```
            # Instantiate the agent
            instance = agent_cls()

            # If needed, we can check or set a system prompt here:
            # if not instance.is_ready:
            #     instance.instruct(SystemMessage("You are ..."))

            # Register this instance with the router
            self.router.register(Role(name=role, agent=instance))
            return agent_cls

        return decorator

    def process(self, role: str, conversation: list[Message]) ->
AssistantMessage:
        """
        A simple convenience method to forward the conversation
        to the router and return the AssistantMessage result.
        """
        return self.router.navigate(role, conversation)
```

Here's the package structure:

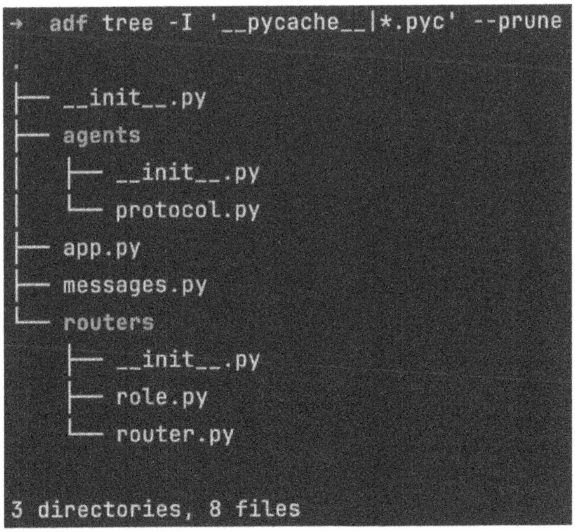

```
→  adf tree -I '__pycache__|*.pyc' --prune
.
├── __init__.py
├── agents
│   ├── __init__.py
│   └── protocol.py
├── app.py
├── messages.py
└── routers
    ├── __init__.py
    ├── role.py
    └── router.py

3 directories, 8 files
```

Figure 6.1: Package structure

This is the first real example of a fully functioning application built on top of our framework. By this point, we've extracted abstractions for messages, agents, routing, and the application context. What we now have in main.py is not just a demo – it's a clean, production-ready entry point that communicates intent clearly and hides the complexity behind the framework's design.

Let's go through this example step by step.

We start by defining a base agent class, GPT4oMiniAgent, which is an implementation of our Agent protocol. This agent does the following:

- Holds a system_prompt, which is required to shape the behavior of the model
- Converts domain-level message types (such as UserMessage, SystemMessage, etc.) into OpenAI's raw schema
- Sends the conversation to OpenAI's gpt-4o-mini model
- Wraps the model's response in our AssistantMessage abstraction

This base class doesn't know it's being used by a poet or a critic – it's generic and reusable:

```python
class GPT4oMiniAgent(Agent):
    client: OpenAI
    system_prompt: SystemMessage

    @staticmethod
    def _convert_to_openai_message(msg: Message) -> Any:
        match msg:
            case SystemMessage():
                return {"role": "system", "content": msg.content}
            case AssistantMessage():
                return {"role": "assistant", "content": msg.content}
            case UserMessage():
                return {"role": "user", "content": msg.content}
            case _:
                raise ValueError(f"Unsupported message type: {type(msg)}")

    def generate(self) -> AssistantMessage:
        """

        Prepends the default system prompt, converts all messages
        to OpenAI schema, calls the model, and returns an
AssistantMessage.
```

```
        """

        openai_messages = [self._convert_to_openai_message(self.system_
prompt)]

        for msg in self.messages:
            if openai_message := self._convert_to_openai_message(msg):
                openai_messages.append(openai_message)


        # Send to OpenAI
        response = self.client.chat.completions.create(
            model="gpt-4o-mini",
            messages=openai_messages,
            temperature=0.7,
        )
        return AssistantMessage(content=response.choices[0].message.
content or "")



@app.register(role="poet")
class PoetGPT4oMiniAgent(GPT4oMiniAgent):
    client = OpenAI(api_key=app.settings.openai_api_key)
    system_prompt = SystemMessage("You are a poet")



@app.register(role="critic")
class CriticGPT4oMiniAgent(GPT4oMiniAgent):
    client = OpenAI(api_key=app.settings.openai_api_key)
    system_prompt = SystemMessage("You are a critic of poetry")
```

In the main() function, we simulate a simple but realistic multi-turn agent scenario:

1. A user starts a conversation with the "poet" agent to generate a haiku.

2. The haiku is passed to the "critic" agent for evaluation.

3. The critic's feedback is used to refine the original haiku by returning to the "poet":

```
# Step 1: build conversation
conversation = [UserMessage("Create a haiku")]

# Step 2: direct to "poet" agent
answer = app.process("poet", conversation)
```

```
print("Poet answer:", answer)


# Step 3: user then asks for a critique
conversation.append(answer)
conversation.append(UserMessage("Can you critique the haiku?"))


# Step 4: direct to "critic" agent
response = app.process("critic", conversation)
print("Critic answer:", response)
# Step 5: Improve the haiku
conversation.append(response)
conversation.append(UserMessage("Can you improve the haiku?"))
# Step 6: direct to "poet" agent again
response = app.process("poet", conversation)
print("Improved haiku:", response)
```

Here's what the use of the framework gave us, both technically and in terms of developer experience:

- **Separation of concerns:** The agent logic (GPT4oMiniAgent) is completely decoupled from how the role is routed or how the application is configured. This keeps our mental model clean.

- **Declarative role registration:** Thanks to @app.register(role=...), agents are auto-registered just like Flask routes. There's no need to manually update dictionaries or write additional glue code – just subclass and decorate.

- **Clean configuration:** The Application.settings namespace provides an easy place to stash environment-specific data (such as openai_api_key) that all agents can access. There's no hardcoded config logic in the agents themselves.

- **Testability and extensibility.**

With this architecture, it's trivial to do the following:

- Add unit tests for Agent.generate()
- Substitute models (e.g., use Ollama or Azure)
- Log inputs and outputs per role
- Add caching, retries, or parsing logic – without touching the application logic

The final `main.py` is extremely concise – but powerful. A developer using the framework doesn't need to understand the internals of routing or schema conversion to create a working multi-agent LLM application.

In summary, this application is the first practical payoff of our framework effort. It gives us a clean structure, ready for scaling and production deployment.

Packaging and distributing

One of the most exciting developments in Python tooling in recent years is the emergence of uv – a next-generation package and project manager that's redefining how Python developers manage dependencies, environments, and builds.

uv is a modern, high-performance Python package manager and installer written in Rust. It serves as a drop-in replacement for traditional Python package management tools such as `pip`, offering significant improvements in speed, reliability, and dependency resolution.

uv is designed with performance in mind. Benchmarks show that uv can be 10–100 times faster than traditional tools such as `pip` and `pip-tools`. This speed boost is achieved through efficient dependency resolution, parallel downloads, and a global package cache that avoids redundant installations.

uv consolidates the functionality of multiple tools:

- **Dependency management**: Replaces `pip` and `pip-tools` for installing and locking dependencies
- **Environment management**: Supersedes `virtualenv` and `pyenv` by handling virtual environments and Python versions
- **Script execution**: Offers capabilities similar to `pipx` for running Python scripts with isolated dependencies
- **Project management**: Provides features akin to `poetry` and `twine` for building and publishing packages

For more information, visit the official uv documentation at `docs.astral.sh/uv` and the GitHub repository at `github.com/astral-sh/uv`.

To kickstart a new Python project with uv, you can use the `uv init` command. This command sets up a standardized project structure, including essential files such as `pyproject.toml` and `README.md`, and initializes a virtual environment. This approach streamlines project setup, ensuring consistency and best practices from the outset.

By default, uv init sets up the project as an application. If you intend to create a library instead, you can use the --lib flag:

```
uv init --lib
```

To enhance the quality, maintainability, and reliability of your Python projects, integrating a suite of development tools is essential. Tools such as ruff, pytest with coverage support, and mypy can significantly improve your code base by providing linting, testing, and static type checking capabilities. Here's how you can incorporate these tools into your project.

ruff is a lightning-fast Python linter and formatter written in Rust. It supports a wide range of linting rules and can automatically fix many issues. ruff can replace several traditional tools, such as Flake8, isort, and Black, streamlining your development workflow.

To enhance your Python project's code quality, integrating tools such as mypy for static type checking and pytest with coverage support is essential. These tools help catch errors early and ensure your code is well tested. Here's how you can set them up:

```
uv add --dev mypy pytest pytest-cov ruff
```

Add a dummy agent:

```python
from adf.agents import Agent
from adf.messages import SystemMessage, Message, AssistantMessage


class DummyAgent:
    # Provide the required attributes.
    system_prompt = SystemMessage("dummy prompt")
    name = "dummy_agent"

    def generate(self, messages: list[Message]) -> AssistantMessage:
        # For testing purposes, simply join all message contents with a
separator.
        combined = " | ".join(str(msg) for msg in messages)
        return AssistantMessage(content=f"Dummy response: {combined}")
```

To test our framework, we added just a few simple tests:

```python
import pytest

from adf.app import Application
from adf.messages import UserMessage, SystemMessage, AssistantMessage
from adf.routers.role import Role
from adf.routers.router import RoleRouter, RoleIsNotRegisteredError
from tests.conftest import DummyAgent


def test_role_router_navigate_success():
    """
    Test that RoleRouter properly routes a conversation when the role is
    registered.
    """
    # Initialize the router and register a dummy role.
    router = RoleRouter()
    dummy_role = Role(name="test", agent=DummyAgent())
    router.register(dummy_role)

    # Build a test conversation.
    conversation = [SystemMessage("Test system"), UserMessage("Test
user")]
    result = router.navigate("test", conversation)

    # Verify that the returned message is an AssistantMessage with the
expected content.
    assert isinstance(result, AssistantMessage)
    assert "Dummy response:" in result.content


def test_role_router_navigate_unregistered():
    """
    Test that navigating to an unregistered role raises
RoleIsNotRegisteredError.
    """
    router = RoleRouter()
```

```
    conversation = [SystemMessage("Test system"), UserMessage("Test
user")]

    with pytest.raises(RoleIsNotRegisteredError):
        router.navigate("nonexistent", conversation)


def test_application_registration_and_process():
    """
    Test that the Application's registration decorator registers an agent,
    and the process method correctly routes the conversation.
    """
    # Create an Application instance.
    app = Application(name="test_app")

    # Use the decorator to register a dummy agent under the role "dummy".
    @app.register(role="dummy")
    class DummyAgentForApp(DummyAgent):
        system_prompt = SystemMessage("App dummy prompt")

    # Build a sample conversation.
    conversation = [UserMessage("Hello")]
    result = app.process("dummy", conversation)

    # Verify that the result is an AssistantMessage and that dummy
response is present.
    assert isinstance(result, AssistantMessage)
    assert "Dummy response:" in result.content
```

Linters checks:

```
(4.Packaging) →  4.Packaging git:(main) ruff format --check
8 files already formatted
(4.Packaging) →  4.Packaging git:(main) ruff check
All checks passed!
(4.Packaging) →  4.Packaging git:(main) mypy .
Success: no issues found in 10 source files
```

I strongly recommend setting up **continuous integration** (**CI**), for example, with GitHub Actions, to automatically run tests and linters and handle package publishing to private or public repositories. This greatly increases the reliability and maintainability of your code base, ensuring all changes are validated before they reach production. However, CI configuration is beyond the scope of this book. In open source projects, CI is not just a best practice – it's practically a necessity for managing contributions from many people. CI servers automatically build and test the software whenever code is committed or a pull request is opened, providing immediate feedback on integration issues. Modern open source frameworks typically use services such as GitHub Actions, GitLab CI, or CircleCI to run their test suites on multiple platforms. For example, Django's CI pipeline runs an extensive matrix of tests across supported Python versions, database backends, and operating systems to ensure that a change doesn't break compatibility. Every proposed code change must pass all these checks before it's merged. By catching integration problems (failing tests, lint errors, etc.) early, the project maintains a stable main branch despite rapid iterative development.

Run tests:

```
uv run pytest
```

This is our test coverage:

```
Name                         Stmts   Miss   Cover   Missing
--------------------------------------------------------------
adf/__init__.py                  0      0    100%
adf/agents/__init__.py           2      0    100%
adf/agents/protocol.py           6      0    100%
adf/app.py                      20      0    100%
adf/messages.py                 17      1     94%   35
adf/routers/__init__.py          3      0    100%
adf/routers/role.py              6      0    100%
adf/routers/router.py           14      0    100%
--------------------------------------------------------------
TOTAL                           68      1     99%
```

Figure 6.2: Test coverage

For an improved development experience, you may also want to configure **pre-commit hooks**. These tools run linters, formatters, and type checkers automatically before every commit, catching issues early and enforcing consistent coding standards across your team.

Code review tools integrated into these platforms (such as GitHub's review interface) make the review process efficient, with inline comments, suggestions, and the ability to require certain checks (tests passing and approvals given) before merge. Many projects also enable bots for routine tasks – for example, a bot that automatically labels new issues, or one that pings reviewers if a pull request is stale. Some use continuous quality tools: for example, coverage reporting services that comment on a pull request if coverage drops, or security scanners that alert of vulnerable dependencies. These automations act like additional team members, handling XP chores (such as running all tests and checking standards) so humans can focus on creative work.

As for packaging, I'll stop short of automation and simply build the package manually using the following:

```
uv build
```

This command generates your distribution files, ready for publishing or installation. uv serves as a fast, modern alternative to setuptools and poetry, handling everything from dependency resolution to packaging in a single binary. For more information about its full capabilities, refer to the official documentation at https://docs.astral.sh/uv/.

Libraries and transports

It's time to evolve our toy framework into a production-ready skeleton.

We'll integrate two building blocks:

- An **OpenSearch-backed vector store** for fast **k-nearest neighbors (kNN)** retrieval
- An **HTTP transport layer** that exposes each agent as a REST endpoint

With these pieces in place, the architecture moves from "demo" to something a real application can stand on.

Let's first define the embeddings protocol and its implementation:

```python
from collections.abc import Iterable, Sequence
from typing import Protocol


class Embeddings(Protocol):
    """Turns text into one or more dense vectors."""

    dimensions: int
```

```
    def embed(self, texts: Iterable[str]) -> Sequence[Sequence[float]]:
        """Turns text into one or more dense vectors."""
```

Then, establish a protocol for integrating the OpenAI embeddings model with the OpenSearch vector database:

```python
class OpenAIEmbeddings(Embeddings):
    """OpenAI embedding model."""

    dimensions = 768
    model: str = "text-embedding-3-small"
    openai_client: OpenAI
    batch_size: int = 100

    def embed(self, texts: Iterable[str]) -> Sequence[Sequence[float]]:
        out = []
        for chunk in self._chunk(texts, self.batch_size):
            out.extend(self._call(chunk))
        return out

    @staticmethod
    def _chunk(it: Iterable[str], n: int) -> Iterable[list[str]]:
        chunk = []
        for item in it:
            chunk.append(item)
            if len(chunk) == n:
                yield chunk
                chunk.clear()
        if chunk:
            yield chunk

    def _call(self, batch: list[str]) -> list[list[float]]:
        resp = self.openai_client.embeddings.create(model=self.model,
input=batch, dimensions=self.dimensions)
        return [d.embedding for d in sorted(resp.data, key=lambda d:
d.index)]
```

And vector store protocols and it's implementation:

```python
from collections.abc import Iterable
from typing import Protocol

from adf.rag.vectorstore.embeddings.protocol import Embeddings

class VectorStore(Protocol):
    """Stores vectors, returns texts of the most similar items."""

    embeddings: Embeddings

    def index(self, texts: Iterable[str]) -> None:
        """Stores vectors, returns texts of the most similar items."""

    def search(self, query: str, k: int = 5) -> list[str]:
        """Returns texts of the most similar items."""



@dataclass
class OpenSearchVectorStore(VectorStore):
    """OpenSearch vector store."""

    os: OpenSearch
    index_name: str

    def ensure_index(self) -> None:
""" Check if an index and mappings are created """
        if not self.os.indices.exists(self.index_name):
            self.os.indices.create(
                self.index_name,
                body={
                    "mappings": {
                        "properties": {
                            "vector": {
                                "type": "knn_vector",
```

```
                                      "dimension": self.embeddings.dimensions,
                                      "method": {"name": "hnsw", "engine":
"nmslib"},
                            },
                            "text": {"type": "text"},
                        }
                    }
                },
            )


    def index(self, texts: Iterable[str]) -> None:
        vectors = self.embeddings.embed(texts)
        bulk_body = []
        for text, vec in zip(texts, vectors, strict=False):
            _id = str(uuid.uuid4())
            bulk_body.extend(
                [
                    {"index": {"_index": self.index_name, "_id": _id}},
                    {"vector": vec, "text": text},
                ]
            )
        self.os.bulk(bulk_body, refresh=True)



    def search(self, text: str, k: int = 5) -> list[str]:
        vector = self.embeddings.embed([text])[0]
        resp = self._os.search(
            index=self.index_name,
            body={
                "size": k,
                "query": {"knn": {"vector": {"vector": vector, "k": k}}},
                "_source": ["text"],
            },
        )
        return [hit["_source"]["text"] for hit in resp["hits"]["hits"]]
```

To implement the transport layer, the application context should be extended with the FastAPI component. First, define the message formats:

```python
class _MessageIn(BaseModel):
    role: str
    content: str

    def to_domain(self) -> Message:
    if self.role == "user":
        return UserMessage(self.content)
    if self.role == "system":
        return SystemMessage(self.content)
    if self.role == "assistant":
        return AssistantMessage(self.content)
    msg = f"unknown role {self.role}"
    raise ValueError(msg)



class _AnswerOut(BaseModel):
    content: str
```

The next step involves registering the appropriate routes and assigning the corresponding roles:

```python
def decorator(agent_cls: type[T]) -> type[T]:
    instance = agent_cls()
    self.router.register(Role(name=role, agent=instance))

    base_path = f"/{role}"

    @self.fastapi.post(base_path, response_model=_AnswerOut,
tags=["agents"])
    async def _dialog(messages: list[_MessageIn]) -> _AnswerOut:
        try:
            answer = self.process(role, [m.to_domain() for m in messages])
        except Exception as exc:  # pragma: no cover
            raise HTTPException(500, str(exc)) from exc
        return _AnswerOut(content=str(answer))
```

```
        if isinstance(instance, RagMixin):

            @self.fastapi.post(f"{base_path}/index", response_model=_
    AnswerOut, tags=["agents"])
            async def _index(documents: list[Document]) -> _AnswerOut:
                try:
                    instance.index_documents(documents)
                except Exception as exc:  # pragma: no cover
                    raise HTTPException(500, str(exc)) from exc
                return _AnswerOut(content="Documents indexed successfully.")

        return agent_cls

    return decorator
```

We can now use our framework in this manner:

```
if __name__ == "__main__":
    import uvicorn
    uvicorn.run(app.fastapi, host="0.0.0.0", port=8000)
```

While this example lays the groundwork for understanding basic mechanics, it's still far from resembling a real-world development process. In practice, effective software delivery also requires solid organizational principles to structure collaboration, workflows, and decision-making at scale.

Embracing agile principles for responsive development

Open source framework projects often mirror Agile and **Extreme Programming (XP)** values: iterative releases, early and frequent feedback, and high code quality. But open source teams are often geographically distributed, have no single on-site customer, and communicate asynchronously.

Agile emphasizes frequent delivery of working software and readiness for change. In open source, this appears as "release early, release often." Users act as stakeholders, providing immediate feedback via issues or pull requests, thus creating a tight feedback loop.

This enables quick feedback from users and contributors on new features or fixes. Unlike a traditional Agile team that might have a product owner providing requirements, open source projects treat their user community as the customer. Active users report issues, request enhancements, and even contribute code – effectively serving the role of stakeholders in directing development. The result is a tight feedback loop: maintainers iteratively implement changes and users immediately try them out and give input via issue trackers, forums, or chat.

As we complete the initial design of our agent framework and demonstrate it in a working application, we enter a new phase: **iterative, production-informed development**. Rather than assuming all features in advance, we treat the current implementation as a functional prototype – one that's stable enough to be adopted in real-world applications. These applications serve not only as a proof of concept but also as valuable **feedback loops**. Developers using the framework surface missing abstractions, edge cases, or specialized needs that we may not have initially considered.

While open source adoption can begin even before a framework is feature-complete, it's critical that the current version solves at least one problem from end to end. A partially implemented framework becomes viable for early adopters in the following instances:

- It addresses a real use case fully (e.g., implements an agent that completes a specific task with minimal friction)
- Its interfaces are stable and composable
- Gaps are clearly documented so that downstream developers can extend or customize behavior where needed

From there, we extend the core iteratively: introducing **reference implementations** (e.g., tested and recommended agent classes), as well as **optional libraries** that bring in support for external APIs and ecosystems – such as OpenAI, Gemini, Claude, or AWS Bedrock. The core remains small and stable, while external functionality is layered through modular packages. This model ensures a clear boundary between framework and integration code, allows different teams to contribute new capabilities without touching core internals, and supports a "batteries optional" philosophy – the framework works out of the box but can grow indefinitely in power.

Another aspect of feedback loops in open source is the practice of releasing preview or beta versions. Many frameworks (such as Django) publish release candidates for upcoming versions and call on the community to test them.

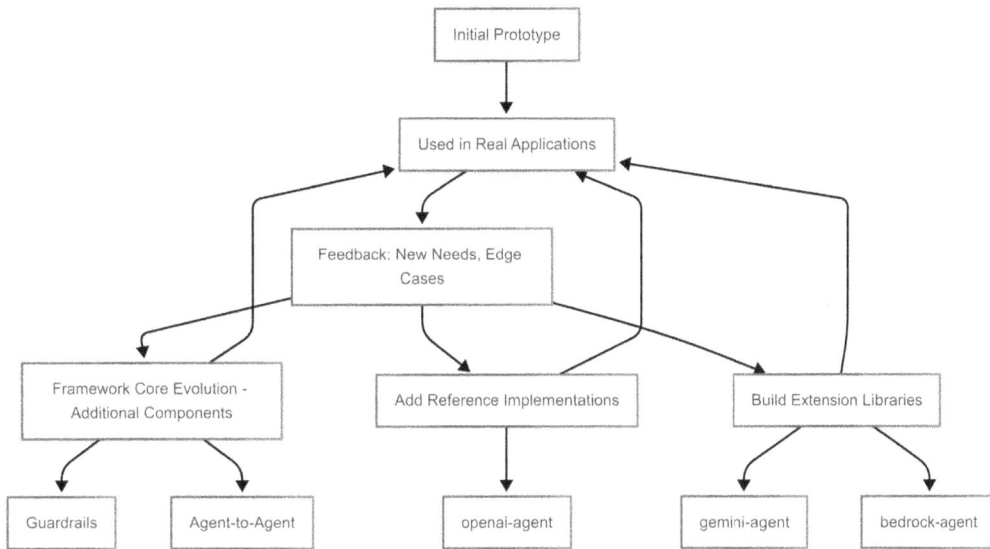

Figure 6.3: Evolution of a framework

This mirrors the XP idea of "rapid feedback" by exposing work in progress to real users early. Problems can be identified before final release, and the project can course-correct if needed. Indeed, open source development relies on the idea that *given enough eyes, all bugs are shallow* – wide community exposure leads to bugs being found and fixed faster. In Agile terms, the community acts as an extended QA and feedback team. Researchers have noted that presenting code changes to many developers and users (as open source projects do) is an effective form of peer review that catches issues early, reinforcing the value of frequent iterations and review cycles.

Open source development exemplifies the XP concept of **collective code ownership**. No single developer "owns" a component of the framework; instead, the code is collectively owned and maintained by the community. This philosophy is evident in how open source projects grant commit rights and handle contributions. Core teams are usually small, but they act more as stewards than exclusive owners – they review and merge contributions from anyone in the community. Over time, frequent contributors are often invited to become core committers themselves. The Django project's governance, for example, ensures that there are always multiple maintainers (called mergers) to spread knowledge and avoid over-burdening individuals. There is even an explicit goal to prevent burnout by having a minimum of three active mergers and no upper limit, emphasizing that responsibility for the code base should be distributed, not concentrated. This broad ownership model means any qualified person can fix a bug or improve a module, regardless of who originally wrote it – fostering a sense of collective responsibility for quality.

Shared code ownership does come with the need for clear **coding standards and processes**. Most frameworks define a style guide (PEP 8 for Python projects, ESLint/Prettier configs for JavaScript, etc.) and use automated linters/formatters to ensure consistency. They also often require that significant changes go through a design discussion (e.g., Django's DEP – **Django Enhancement Proposal** – process for major features) so that the architecture remains coherent. In essence, while everyone can contribute, the community agrees on the rules of contribution and design upfront. This balance of openness and control allows many hands to work on the code base without it degenerating into chaos.

Drawing from the preceding exploration, several key factors emerge that help open source framework teams stay responsive to users and maintain code excellence over time:

- **Comprehensive automated testing**: A strong automated test suite (with unit, integration, and system tests) is the safety net for fast iteration. It allows fearless refactoring and frequent releases because regressions are caught early. High coverage and CI enforcement of tests ensure that contributions improve the project without breaking it. Studies show TDD and thorough testing directly improve quality in open source, and successful projects such as Django treat tests as non-negotiable for every change.

- **CI pipelines**: Investing in reliable CI infrastructure pays huge dividends. CI provides immediate feedback on each commit, enforcing a standard of "no broken builds." It also enables multiple-platform support and quick compatibility fixes. By automating builds, tests, linting, and even deployments, the project reduces manual effort and errors. Modern CI tools (GitHub Actions, etc.) integrated with version control are a big enabler for distributed teams, keeping everyone informed of build status and freeing maintainers from running tests themselves.

- **Strong code review and coding standards**: A culture of thorough code reviews not only improves code quality but also spreads knowledge. Requiring at least one other person to approve a change (as many projects do) prevents blind spots. Clear coding standards and style guides (often enforced by linters/formatters in CI) mean that when code from many authors comes together, it appears consistent and is easier to maintain. Respectful, constructive code reviews also serve as mentorship, upgrading the skills of contributors over time – a virtuous cycle for the community.

- **Frequent releases and feedback incorporation**: Releasing updates regularly (with clear release notes) keeps the community engaged and provides constant feedback. "Release early, release often" prevents backlog bloat and allows the project to course-correct quickly if a change is not well received. It also gives users confidence that the project is active and responsive. Even if not every release is packed with features, the habit of frequent small releases is healthier than infrequent big-bang releases. Many frameworks adopt semantic versioning and schedule periodic minor releases, which establishes a rhythm the community can rely on.

- **Transparent road mapping and issue tracking**: Openness about what the team is working on and what is planned builds trust with users. Public roadmaps, or at least a curated set of "important upcoming issues," help focus the community's efforts. It also invites early feedback – if users see a change coming, they can voice concerns or excitement, guiding the implementation. Effective use of an issue tracker, with labels and milestones, turns it into a collaborative to-do list that anyone can contribute to. This aligns with Agile backlog grooming but in a public, crowdsourced manner.

- **Tooling to support distributed work**: Successful projects reduce friction for contributors. Scripts to set up a dev environment, run tests locally (as FastAPI provides), or generate documentation make it easier for anyone to jump in. Integration of docs with code (such as FastAPI testing its documentation examples as part of the test suite) ensures documentation stays up to date and lowers user support burden. Communication tools (chat and forums) for quick help and CI bots for routine tasks all improve the contributor experience. When contributing feels smooth and rewarding, more people participate – increasing the project's bus factor and resilience.

Summary

In this chapter, we delved into essential techniques for effectively prototyping ADFs. The process begins by identifying and abstracting reusable patterns from concrete applications, which serve as the foundation for a robust framework. Through iterative refinement, we introduced structured message types and clear execution flows, evolving from minimal working examples to comprehensive, composable agent-oriented structures.

Key concepts included defining core abstractions, employing role-based routing for dynamic and specialized agent interactions, and structuring the framework into a cohesive, reusable Python package. The chapter also emphasized best practices using modern Python tooling such as uv for dependency management, pytest for automated testing, and ruff for linting and code quality.

Furthermore, we highlighted Agile principles, emphasizing frequent feedback loops, transparent community-driven development, CI, and robust automated testing strategies. The importance of a **secure system development life cycle (SSDLC)** was underscored, recommending proactive security measures, tooling integration across different language ecosystems, secure CI/CD practices, and clear incident response and vulnerability disclosure procedures.

By mastering these techniques, you will be capable of developing frameworks that are not only functional and efficient but also resilient and secure, able to adapt effectively to emerging technological challenges.

In the next chapter, we build on the foundational architecture and modular principles explored previously, and shift our focus toward practical implementation. This includes defining agent roles, implementing dynamic prompt flows, and integrating role-specific behavior across the framework. The goal is to evolve our ADF from a modular skeleton into a flexible, intelligent system that adapts to context and user needs. By the end of the chapter, you'll be equipped to build extensible workflows that support smart reasoning, stateful interaction, and scalable component orchestration.

Unlock this book's exclusive benefits now

Scan this QR code or go to packtpub.com/unlock, then search this book by name.

Note: Keep your purchase invoice ready before you start.

7

Documenting and Releasing a Framework

Building the framework in the lifecycle of an **application development framework (ADF)** is only the beginning. Proper documentation and release management are paramount to ensure its long-term success and adoption. Without well-documented features and a structured approach to managing releases, even the most innovative frameworks can fail to deliver their intended value.

This chapter provides a comprehensive guide to creating adequate documentation and implementing robust release management practices. By focusing on tools, platforms, and best practices, we aim to help you make an ADF that is not only functional but also user-friendly, transparent, and easy to maintain.

As we know, the primary purpose of frameworks is to deal with systems complexity and simplify application developers' work, and documentation is clearly a significant contributor to this mission.

Meanwhile, strategic release management ensures that updates are predictable, stable, and well-communicated, fostering trust and confidence among users.

Drawing on insights from successful ADF projects, this chapter covers the tools and methodologies needed to build strong documentation and manage releases effectively. From leveraging GitLab Pages and Sphinx for documentation to mastering API documentation and adopting versioning strategies, you will learn how to make your framework an indispensable asset to your organization and its developers.

This chapter will cover the following topics:

- Establishing a robust documentation foundation
- Step-by-step guide: Building and maintaining ADF documentation
- Developing and optimizing API documentation for clarity and usability
- Implementing effective versioning and release strategies

With these capabilities, your ADF will not only deliver on its promises but also inspire confidence and trust among its users and stakeholders.

Establishing a robust documentation foundation

The success of any ADF depends not only on its technical capabilities but also on how easily developers can adopt and integrate it into their workflows. The primary purpose of ADF documentation is to ensure that application developers can use the framework efficiently and autonomously. Well-structured and accessible documentation minimizes reliance on framework developers, preventing them from becoming a bottleneck in ADF adoption.

When application developers struggle to find the information they need, they either abandon the framework in favor of alternatives or continuously seek support from the framework team. Both scenarios slow down adoption and reduce the framework's overall impact. By providing clear, actionable documentation, ADF developers empower their users to explore, integrate, and extend the framework independently, leading to greater efficiency and smoother onboarding.

Good documentation is not merely an auxiliary feature but a core enabler of the framework's intended value. It guides developers through best practices, prevents common pitfalls, and aligns expectations about how the framework should be used. Moreover, it enhances the perception of professionalism and stability, increasing the likelihood of adoption within an organization.

Beyond onboarding, documentation plays a crucial role in ensuring long-term maintainability. As teams change and projects evolve, having a reliable knowledge base prevents the accumulation of technical debt and reduces the risk of knowledge silos. In this way, robust documentation directly contributes to the sustainability of the ADF.

Documentation as a continuation of an ADF

Documentation is not an isolated "optional" piece of deliverables. It is a component of an ADF; it is a natural extension of the framework itself. A well-documented framework reduces friction for new adopters, supports efficient collaboration among teams, and improves engineering efficiency. In this sense, documentation should be considered part of the ADF's architecture, just like its core abstractions and API design.

Framework Documentation Maturity Ladder

Docs & guidance

If a process is essential but not yet automated, it should be well-documented to provide a guidance

Validation

if we need to ensure that a non-automated process is in place, we can add validation for manual parts (static checks, strict formats, regexp, assertions, runtime validation)

Automation

repetitive and error-prone tasks should be covered by scripts providing shortcuts to the correct process implementation (e.g. Django management commands, or console commands in other frameworks)

Implementation

if a process is fully integrated in ADF implementation, it may no longer require extensive documentation beyond high-level conceptual guidance and auto-generated reference docs

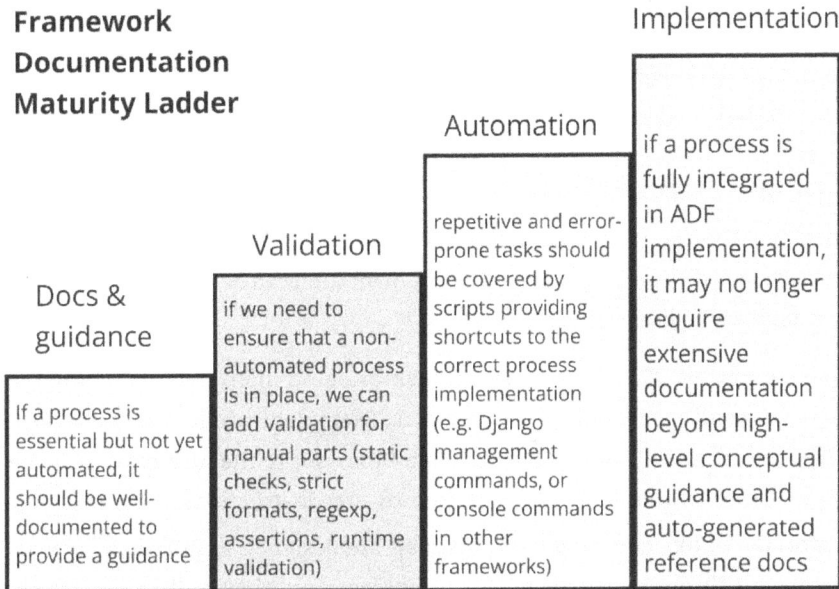

Figure 7.1: From documentation to a framework maturity ladder

I would suggest looking at ADF documentation as a "phase zero" framework implementation: when there is no framework code yet, but guidance on how to build an application according to the future framework structure and principles.

To continue developing this perspective, there might be the following heuristic for prioritizing documentation efforts as the documentation-to-automation maturity ladder:

- **Documentation:** If a process is essential but not yet automated, it should be well documented to provide guidance

- **Validation:** If we need to ensure that a non-automated process is in place, we can add validation for manual parts (static checks, strict formats, and runtime validation)

- **Automation:** If a documented process is repetitive and error-prone, it should at least be covered by scripts providing shortcuts to the correct process implementation (such as management commands in Django or console commands in many other frameworks that are run manually outside of the ADF-driven implementation flow)

- **Implementation (integration):** If a process is fully integrated in the ADF implementation, it may no longer require extensive documentation beyond high-level conceptual guidance, as well as automation to be run aside of the ADF

This approach helps focus documentation efforts on areas that truly need clarification – those parts of the framework that cannot be automated or require human decision-making. By treating documentation as an evolving asset rather than a static one, ADF developers can avoid overloading users with unnecessary details while ensuring that essential concepts remain accessible.

Types of documentation

Not all documentation serves the same purpose, and understanding its different types can help create a well-balanced knowledge base. ADF documentation can be categorized into four primary types, each addressing distinct needs:

- **How-to guides**: These are practical, task-oriented instructions that help developers achieve specific goals using the framework. Examples include "How to Set Up Your First ADF Project" and "How to Add a Custom Processor to the ADF Pipeline." These guides should be concise and focused, with step-by-step instructions and real-world examples.

- **Tutorials**: Unlike how-to guides, tutorials are designed to introduce new users to the framework through structured, progressive learning. They walk the user through a complete use case, helping them build confidence in the framework's capabilities. A well-crafted tutorial answers the question, "Where do I start?" and should prioritize accessibility over comprehensiveness. This kind of document is also known as "Hello World" guides.

- **Reference documentation**: This is the technical backbone of ADF documentation, covering API specifications, configuration parameters, and internal architecture details. It should be exhaustive and precise, offering answers to developers who already know what they are looking for. Automated documentation generation tools such as Sphinx (for Python) or Docusaurus (for JavaScript) can ensure that reference materials remain up to date with the framework's code base.

- **Explanations and conceptual documentation**: This type of documentation offers the theoretical context, design rationales, and architectural principles behind the framework. It aids developers in understanding why the ADF functions as it does. Unlike reference documents, which address "What does this do?" and how-to guides that tackle "How do I do this?", conceptual documentation responds to "Why is it designed this way?".

Each type of documentation plays a unique role in supporting ADF adoption. A balanced approach ensures that developers can smoothly transition from onboarding to mastery, with each piece of documentation fulfilling a clear purpose.

By aligning your documentation strategy with your framework's maturity, you ensure that developers get the information they need when they need it most, from getting started with a simple tutorial to understanding deep architectural concepts for advanced integration.

Documentation focus by ADF maturity level

Documentation Type	Level 2: MVF	Level 3: Bullet-proof	Level 4: Advanced	Level 5: Ecosystem
Explanations/ conceptual docs	Basic (README)	Growing importance of extensibility	**Critical** for architects and senior developers	Foundational; guides the entire ecosystem
Tutorials	**Critical** for initial adoption and "Hello World"	Still vital for onboarding; more topics appear	Specialized tutorials for complex features	The community may contribute diverse tutorials
How-to guides	Minimal; often covered by the tutorial	**Essential** for new features and common tasks	Numerous guides for advanced integrations	Covers a vast range of use cases, often by the community
Reference documentation	Foundational but can be minimal (auto-gen)	Must be robust, accurate, and well-maintained	Exhaustive and versioned	Comprehensive, searchable library

Table 7.1: Document focus by ADF maturity level

Automating documentation generation

Automating the generation of API documentation ensures that it remains consistent with the code base, reducing the risk of discrepancies and outdated information. Several tools can assist this process by extracting information directly from the source code or standard specifications to produce comprehensive documentation.

The following are some tools that facilitate this process. Please use the list as an example of what you might need, not as a recommendation or promotion of particular vendors:

- **Sphinx** (`https://www.sphinx-doc.org/`): Sphinx is a documentation generator that transforms **reStructuredText (reST)** files into various output formats, including HTML and PDF. Originally created for Python documentation, it has been adopted by many projects for its extensibility and support for automatic code documentation. Usage examples include the following:

    - **Python**: The official Python documentation is built using Sphinx, showcasing its capability to handle large and complex documentation needs
    - **Django**: Django employs Sphinx to generate comprehensive documentation for its web framework, aiding developers in understanding and utilizing its features

- **YARD** (`https://yardoc.org/`): YARD is a documentation generation tool for the Ruby programming language. It enables users to generate consistent, usable documentation that can be exported to various formats easily. YARD supports extending for custom Ruby constructs, such as custom class-level definitions. Usage examples include the following:

    - **Ruby on Rails**: Many Ruby on Rails projects utilize YARD to maintain clear and concise API documentation, facilitating better collaboration and code maintenance
    - **Puppet**: Puppet uses YARD to document its code base, providing users with accessible and well-structured documentation

- **Javadoc** (`https://docs.oracle.com/javase/8/docs/technotes/guides/javadoc/index.html`): Javadoc is a documentation generator for generating API documentation in HTML format from Java source code. It parses the declarations and documentation comments in a set of source files to produce a corresponding set of HTML pages describing the classes, interfaces, constructors, methods, and fields. Usage examples include the following:

    - **Java standard library**: The official Java API documentation is generated using Javadoc, providing a consistent and comprehensive reference for developers
    - **Android SDK**: The Android SDK utilizes Javadoc to document its classes and methods, aiding developers in building Android applications

- **DocFX** (`https://dotnet.github.io/docfx/`): This is a modern, open source documentation generation tool for .NET projects, including C#. It builds documentation from both triple-slash code comments (`///`) in your source code and from separate Markdown files, creating a unified documentation website. Usage examples include the following:

- **.NET**: Microsoft uses DocFX to generate the official .NET reference documentation, showcasing its scalability for large projects
- **Unity projects**: Developers using the Unity engine often leverage DocFX to create documentation for their C# scripts and game logic

- **TypeDoc** (`https://typedoc.org/`): This is a popular documentation generator specifically for TypeScript projects. It reads JSDoc or TSDoc comments from your TypeScript source code and generates a static HTML website detailing your project's modules, classes, interfaces, and methods. Usage examples include the following:

  - **RxJS**: This widely used reactive programming library uses TypeDoc to generate its extensive and well-structured API documentation
  - **Angular libraries**: Many libraries within the Angular ecosystem rely on TypeDoc to automatically generate clear API documentation from their TypeScript source

- **Doxygen** (`https://www.doxygen.nl/`): Doxygen is a documentation generator for various programming languages, including C++, C, Java, and Python. It extracts comments from the source code and generates documentation in multiple formats, such as HTML and LaTeX. Usage examples include the following:

  - **Drupal**: Drupal uses Doxygen to generate its extensive documentation, assisting developers in understanding and utilizing the framework effectively
  - **OpenCV**: OpenCV employs Doxygen to maintain its API documentation, providing clear guidance for developers working with computer vision libraries

Implementing these tools involves integrating them into the development workflow, ensuring that documentation is generated automatically as part of the build or deployment process. This practice guarantees that the documentation reflects the current state of the API, providing developers with accurate and reliable resources.

This kind of tool is a "must-have" setup for any framework, corporate or open source.

Using source control systems for documentation publishing and hosting

For teams that prefer a fully integrated workflow, documentation can be published and hosted using source control systems such as GitHub, GitLab, and Azure DevOps. These platforms provide built-in solutions for hosting documentation alongside source code, ensuring that documentation remains synchronized with development efforts.

We also recommend choosing this option as the first choice for early-stage development to leverage your current well-known toolset and minimize investment in new technology.

- **GitHub Pages**: GitHub Pages is a free static site hosting service that can publish Markdown-based documentation directly from a GitHub repository. Examples include open source projects that use GitHub Pages with Jekyll to host API documentation.

- **GitLab Pages**: Similar to GitHub Pages, GitLab Pages allows developers to host static websites directly from a GitLab repository. Usage examples include the official GitLab documentation, which is hosted using GitLab Pages.

- **Azure DevOps Wiki**: Azure DevOps includes a built-in Wiki feature that allows teams to create and maintain technical documentation within their DevOps projects. Usage is mainly around enterprise DevOps teams: they often use Azure DevOps Wiki for API and internal process documentation. Refer to the guide on how to publish auto-generated docs from your code repository to the wiki: `https://learn.microsoft.com/en-us/azure/devops/project/wiki/publish-repo-to-wiki`.

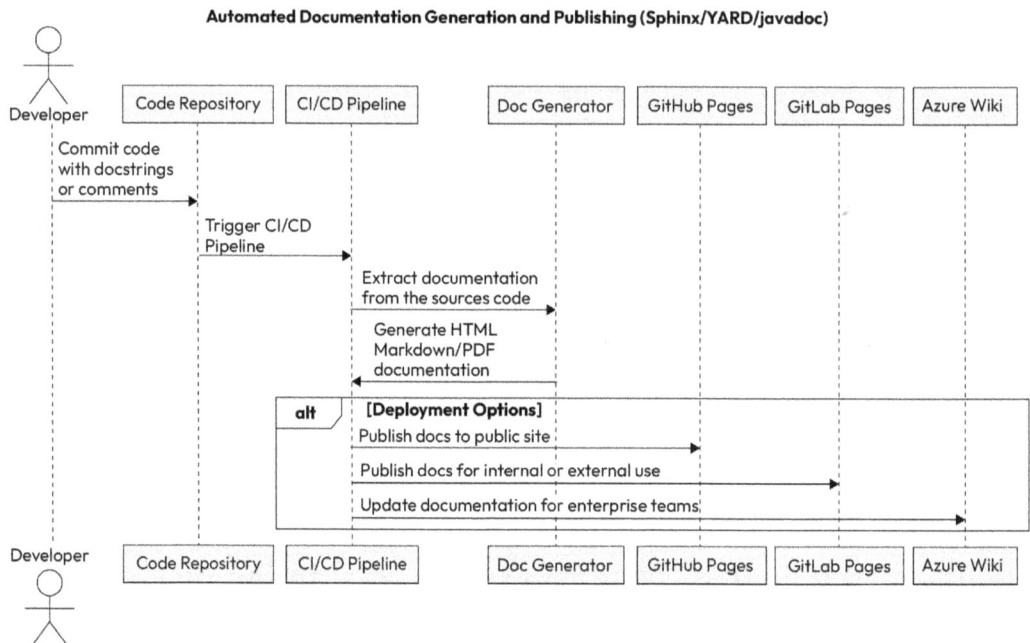

Figure 7.2: Document generation sequence diagram

Let's look at how it works:

- Developers commit new code with embedded documentation comments.
- The repository (GitHub, GitLab, or Azure DevOps) triggers the CI/CD pipeline.
- CI/CD invokes a documentation generator (Sphinx, YARD, Javadoc, Swagger, etc.).
- The generated documentation is formatted (HTML, Markdown, PDF, or interactive API docs).
- The CI/CD system publishes the docs to one of the deployment targets:

    - GitHub Pages (for open source and public projects)
    - GitLab Pages (for internal and external documentation)
    - Azure DevOps wiki (for enterprise collaboration)
    - End users (developers, architects, and stakeholders) access the latest documentation.

This set of tools covers both corporate-owned ADFs that are not intended to be published (yet), as well as OSS ones.

End-to-end generation, publishing, and hosting

Alternative tooling, focused on complementary documentation, is available for documenting mature frameworks ready to become a core of runtime platforms (see the next section for details). Several tools support this workflow, providing automated pipelines for effectively generating, publishing, and hosting documentation:

- **Docusaurus** (`https://docusaurus.io/`): Docusaurus is an open source static site generator optimized for documentation websites. It supports Markdown and provides features such as versioning, localization, and search, making it easy to maintain high-quality documentation for long-term projects. Usage examples include the following:
- **Meta (Facebook)**: Meta uses Docusaurus to ensure structured and searchable docs for several of its open source projects
- **React Native**: This employs Docusaurus to maintain its documentation website, offering developers an intuitive and well-organized reference
- **MkDocs** (`https://www.mkdocs.org/`): MkDocs is a fast, simple static site generator geared toward project documentation. Written in Python, it supports Markdown, various themes, and plugins. It integrates well with Git-based workflows, making it ideal for version-controlled projects. Usage examples include the following:

- **Material for MkDocs:** This is a popular extension used by many open source projects to create sleek and modern documentation portals
- **Python libraries:** Various Python projects use MkDocs for lightweight yet effective documentation
- **Document360** (`https://document360.com/`): Document360 is a cloud-based knowledge management platform designed for creating, publishing, and maintaining technical documentation. It supports Markdown, WYSIWYG editing, version control, and role-based access. It also has a free tier and supports start-ups and individual contributors. Usage examples include the following:
- **Microsoft Azure:** This uses Document360 for internal and external API documentation
- **Harvard University:** This employs Document360 to manage API documentation across multiple teams
- **ReadMe** (`https://readme.com/`): ReadMe is a documentation-as-a-service platform that provides an interactive and user-friendly experience for API consumers. It includes an API explorer, real-time updates, and analytics to track how documentation is being used. Usage examples include the following:
- **Intercom:** This uses ReadMe to provide developers with dynamic API documentation
- **Segment:** This leverages ReadMe for structured API documentation and user-friendly navigation

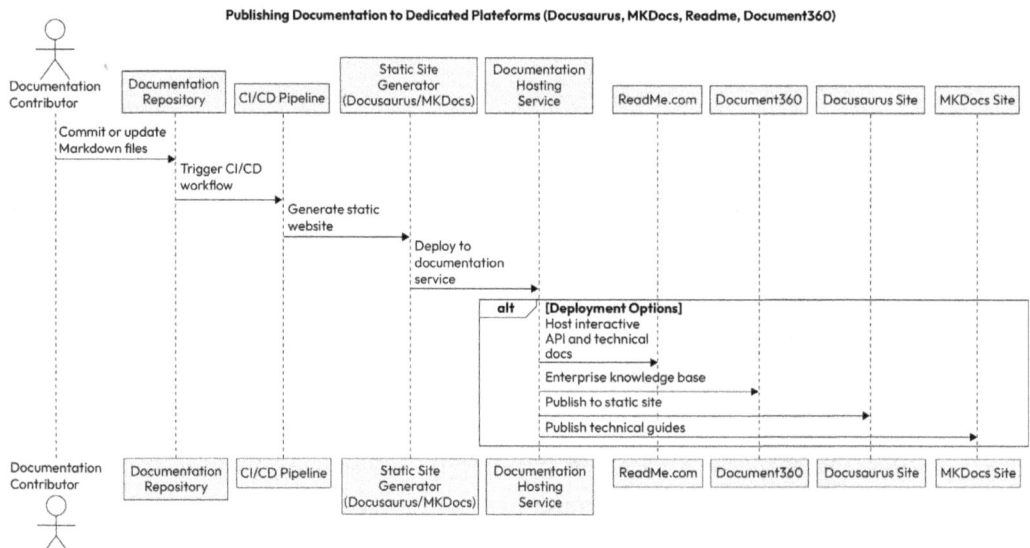

Figure 7.3: Static site generation sequence diagram

⚲ Quick tip: Need to see a high-resolution version of this image? Open this book in the next-gen Packt Reader or view it in the PDF/ePub copy.

🔒 The next-gen Packt Reader and a free PDF/ePub copy of this book are included with your purchase. Scan the QR code OR visit packtpub.com/unlock, then use the search bar to find this book by name. Double-check the edition shown to make sure you get the right one.

Navigation and search for ADF documentation

Even the most well-written documentation is useless if users cannot find the information they need quickly. Effective **navigation and search capabilities** are essential for making ADF documentation accessible, ensuring that developers, architects, and other stakeholders can efficiently locate relevant guides, references, and tutorials. Without a structured approach to organizing content and robust search functionality, documentation can become a bottleneck instead of a productivity booster.

Structuring navigation for ADF documentation

A well-structured documentation portal should be **hierarchical and task-oriented**, catering to both **new users** (who need tutorials and onboarding guides) and **experienced users** (who require quick access to reference documentation and advanced use cases). A common approach is to divide documentation into **four primary sections**:

- **Getting started**: Tutorials, quick-start guides, and installation instructions
- **Core concepts**: Architectural overviews, fundamental principles, and best practices
- **How-to guides**: Step-by-step solutions for specific tasks and integrations
- **API/reference documentation**: Automatically generated function and method references

Many frameworks, such as **Django** and **Spring Boot**, use this structured approach to ensure logical progression from beginner-friendly tutorials to advanced technical references.

Enhancing search with indexing and metadata

For larger documentation sets, full-text search with indexing is critical. Tools such as Algolia Search (used in Docusaurus), Elasticsearch, or Lunr.js (for MkDocs and Jekyll sites) significantly improve searchability in the following ways:

- Providing instant, predictive search suggestions as users type
- Indexing Markdown and API documentation content, ensuring quick retrieval
- Supporting filters by category (e.g., API methods vs. troubleshooting guides)

Many modern documentation platforms, such as ReadMe.com, Document360, and GitBook, integrate context-aware search, allowing users to refine queries based on documentation type, making it easier to locate code snippets, tutorials, or deep-dive explanations.

Cross-linking and contextual navigation

Beyond search, effective **internal linking** ensures users naturally discover related topics. Some best practices include the following:

- "See Also" sections linking related documentation pages
- Breadcrumb navigation to help users track where they are within the hierarchy
- Inline tooltips that define key terms without requiring users to leave the page

For example, **Kubernetes documentation** effectively uses **deep linking** to connect high-level concepts with CLI references, enabling seamless transitions between conceptual overviews and practical commands.

By implementing intuitive navigation, powerful search capabilities, and structured cross-linking, ADF documentation can become a highly usable, developer-friendly resource, reducing onboarding time and minimizing support requests.

Step-by-step guide: Building and maintaining ADF documentation

Creating and maintaining high-quality documentation for an ADF requires a structured and iterative approach. This guide outlines key activities to ensure that documentation remains clear, comprehensive, and up to date while supporting different stakeholders, from architects to application developers. Without clear, structured, and regularly updated documentation, even the most well-designed frameworks risk low adoption rates and increased maintenance burdens. In this section, we outline the key activities required to build and sustain an effective documentation system, covering high-level conceptual descriptions, architecture references, practical guides, automated reference documentation, and ongoing maintenance strategies.

Creating a concept-level description

This is a high-level overview of the ADF, typically stored as a README.md file in the repository root or a landing page of the dedicated ADF website.

The first step in documentation is establishing a concept-level description that provides a big-picture view of the framework. This document should be tailored for CTOs, architects, and senior engineers, giving them insights into the following:

- **The purpose of the ADF**: Why was this framework created, and what problems does it solve?
- **Core principles and design philosophy**: What fundamental ideas guide its development? What architectural patterns, best practices, and trade-offs have been made?
- **Key capabilities and limitations**: What can developers expect from the framework?
- **How the ADF fits into the broader system landscape**: How does this ADF fit within existing software systems?

For example, Django's official README file succinctly introduces it as "a high-level Python Web framework that encourages rapid development and clean, pragmatic design," immediately setting expectations for potential adopters. Similarly, React's documentation provides a brief but powerful summary of why a developer might choose it, highlighting its declarative nature and component-based architecture.

Here are some best practices:

- Keep this document **concise but informative,** focusing on what the framework does rather than how it works in detail. Avoid including every link and reference; this is not intended as an index for your ADF documentation.
- Incorporate diagrams as needed (utilizing Mermaid.js, PlantUML, or Excalidraw for visual representation), but limit them to conceptual-level illustrations. Detailed architectural descriptions and diagrams should be included in the reference materials.
- Make sure the document is version-controlled and updated simultaneously with significant ADF changes updates.

As a bonus, you can always add some fancy promo materials as concept-level documentation to present your ADF as a genuine informational product. Examples of such promo landings can be found at `https://react.dev` and `https://nestjs.com/` (the cat picture is awesome!); they are designed to "sell" the framework rather than present its capabilities.

Providing architecture references

The description focuses on detailed software system models built on top of your ADF.

For architects and technical leads evaluating the framework, providing **architectural references** that show how real-world applications are structured using the ADF is crucial. These references help teams understand best practices and guide them in implementing the framework correctly.

This type of documentation is frequently overlooked, and its importance is underestimated.

Key elements to include in architecture documentation include the following:

- **Diagrams that illustrate system structure, core system components, and their interactions, and where the ADF fits in**: Use tools such as Mermaid.js, PlantUML, or `diagrams.net` (formerly `draw.io`) to create clear visual representations of application components and their interactions.
- **Deployment models**: Show different environments where the ADF can be deployed (e.g., microservices, monolithic applications, cloud-based, or on-premises).
- **Case studies and sample implementations**: Provide real–world examples or at least sample app architecture designs of projects that effectively utilize the ADF. In the case of an internal framework, it is worth listing all existing implementations based on your ADF here, with links to their respective architecture design documentation.

For instance, Kubernetes documentation provides **detailed architecture diagrams** to explain its core components, such as Pods, Nodes, and clusters, making it easier for engineers to grasp its internal workings. Similarly, Spring Boot includes **deployment scenarios** illustrating how its framework integrates within microservice architectures.

Adding known limitations and constraints can add tremendous value: application developers always prefer to know such information in advance instead of discovering it during the production system roll-out.

For example:

- **Concurrency model limitation (Node.js)**: It is part of the Node.js design philosophy that an API should always be asynchronous, even where it doesn't have to be. This piece of documentation clearly explains some unwanted consequences of this approach: `https://nodejs.org/en/learn/asynchronous-work/event-loop-timers-and-nexttick#why-would-that-be-allowed`.
- **React's effect**: "You might not need an Effect" `https://react.dev/learn/synchronizing-with-effects#you-might-not-need-an-effect`.

Excellent frameworks build trust by being transparent about their trade-offs.

Here are some best practices:

- Break down complex diagrams into multiple layers (e.g., high-level system architecture, component diagrams, and data flow). Using the C4 model might be efficient here.
- If relevant, offer multiple architecture variations for different use cases (e.g., serverless, containerized, and monolith-to-microservices transition).
- Ensure that documentation includes trade-offs and alternative solutions when applicable.

Writing tutorial guides for ADF adoption

These are comprehensive, step-by-step onboarding guides for new users. Often, the first information source is for application developers who want to try the ADF or build a "proof of concept."

Tutorials are **critical for onboarding new developers** with step-by-step instructions. The goal is to guide a user from installation to a fully functional implementation of the framework-based application. Tutorials are essential for lowering the learning curve and accelerating adoption. These guides should take a progressive learning approach, from basic usage to advanced capabilities.

A well-structured tutorial should include the following:

- **Introduction**: What the tutorial covers and what knowledge is expected beforehand.
- **Setup and prerequisites**: Instructions for installing dependencies, configuring environments, and getting started.
- **Building a basic application**: A small but meaningful example that demonstrates core ADF functionalities. Ideally, it should also hint at the ideal application type your ADF is aimed at structuring.

- **Exploring key features**: Progressive learning that introduces additional concepts in a logical sequence.

- **Troubleshooting and next steps**: Common issues, debugging techniques, and where to go from here.

For example, Flask's **Quickstart** tutorial walks new users through building a simple web app step by step and demonstrates key features such as routing, templates, and database integration. Similarly, Vue.js provides **interactive tutorials** that allow users to experiment with code snippets directly in the browser.

> Hint: There are new generations of tooling designed to help with this kind of documentation. Take a look at https://www.guideflow.com/.

For frameworks that involve a significant user interface component, creating and maintaining visual tutorials can be labor-intensive. A new generation of tooling is available to address this challenge. Tools such as Guideflow, Scribe, Tango, Guidde, and Dubble can automate and significantly simplify the task of keeping visual documentation (especially screenshots and click-throughs) synchronized with your evolving software.

These tools typically function by recording a user's interaction with a web application. Each click, input, or navigation step is automatically documented with a corresponding screenshot and textual instruction. This process largely eliminates the need for manual image capture, annotation, and formatting, offering several advantages:

- **Create**: The primary benefit is the rapid conversion of a manual process into a visually structured walkthrough, saving considerable time.

- **Update**: Instead of recreating an entire guide when a UI element changes, you can often rerecord only the affected section. Some tools even offer **smart update detection**, notifying you when a UI element appears to have changed so you can proactively recapture that step.

- **Publish**: The output from these tools can typically be embedded directly into documentation platforms such as Confluence, Notion, and GitHub, or exported to Markdown for use in custom documentation sites.

It is important to recognize that these tools are reactive, not fully autonomous. They do not proactively monitor your application for UI changes. The documentation author must still initiate a recapture or visually validate that the guides remain accurate after a new software release.

For frameworks with a rapidly changing UI, the following best practices are recommended:

- Version your guides. Align your documentation versions with your product releases (e.g., have distinct guides for v1.3.2 and v1.4.0 of your framework).

- Mark outdated content. If a guide becomes partially outdated, clearly mark the affected steps with a warning until they can be re-recorded and updated.

- Ensure that each step builds upon the previous one to avoid overwhelming new users.

- Use screenshots and sample outputs to confirm the expected results.

- Include troubleshooting tips at each step.

- Encourage contributions by allowing users to submit feedback and improvements.

- Where possible, provide copy-paste-ready code snippets (as the default way to provide guidance) and interactive sandboxes (as an advanced method more applicable to high-maturity frameworks or platforms).

How-to guides for specific scenarios

How-to guides are step-by-step solutions for advanced usage, integrations, migrations, and edge cases.

Unlike tutorials, which focus on general onboarding, how-to guides address specific, real-world tasks that developers commonly encounter. These guides should be short, task-focused, and solution-oriented, allowing application developers to find and apply relevant information quickly.

Examples of useful how-to guides include the following:

- **Handling authentication and authorization**: Covering integrations with specific identity providers, including advanced tasks such as enabling **single sign-on (SSO)** or **multi-factor authentication (MFA)**

- **Extending the ADF with plugins**: Showing how to customize or enhance the framework's capabilities most efficiently

- **Migrating from another framework to your ADF**: Providing necessary steps for converting the code base and importing the framework configuration

- **Deploying and scaling applications built with the ADF**: Offering practical advice for production readiness, including highly available configuration, request routing, and secure framework secrets and keys

For example, Django's documentation includes dedicated guides for deployment, database migrations, and testing, ensuring that users can easily access relevant knowledge when needed.

Here are some best practices:

- Format guides as a list of repeatable steps with clear inputs and expected outcomes. They do not necessarily need to be visually rich and detailed like tutorials, because we assume the application developer is already familiar with basic ADF functions.

- Link to related documentation where necessary (e.g., API references and architecture reference).

- Include expected outcomes and validation checks.

Generating and maintaining reference documentation

Reference documentation provides **detailed technical specifications** for the ADF's components, including APIs, configuration options, and internal mechanisms. Unlike tutorials and how-to guides, reference documentation is often **generated automatically** from source code to ensure accuracy and consistency.

Based on the tools discussed earlier, consider the following:

- **Select the proper documentation tooling**: Based on the programming language and framework needs, choose tools such as Sphinx (Python), YARD (Ruby), Javadoc (Java), or Swagger/OpenAPI (REST APIs).

- **Ensure the code is adequately commented**: Use structured docstrings that documentation generators can process into readable formats. Hint: you can either generate docstrings with a coding copilot or an AI-powered IDE, or vice versa, generate code based on a proper function's description. Here is an example:

```python
def add_user(name: str, email: str) -> bool:
    """

    Adds a new user to the system.
    Args:
        name (str): The full name of the user.
        email (str): The user's email address.
    Returns:
        bool: True if the user was added successfully, otherwise
False.
    Raises:
        ValueError: If the email is invalid.
    """

    # Function implementation here
```

- **Automate documentation updates with CI/CD pipelines**: Configure workflows in GitHub Actions, GitLab CI/CD, or Azure DevOps to regenerate and publish documentation whenever changes are pushed.

For example, FastAPI automatically generates interactive API documentation using Swagger UI and Redoc, ensuring that users always have up-to-date reference material without extra effort.

Here are some best practices:

- Use a consistent docstring style (Google-style, NumPy-style, or Javadoc format).
- Enable search functionality in generated documentation to improve usability.
- Set up automated daily or per-commit builds to keep API documentation synchronized with the latest code changes.
- Store generated documentation alongside versioned releases for historical reference. Please note that this advice is mostly relevant to the reference documentation, as we might not want to store lots of duplicated user guides, tutorials, and other artifacts that are not required to be synchronously updated each time we increment a version.

Ongoing maintenance and documentation strategy

Documentation is a **living asset** and must evolve alongside the ADF. The best way to ensure long-term effectiveness is to integrate documentation into the **development cycle** rather than treating it as an afterthought.

Key strategies for ongoing maintenance include the following:

- Make documentation updates part of the release process. Even if some of your documents are not autogenerated ones, use a release checklist to quickly review your documentation and ensure it is still relevant.
- Track documentation issues and improvements using GitHub/GitLab issues or Jira.
- Encourage community contributions by making documentation open source.
- Analyze user engagement to identify gaps in existing documentation.
- Monitor analytics to see which documentation pages are most used or need improvement.
- Host periodic "documentation sprints" to refine and clarify complex topics.

By treating documentation as a first-class citizen in software development, ADF developers can create a sustainable, developer-friendly experience that promotes adoption and long-term success.

An ADF can provide a seamless, intuitive, and productive developer experience by combining high-level conceptual documents, detailed architecture references, practical guides, and automated API documentation. To summarize the chapter content, please see the following diagram, which incorporates tools and artifacts in a single model:

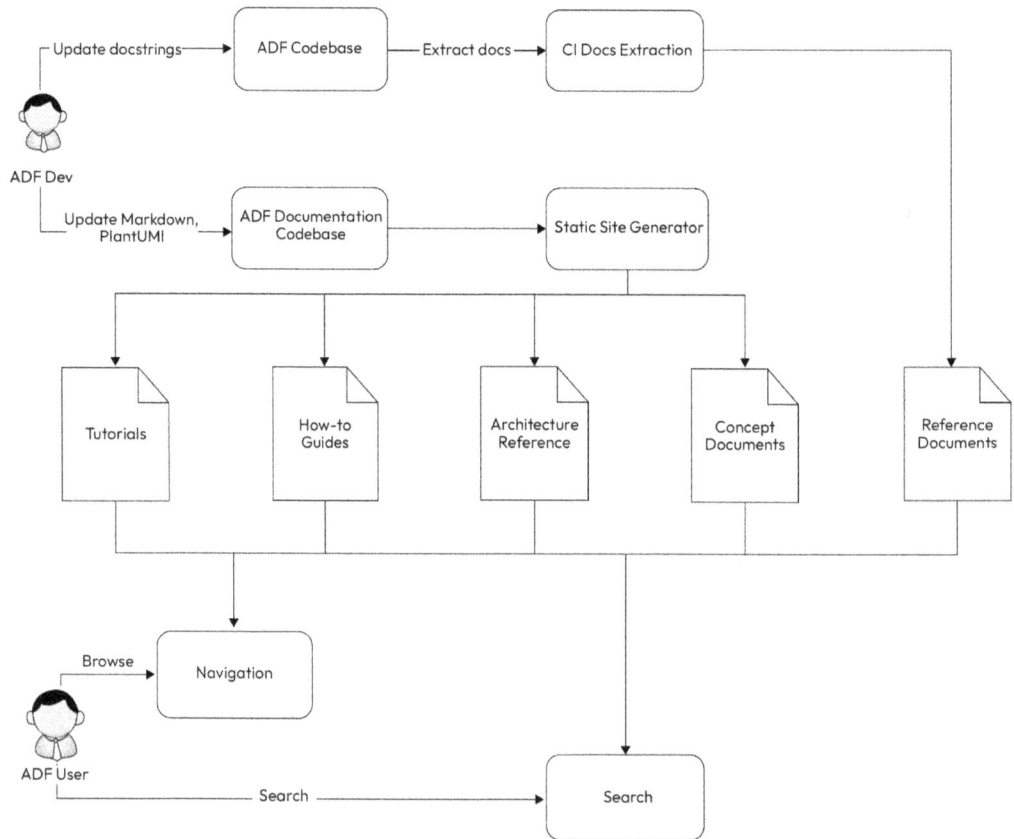

Figure 7.4: Documentation tools and artifacts

By leveraging these tools and platforms, teams can establish a robust workflow for generating, publishing, and maintaining API documentation, ensuring that it remains accessible, up-to-date, and aligned with the framework's evolution.

> Hint: You can use the "Step-by-step guide" section as an extended prompt for your favorite LLM, copilot, or AI agent that has access to your code base to generate the first draft of your documents.

As an inspirational example, we built a production-level quality custom integration framework documentation website in two hours with Cursor (`https://cursor.com`, an AI-powered IDE) and Fumadocs (`https://fumadocs.vercel.app/`, a documentation framework) on top of the Vercel platform. The framework is the "PandaConnect" prototype, hosted at `https://pandaconnect-iota.vercel.app/`.

Developing and optimizing API documentation for clarity and usability

Although we described general documentation best practices in the previous section, the API documentation is worth additional refinement.

To fully understand the importance of API documentation in the context of an ADF, we must first clarify how APIs relate specifically to an ADF. Traditionally, API documentation refers to comprehensive references for a fixed set of endpoints that frameworks directly expose, such as RESTful routes, RPC calls, or library methods. However, when we discuss APIs within the ADF domain, we refer to something notably different.

Typically, an ADF itself does not provide static, built-in APIs. Instead, its core value lies in the infrastructure, tooling, and patterns it provides, empowering application developers to define, implement, and manage their own domain-specific APIs. In other words, the APIs produced by an ADF are an emergent property shaped by how developers choose to implement their applications within the provided framework.

This critical distinction gives rise to two distinct documentation needs:

- Clearly documented methods and guidelines explaining how application developers can define and implement their own APIs within the ADF's context
- Well-defined interfaces, tooling, and recommended practices enabling application developers to build comprehensive documentation for the APIs they create

Let's explore each of these documentation areas in more detail.

Documenting how to define and implement APIs

The primary goal of an ADF is to facilitate the creation of application-specific logic, enabling developers to expose domain objects, controllers, or services as API endpoints. Therefore, documentation provided by ADF authors should carefully illustrate how to define these endpoints within the constraints and patterns of the framework.

Why does this matter? Without clear, structured guidance, application developers risk implementing inconsistent or inefficient endpoints, leading to brittle interfaces and unintended technical debt. Clear documentation mitigates these risks by providing developers with reliable instructions, recommended patterns, and practical examples.

For example, suppose the ADF uses a web framework resembling Django. In that case, the framework's documentation should explicitly describe how developers define views or controllers, how these are linked to routes, and how the corresponding URL routing definitions are created and managed. Similar guidelines apply across different types of frameworks, whether frontend, backend, or hybrid.

Supporting application developers in creating their own API documentation

After application developers successfully implement their APIs using the ADF, the next challenge arises: producing clear, maintainable documentation of these domain-specific endpoints. If consumers of these APIs – be they internal teams or external partners – cannot easily understand how to use them, the APIs themselves will quickly become ineffective, no matter how well engineered they might be.

To help developers succeed in this critical step, ADF authors should provide robust guidance and tooling recommendations that simplify API documentation. Consider the following approaches.

Schema-driven versus code-first approach

Application developers often document APIs using one of two general approaches: schema-driven or code-first.

Schema-driven approaches leverage a **domain-specific language** (**DSL**) or a configuration format (such as YAML or JSON) to define APIs explicitly. From these definitions, the ADF can automatically generate boilerplate code, API stubs, or interactive documentation. Tools such as OpenAPI or AsyncAPI specifications are popular for such approaches.

Code-first approaches, on the other hand, allow application developers to define APIs directly through source code annotations, decorators, or docstrings within the project's programming language (for instance, Python, TypeScript, or Java). The ADF can then parse these annotations to generate API documentation automatically.

Both approaches are viable, and the choice depends on the ADF's architectural context and developer preferences. However, we would not recommend trying to cover both options to avoid confusion – help your users decrease cognitive load by narrowing down the number of decisions they have to make when integrating your framework!

Integration with common documentation tools

The ADF documentation should encourage integration with widely used API documentation generation tools. Some effective options include the following:

- **For RESTful APIs**: Recommend OpenAPI (Swagger UI, Redoc) or RAML, offering built-in tools or adapters within the ADF for automatic schema generation.
- **For internal or library APIs**: Recommend documentation generators such as Sphinx for Python projects or TSDoc for JavaScript/TypeScript-based ADFs, with configuration samples and scripts provided by the ADF.
- **For command-line interfaces**: Include examples of integrating CLI documentation tooling such as Click or docopt, showing how application developers can create clear, helpful documentation embedded directly within their tools.

Enhancing developer productivity through integrated tooling

Please note that the following recommendations are mostly relevant to a highly mature framework. Rather than integrating API docs tooling, you can make many more critical improvements in a framework of one, two, or three maturity levels.

Beyond simply recommending external tools, consider how your ADF can actively support application developers by embedding or integrating a convenient API documentation tool directly within the framework itself. The following practices significantly enhance developer productivity and experience:

- Providing built-in scripts or commands that automatically generate or update API documentation during builds or deployments
- Offering documentation generation as part of the CI/CD pipeline, so every API change immediately triggers documentation updates

Interactive documentation features are also invaluable. Tools such as interactive playgrounds, request simulators, and auto-generated cURL commands or code snippets improve usability and reduce the onboarding time required for API consumers.

Several successful frameworks exemplify these principles:

- **FastAPI**: This modern Python framework automatically generates interactive API documentation from your code. By using Python type hints, FastAPI creates a live, interactive Swagger UI and Redoc interface where developers can not only read about endpoints but also test them directly in the browser. This is a core feature, not an add-on, making documentation an inseparable part of the development process. You can learn more in the FastAPI documentation: `https://fastapi.tiangolo.com/features/#automatic-docs`.

- **Django REST Framework (DRF)**: DRF includes `BrowsableAPIRenderer`, which creates a user-friendly HTML representation of your API. This interface is not static; it allows developers to browse API resources and even submit `POST`, `PUT`, or `DELETE` requests through web forms, providing an invaluable tool for exploring and debugging the API without needing a separate client. See the feature on the DRF Browsable API at this link: `https://www.django-rest-framework.org/topics/browsable-api/`.

- **Ruby on Rails**: Rails provides several built-in commands that enhance productivity by self-documenting the application. The `rails routes` command, for example, inspects the application's routing configuration and outputs a complete list of all available URL endpoints, their corresponding controller actions, and HTTP methods. This serves as instant, accurate documentation for the application's surface area.

- **NestJS (with Swagger plugin)**: This Node.js framework offers a dedicated `@nestjs/swagger` module that deeply integrates with the framework's architecture. By adding decorators to controllers and models, developers can automatically generate a comprehensive OpenAPI (Swagger) specification and a rich interactive UI. This demonstrates how a framework can provide a seamless, officially supported pathway for creating powerful documentation with minimal effort. Explore the integration in the NestJS OpenAPI documentation: `https://docs.nestjs.com/openapi/introduction`.

Summarizing the documentation strategy for ADF-enabled APIs

In summary, because APIs generated from an ADF arise from specific application contexts rather than from the framework itself, ADF authors face two documentation responsibilities:

- Provide detailed, structured instructions for developers on how to create API endpoints within the framework's patterns and capabilities.

- Recommend and support tools and strategies that empower application developers to generate and maintain their own high-quality API documentation effectively. For a proprietary "corporate source" framework, it might be feasible to integrate standard internal documentation tooling to simplify application developers' lives even more.

By clearly distinguishing between these two documentation goals and systematically addressing each, you ensure that developers using your ADF consistently deliver robust, maintainable, and understandable APIs, enhancing both their productivity and the value of your framework.

Implementing effective versioning and release strategies

A structured approach to versioning and release management is essential for the long-term success and maintainability of an ADF. Clearly defined strategies ensure releases are predictable, stable, and easy to adopt, reducing user friction and building stakeholder trust.

This section explores the lifecycle of an ADF release, essential practices such as semantic versioning, deprecation policies, and long-term support, and demonstrates how automation streamlines the release process.

Build and deployment process

Before effective release management can occur, a reliable build and deployment process must be established. This ensures consistency, repeatability, and quality control from initial development to final distribution.

Repository and branching strategy

The build process begins within the source code repository, guided by structured branching strategies such as Git Flow, feature branching, or trunk-based development. These strategies maintain clarity and streamline team collaboration. Creating snapshots or forks supports isolated development environments, enabling teams to experiment without disrupting the primary codebase. After thorough validation and testing, these forks can merge back into the main branch, ensuring minimal disruption.

Corporate ADF specifics here are that forks and snapshots might be restricted to avoid high variability of supported versions and centralize ADF ownership. For an open source ADF, usually, it is the responsibility of application developers to decide how to consume the ADF: as a fork, snapshot, or package.

Build automation

Automating the build process is critical to ensure reliability and efficiency. Here are the key components:

- **Testing and validation**: Integrating tests into build automation helps detect issues early, long before problematic builds reach the production environment. Unit tests are simple, function-bound tests that are easy to write and execute. Integration tests validate interactions between components, while system-level tests ensure comprehensive coverage. Modern AI-powered IDEs and copilots significantly streamline creating and maintaining test suites. Still, manual review of AI-generated test code remains essential due to the technology's novelty and potential inaccuracies.

- **Linting and static analysis**: Early identification of coding issues saves significant time and effort in later stages. Automated linting tools enforce coding standards, consistency, and best practices, helping prevent common coding errors and improving readability and maintainability.

- **Matrix builds**: Ensuring compatibility across various environments, dependencies, and technology stacks is crucial for broad adoption. Matrix builds systematically test the ADF across multiple configurations, identifying compatibility issues early and allowing for proactive resolution.

- **Artifact generation**: Automating artifact generation ensures reproducible and reliable builds. This process packages binaries, compressed archives, or containers ready for distribution, ensuring consistent deployments and reducing manual errors.

Specialized components, such as machine learning or agent-based functionalities, may require tailored build steps to handle unique dependencies, configurations, and deployment requirements properly.

Release and artifact distribution

Following successful builds, artifacts are finalized for release with semantic versioning clearly indicating the version and related metadata. These artifacts are then published through reliable, centralized distribution channels:

- Public registries such as PyPI, Maven, or GitHub Packages
- Internal or enterprise-specific artifact repositories such as Amazon S3 or Artifactory

Centralized artifact distribution ensures that the artifacts are easily accessible, secure, and consistent across the user ecosystem.

Release lifecycle phases

Every successful ADF moves through distinct lifecycle phases, starting with initial exploratory versions, progressing through stable, production-ready releases, and eventually reaching the long-term support stage.

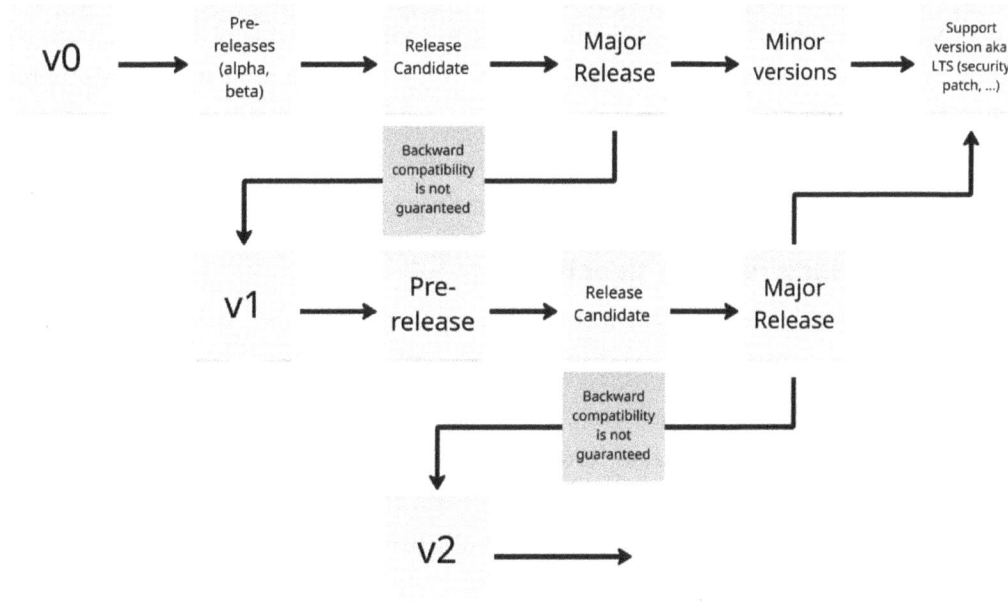

Figure 7.5: Release management flow

- **Initial versions (v0)**: Early releases validate foundational decisions and gather critical user feedback:
- **Alpha releases**: These experimental versions test core functionalities with a limited user group. Think of it as a **proof of concept (PoC)** of the framework you want to test by a trusted circle of early users. So, the alpha release is another way to have **crowdsource testing** for free. Usually, ADF developers do not commit to any support for such builds.
- **Beta releases**: These versions are more stable than alpha, allowing for broader testing of integrations and use cases. ADF developers usually provide limited support for this version.
- **Release candidates (RCs)**: These are nearly final versions intended for extensive validation before the official stable release. This version is optional; some software products jump straight to stable/major versions after beta. Ideally, the ADF could be open for direct contribution to its alpha (and probably beta) users to simplify and speed up the feedback loop.

- **Stable versions (v1, v2, …):** Stable releases represent clearly documented milestones with defined migration paths:

- **Major releases:** These introduce significant enhancements, new features, or breaking changes. Usually, it requires migration or manual work to upgrade, so it is better not to release it too often.

- **Minor versions:** These offer incremental updates and improvements without significant disruptions. It is important to keep minor versions backward compatible to streamline the application upgrade process.

- **Long-term support (LTS):** This provides ongoing security updates and critical fixes for enterprise stability, but no functional changes are made here.

Complementary release practices

Implement additional practices to enhance the clarity, predictability, and reliability of the release process:

- **Change logs:** Document changes, enhancements, and bug fixes to maintain transparency and accountability. **Release Notes** is a commonly used format to keep stakeholders informed.

- **Tracking:** Integrating the task tracker and/or issue tracker with the CI documentation step can achieve some automation.

- **Deprecation strategies:** Clearly communicate feature retirements, providing warnings and migration guides to facilitate smooth transitions.

- **N-2 support policy (or any alternative support policy that goes as deep back in legacy versions as you are comfortable with):** Offer support for the current and two previous major releases, giving users flexibility and time for upgrades.

> **Simplified release management**
>
> Avoid unnecessary complexity, such as shadow releases or feature flags, unless explicitly required, maintaining simplicity and ease of use. It is usually feasible for an ADF to delegate advanced roll-out activities to application developers, so they are responsible for feature flags and shadowing on their side.

Versioning and metadata

Adopt semantic versioning to communicate release changes intuitively, categorizing releases clearly as **major**, **minor**, or **patch**.

When paired with comprehensive documentation, intuitive navigation, and metadata-rich release notes, semantic versioning significantly enhances user accessibility and adoption.

Navigating issue tracking and collaboration platforms

Effective release management doesn't stop at versioning or artifact distribution. An equally important practice is to establish a reliable mechanism for gathering user feedback and tracking issues throughout the lifecycle of your ADF.

Issue tracking platforms are more than just bug-reporting tools. They serve as vital communication channels between framework developers and their users, enabling the exchange of critical insights, enhancement requests, and user experience improvements. Such platforms significantly reduce friction in feedback loops, empowering users to become active participants in the evolution of your framework.

Moreover, a transparent issue-tracking approach can transform user perception by clearly demonstrating your priorities, roadmap items, and commitment to addressing feedback. Publicly tracking issues provides transparency around decisions, helping to set correct expectations about feature timelines, highlighting upcoming improvements, and clarifying the rationale behind prioritization choices.

When selecting an issue tracking solution, it's tempting to gravitate toward feature-rich, complex systems that promise extensive analytics or intricate workflows. However, simplicity should be the guiding principle, especially in the early stages of your ADF lifecycle. Prioritize tools that minimize friction, not just for your team but also for your users. The chosen platform should offer an intuitive, straightforward process for issue submission, commenting, and following progress, without requiring elaborate onboarding or significant learning effort.

Consider the following popular and accessible platforms based on your context:

- For open source or community-driven frameworks, platforms such as GitHub Issues or GitLab Issue Boards are generally preferred. They seamlessly integrate with the code repositories, offer intuitive interfaces, and facilitate transparent community collaboration.
- For enterprise or internal frameworks, consider simple yet versatile tools such as Jira, Azure DevOps, or YouTrack. These platforms balance simplicity with enterprise-grade features such as integration with internal workflows, security considerations, and controlled user access.

Beyond selecting the platform, it is critical to establish clear guidelines on how users should submit issues. Provide concise templates for bug reports, feature requests, and general inquiries to ensure consistent and actionable feedback. Regularly triage and review reported issues, openly communicate planned resolutions, and update issue statuses promptly. Consider linking your issue tracker directly with automated release notes or documentation pipelines, providing immediate visibility into addressed items upon each new release.

Remember, issue tracking platforms are not mere defect repositories – they are collaborative communication hubs that bridge the gap between framework developers and users. By carefully choosing, clearly structuring, and consistently managing these platforms, you significantly enhance the transparency, trust, and ultimately the long-term success of your ADF initiative.

Summary

As you've seen throughout this chapter, documenting and effectively releasing your ADF goes beyond simple instructions – it's foundational to your framework's adoption, usability, and enduring success. Exceptional documentation is a strategic asset that empowers developers, streamlines collaboration, enhances maintainability, and, ultimately, shapes your framework's impact in the software engineering community.

To elevate your ADF's documentation from merely informational to genuinely transformative, start by embracing interactive documentation tools. Tools such as Swagger/OpenAPI, Postman, or Redoc enable developers not only to read but also to actively engage with your APIs. Interactive experiences allow your users to directly explore endpoints, visualize request-response flows, and quickly grasp how your framework behaves in real-world scenarios, significantly reducing their onboarding time and effort.

Further, amplify your documentation effectiveness by automating documentation generation directly from your code base. Adopting tools such as Javadoc, Doxygen, or Sphinx ensures synchronization between your documentation and code, dramatically reducing maintenance effort, preventing discrepancies, and empowering your engineering teams to focus more deeply on building robust features rather than updating manuals.

But don't stop there – ensure your documentation is easily navigable and intuitively organized. Employ visual aids such as flowcharts, diagrams, video walk-throughs, and interactive architectural views to simplify complexity and accelerate comprehension. Clear visuals help succinctly communicate intricate processes and concepts, improving user experience and boosting the developer's productivity when integrating your ADF into their projects.

Finally, consider your documentation a continuous journey rather than a one-time effort. Implement robust feedback loops to capture user insights and pain points regularly. Actively refining your documentation based on this feedback ensures it remains relevant, effective, and aligned with evolving user needs and technological advancements.

Your next step is clear: take immediate action by integrating interactive documentation tools into your ADF workflow, automating documentation processes, enhancing visual communication, and proactively seeking continuous improvement. By embracing these practices, you'll increase the clarity and adoption of your framework and position your ADF as a leader in developer experience and productivity.

After taking care of the documentation and release management topics, we can safely focus on evolving the framework without any significant blockers to ADF adoption and successful use – check the next chapter!

Unlock this book's exclusive benefits now

Scan this QR code or go to packtpub.com/unlock, then search for this book by name. Ensure it's the correct edition.

Note: Keep your purchase invoice ready before you start.

Part 3

Evolving a Framework

Sustaining relevance through continuous improvement

A great framework is not a fixed artifact – it's a living system. This part of the book focuses on how to evolve an ADF beyond its initial implementation. You'll learn how to embed continuous improvement into the lifecycle of your framework, strengthen its adaptability to new contexts, and ensure its long-term relevance and usability.

We explore the essential mindset and practices that enable ADFs to survive and thrive in real-world conditions, including iterating on developer experience, refining control flow, expanding extensibility, and embracing continuous delivery. Along the way, we reflect on what it means to treat a framework not as a finished product, but as an open-ended conversation with your users.

This part has the following chapter:

- *Chapter 8, Evolving a Framework*

8

Evolving a Framework

Congratulations, it seems that you are on track with building your own **Application Development Framework (ADF)**, configuring pipelines, and preparing extensive documentation and developer guidance. What's next?

This chapter shares more ideas, tips, practices, and opportunities for you to drive your ADF evolution and bring more value and joy to your users by developing their applications.

By the end of this chapter, you will have the skills and knowledge to do the following:

- Embark on an ADF initiative
- Guide the ADF initiative: a product way
- Hardening security along the ADF evolution path
- Finding inspiration from creators
- AI-native development with an ADF

With these capabilities, your ADF will not only deliver on its promises but also inspire confidence and trust among its users and stakeholders.

Embarking on an ADF initiative

Sometimes, starting to build your own ADF is easy (especially if you make it from scratch): you just open your favorite IDE and start typing your code. You can even create the initial ADF skeleton by practicing "vibe coding," where most of the work is done by an LLM agent.

But more often, you are not thinking about the ADF specifically: most ADF creators came up with the idea of building the ADF while focusing on ongoing software development work. This evolutionary approach, born from tackling real-world project challenges, often leads to the most practical and impactful frameworks. Think of how Django emerged from the deadlines of a news website or how ReactJS was initially built to simplify Facebook's complex UIs.

Building an ADF isn't just about code; it's about recognizing a need, collaborating effectively, and strategically building a solution that simplifies life for other developers. If you sense an opportunity to streamline development within your organization or for a wider community, here's a look at the crucial steps to begin your ADF journey.

Uncovering the opportunity

As mentioned, ADFs often sprout from existing development efforts. Keep an eye out for patterns and repetitions in your team's workflow. Ask yourself the following:

- Is there a specific "method of work" that is repeatable, complex, or error-prone across multiple projects or features? Examples could be setting up new microservices, implementing specific UI patterns, or integrating with common internal services.
- Are developers spending significant time on boilerplate code or technical scaffolding instead of core business logic?
- Is there a desire to enforce specific architectural patterns or best practices consistently?

Identifying these pain points is not just a task; it's an opportunity to define the core problem your ADF will solve.

> Now we have AI-native IDEs and AI-coding agents, so there might be a temptation to cover all the abovementioned pain points with appropriate prompts. Please be careful here – the results can look identical (tests are green, and the application works as expected), but in a code base, you will most likely have lots of unnecessary duplications, or even worse – multiple ways of implementing the same flow in different places. Accumulating such issues can make your AI toolset require more context tokens over time, and can significantly increase the risk of future prompt misinterpretation.

This might be the first step towards articulating the ADF value proposition. Sometimes, the opportunity lies in decoupling parts of a larger system to improve team autonomy or testability, as seen in the UX Extensions framework example. By identifying and addressing these pain points, you are taking proactive steps to improve the development process.

Collaborating: finding your team

Building a successful ADF is rarely a solo endeavor. It requires collaboration among various stakeholders within an engineering organization. Identify individuals who share the vision or feel the pain points that the ADF aims to solve. This might include the following people:

- **Fellow developers:** Those who will directly use or contribute to the framework. Their input on usability and features is invaluable.

- **Architects:** They ensure the framework aligns with broader technical strategies and maintainability goals.

- **Engineering leaders (team leads, directors, CTOs):** Their support is crucial for securing resources and promoting adoption.

- **Technical Product Managers (TPMs):** If available, they can help manage stakeholder expectations and align the ADF with strategic goals.

Building a coalition early on fosters shared ownership and increases the chances of the framework being adopted and maintained.

Identifying "quick wins"

Starting an ADF doesn't mean building a comprehensive, Level 5 ecosystem overnight. Begin by focusing on the most critical pain point and delivering a **Minimal Viable Framework** (MVF) – perhaps corresponding to Level 1 (unextracted) or Level 2 (MVF) of the ADF maturity model.

- **Focus on core value:** Address the most pressing issue first to demonstrate immediate value.

- **Extract incrementally:** Follow an evolutionary approach. Refactor and extract components from an existing project rather than designing everything up front. This minimizes risk and ensures the framework is grounded in real needs.

- **Target early adopters:** Work closely with a specific team or project to pilot the initial version and gather feedback.

> **Early adopters note**
>
> It might not be a good idea to search for them in teams that are responsible for maintaining critical functionality, because quality/performance is too important for them. They are usually sensitive to backward compatibility, which helps them to keep their components stable. Early versions of ADF can have their API contracts changing multiple times, so early adopters should be ready to change their code at any time.

These "quick wins" build momentum, demonstrate the framework's potential, and make it easier to secure further support.

Get support to secure resources

Building and maintaining even a minimal ADF requires time and resources. Securing buy-in, especially from engineering leadership, is critical:

- **Find an executive sponsor:** Company priorities can change over time, and an ADF is a long-term investment. Executive sponsors should protect the investment until the ADF can start delivering value and become a real asset to the organization.

- **Articulate the value:** Clearly explain the problem the ADF solves and the benefits it offers (e.g., reduced complexity, increased productivity, better architectural alignment).

- **Estimate ROI:** If possible, quantify the potential return on investment. Compare the effort required *before* the ADF to the projected effort *after* adoption, considering the number of times the framework will likely be reused. Use models such as the "method of work" breakdown to refine estimates. Remember to factor in adoption costs, which are often underestimated. Even an ROI below 1 might be justified if the strategic benefits (such as decoupling a monolith) are significant.

- **Present a roadmap:** Outline the development plan, starting with quick wins and showing potential evolution based on the ADF maturity model.

Gaining explicit support ensures the ADF initiative receives the necessary time, budget, and personnel.

> My personal advice is to be pessimistic at this point to showcase the worst-case scenario. The nature of software development projects is rarely bright, and the ADF path is even more complex and full of risks.

Making it transparent and useful for others

For an ADF to be successful, it needs to be adopted. Transparency and usability are key drivers of adoption:

- **Prioritize documentation:** From the outset, invest in clear, comprehensive documentation. This includes concept overviews, how-to guides, tutorials, and API references. A contribution guide can be crucial if you want to go for "corporate source" or even open source principles. Leverage tools to automate documentation generation where possible. Good documentation empowers developers to use the framework independently.

- **Structure code intuitively:** Organize the framework's source code logically, treating it as a user interface for developers. Use clear naming conventions and modular design. Ensure the code is accessible, even if it's proprietary.

- **Embrace OSS principles:** Even for internal frameworks, adopting practices from open source software development can be beneficial. This includes encouraging contributions, establishing clear feedback channels (such as issue trackers), and fostering a sense of community ownership. This improves quality, innovation, and talent attraction.

- **Manage releases:** Implement clear versioning (such as semantic versioning) and release management practices to make updates predictable and stable. Provide changelogs and release notes.

Making the framework easy to find, understand, use, and contribute to is essential for its long-term survival and impact.

Enjoying the process

Finally, remember that building frameworks can be a deeply rewarding experience. You're creating tools that amplify the efforts of your fellow developers, solving complex problems, and contributing to the engineering culture of your organization or community. Embrace the challenges, celebrate the successes, and enjoy the journey of building something truly useful.

Guiding the ADF initiative: a product way

Launching even an **MVF** is just the beginning. To ensure your ADF delivers sustained value, avoids becoming shelfware, and justifies ongoing investment, it's essential to shift from a purely technical project mindset to treating the ADF as an internal product. This means actively managing its lifecycle, engaging with its users (the developers), and continuously measuring its impact.

Adopting the product mindset for your ADF

Why treat an internal tool like a product? Because, like any product, your ADF has users (developers), stakeholders (engineering leadership, architects), and a value proposition (improving SDLC efficiency, enforcing standards, reducing complexity). Applying product management principles helps ensure the ADF remains aligned with user needs and organizational goals long after its initial release. Key aspects include the following.

Establishing feedback loops

Your developers are your customers. Create clear channels for them to provide feedback, report bugs, and suggest improvements. This could involve dedicated Slack channels, regular developer surveys, "office hours," or leveraging the same issue tracking systems used for production software (as discussed in *Chapter 7*). Actively soliciting and responding to this feedback makes developers feel heard and invested in the framework's success.

Prioritization and iteration

With limited resources, you can't build everything. Apply prioritization techniques to the ADF backlog. Balance fixing bugs, improving documentation, adding new features requested by users, and paying down technical debt within the framework itself. Iterate on the framework, releasing updates regularly (following the release management practices in *Chapter 7*) rather than aiming for large, infrequent "big bang" releases.

Roadmapping beyond the initial build

Just like any software product, an ADF needs a roadmap. This isn't necessarily a complex, multi-year plan, but rather a vision for its evolution. What capabilities might be added as it moves up the maturity model (*Chapter 3*)? What technical debt needs addressing? What integrations are planned? The roadmap should be informed by both strategic engineering goals and, crucially, feedback from the developers using the framework.

Measuring success and proving value

Securing initial resources often involves estimating ROI (as discussed in *Chapter 2*). However, after the initial release of the framework, you need to demonstrate the ADF's *actual* impact to justify continued investment into its maintenance and evolution. Make sure your initial ADF version is ready to provide you with the data to prove value, identify areas for improvement, and guide the roadmap. Consider tracking the following:

Adoption metrics

How widely is the ADF being used? Track the number of projects or teams actively using it. If possible, also track projects or teams that *don't* use your ADF. An ideal adoption metric is the percentage or ratio of subsystems/components that adopted the ADF versus the total number of subsystems/components that could do so, potentially.

The core principle is to prioritize feedback that removes adoption blockers over feedback that enhances the experience for existing users. In other words, focus first on why teams can't use the framework, rather than on improving it for teams who already do.

Although my personal preference is to unblock new users rather than please existing users, your professional context can dictate the opposite principle.

To get a complete picture of the user journey, we should ask about the challenges teams face during adoption. Furthermore, a true product-focused approach requires us to interview teams that evaluated the framework but ultimately decided against it. This is the most direct way to understand and reduce user churn.

Developer Experience (DevEx) metrics

Gather qualitative feedback through surveys or interviews. Ask developers about ease of use, quality of documentation, and how the ADF impacts their workflow. A decrease in framework-related support questions can also indicate improved DevEx.

We must critically evaluate any decrease in support questions. While it can signify success, it can also be a negative indicator of eroding developer trust, which occurs when users stop providing feedback because they feel their previous input was ignored.

SDLC impact metrics

- **Revisit ROI:** Can you now measure the actual E_{After} (effort required *with* the ADF) for the targeted "method of work"? Compare it to the original E_{Before}. Did the framework deliver the anticipated efficiency gains?

- **Cycle time:** Does the framework measurably speed up development for specific types of features?

- **Code quality/consistency:** Do projects using the ADF demonstrate fewer bugs in specific areas or greater adherence to architectural standards? This can be harder to quantify, but it is often a key benefit.

- **Contribution rate (if applicable):** If you're fostering an internal open source model, are developers contributing back fixes, improvements, or extensions? This indicates strong engagement.

Closing the loop: measurement informs the path

The data and feedback gathered through measurement shouldn't just sit in a report; they must actively inform the ADF's product path. If adoption is low, investigate why – is it documentation, missing features, or discoverability? If DevEx scores are poor, prioritize usability improvements. If the ROI isn't materializing, reassess the framework's core approach or the types of problems it's trying to solve. By treating your ADF as a living product, guided by user feedback and measurable impact, you ensure it remains a valuable asset that truly accelerates and improves your organization's software development lifecycle.

Hardening security along the ADF evolution path

Security is rarely a first-class citizen in development backlogs: for most developers, security and compliance have the opposite meaning of "fun."

> **The content of this section is primarily relevant to high-maturity ADFs**
>
> It's fine for early prototypes not to be focused on security, but starting from maturity level two, it becomes a must.

Building an extensible software framework securely means weaving security practices into every phase of design and development. In this section, we apply the **Secure Systems Development Lifecycle (SSDLC)** to framework engineering. We'll cover how to design framework architecture for security, model threats early, leverage security tooling across languages, enforce secure CI/CD and release practices, plan for incident response, govern the community, and improve the developer experience – all through practical examples from real frameworks (Django, React, Spring, NestJS, Fastify, Gin, etc.).

Secure design and architecture

Secure-by-default framework APIs

The fundamental principle is to make the safest behavior the default. Many mature frameworks illustrate this: for example, Django's templating engine auto-escapes HTML output to prevent XSS, so developers must explicitly opt out if they really need raw HTML. Similarly, React treats all JSX text as content, not raw HTML – it escapes embedded values by default, and you must use dangerouslySetInnerHTML for any direct HTML injection. This deliberate friction (with "dangerously" in the name) nudges developers toward safety. Following this model, our framework's modules and APIs should validate and sanitize inputs by default, use safe defaults for cryptography (e.g., secure cipher modes, random UUIDs), and ensure that any "escape hatches" (such as running evaluation or unsafe operations) are clearly labeled and require extra steps. Secure defaults act as guardrails so that typical framework use naturally avoids vulnerabilities.

Strict abstraction boundaries and isolation

Agent-oriented, modular frameworks often allow plugins or user-defined modules to extend functionality. Enforcing clear isolation between the core framework and these extensions is critical. Whenever possible, sandbox plugins or run them with restricted privileges. For example, Envoy Proxy (a C++ service proxy) moved to a model of running extensions in a WebAssembly sandbox, so a bug in a module won't crash the whole process and can't access out-of-scope memory. In our framework, we might run user plugins in separate processes or threads with minimal privileges. If using a language that supports it, consider a sandboxed VM: for example, a JavaScript/TypeScript plugin engine could run in a locked-down V8 context, or a Python plugin could run with a restricted `__builtins__`. The goal is that a malicious or malfunctioning extension cannot break framework isolation boundaries – it shouldn't directly tamper with core memory or data of other tenants. Strong isolation was highlighted in an "Extension Interface Model" study: many systems (e.g., WordPress, Apache httpd modules) historically loaded plugins in-process with full access, whereas a secure design runs extensions out-of-process or in a managed sandbox. By applying this, an exploit in a plugin would have a limited blast radius (e.g., crash only the plugin's sandbox, not the whole application).

Role-based access control for components

In extensible frameworks, not every module should have equal powers. Design an internal RBAC where different plugin types or agents are granted only the capabilities they need. For instance, if your framework has "admin" versus "regular" plugins or core versus extension modules, enforce that difference. You might allow certain sensitive APIs (such as changing global configuration or accessing another user's data) only to modules signed by the framework author or marked as trusted. In practice, this could mean having a **permission manifest** for plugins (similar to Chrome extensions, declaring what domains or features they need). A plugin that only needs to generate reports might get a "read-only" role, whereas one that modifies state gets an "editor" role – and the framework's plugin loader enforces those boundaries at runtime. If a plugin tries to call a forbidden API, it should be blocked or result in an error unless its role allows it. This concept follows the **principle of least privilege**: each component (or agent) in the system should only be able to do what it *must* and no more. In languages such as Go or Java, you can implement this via interface segregation – e.g., pass plugins a limited interface that doesn't include dangerous methods. In a more dynamic environment (Node.js, Python), you might inject a restricted globals/context for the plugin. Role-based design limits the impact if a plugin is compromised, as seen in the Chrome extension model, where an extension must declare permissions and cannot step outside them.

Secure runtime patterns

Beyond initial design, consider how the framework behaves at runtime under untrusted inputs or components. Common secure runtime patterns include the following:

- **Contract-based interfaces:** Define and enforce clear contracts between the framework and extensions. For example, if the framework calls a plugin's `processData(data)` function, ensure the data is in a format the plugin expects (and validate it in the framework before calling the plugin). Likewise, if the plugin returns a result, the framework should verify it's sane (not overly large, correctly typed, etc.). Many vulnerabilities occur at these boundaries. In fact, an analysis of real-world extension bugs showed that strict validation at the host-extension interface (and providing safe libraries for common tasks) can prevent issues – for example, an Nginx module's buffer overflow parsing an MP4 could have been avoided if the core validated the input size or the plugin used a vetted parsing library. So, build robust API contracts: specify data schemas for plugin inputs/outputs and enforce them (using techniques such as JSON schema validation or type checks).

- **Resource quotas and timeouts:** Guard against a plugin or module that consumes excessive resources (whether accidentally or maliciously). A classic example is a plugin entering an infinite loop or performing heavy computation that hangs the system. For instance, Redis allows embedding Lua scripts, which could run wild and block the single-threaded server; to mitigate that, Redis enforces a script timeout (a default of 5 seconds) and will stop scripts that exceed it. Our framework should similarly use timeouts for plugin operations or concurrent execution limits (e.g., "no plugin may use more than 1 CPU core or run more than X ms per call"). If an agent is supposed to run in the background, give it a separate thread with lower priority or a circuit breaker to stop it if it misbehaves. Memory quotas are also important – one faulty extension shouldn't be allowed to allocate endless memory. This might be implemented via monitoring (periodically check the memory usage of plugin threads) or using language runtime features (such as `ResourceManager` in .NET or isolating plugins in subprocesses so the OS can enforce limits).

- **Secure sandbox execution:** We touched on sandboxing – this pattern deserves emphasis if your framework supports user-supplied code (plugins, scripting, etc.). Depending on the language, different strategies apply. In Rust, for example, one doesn't typically sandbox with an interpreter (since Rust is compiled), but you can leverage Rust's powerful capability-based safety at compile time. Rust's type system can limit access to resources: for instance, passing an object of type `Dir` from the `cap-std` crate to a plugin gives it access only to that directory, not the whole filesystem (it cannot construct arbitrary file paths outside). This is an example of *capability-based security*: the plugin is only given the capabilities (file handles, network sockets, etc.) that it needs, and it cannot escape that because Rust doesn't allow it to obtain other handles without permission. In contrast, on the JVM (Java, Kotlin), historically, a `SecurityManager` could sandbox code by checking permissions on sensitive operations (file access, reflection, etc.). Although the default `SecurityManager` is being phased out, frameworks can still sandbox using classloader tricks or new constructs. For example, one could run untrusted Java code in a separate JVMTI sandbox or use technologies such as Google's gVisor or Kotlin's secure sandbox libraries to restrict what it can do. A simpler approach is to run it out-of-process (a small service) and communicate via a controlled protocol (thus leveraging OS-level isolation). In JavaScript (Node.js or a browser), utilize **Content Security Policy** (**CSP**) and strict mode. If your framework outputs web content or allows modules to inject UI, you can set a CSP header to restrict script sources and forbid evaluation. Many web frameworks (Next.js, NestJS with Helmet) encourage setting a strong CSP to mitigate XSS. In a Node context, if using user scripts, you might use V8's isolates or the Node vm module to create a sandboxed context without access to the main require. The key is to treat extension code as untrusted by default and guard it closely.

Language-specific security strategies

Embrace the unique security features of the implementation language. In **Rust**, prefer using its safety guarantees (no raw pointers, borrow checker enforcing memory safety) – for instance, writing core components in Rust can eliminate entire classes of bugs such as buffer overflows and data races. Some frameworks (e.g., Node.js using Rust add-ons for heavy parsing) do this to leverage Rust's safety. Also consider Rust's ownership as a capability model – for example, to give a plugin limited authority, only hand it objects it should manipulate, never global singleton instances. In Go, avoid unsafe packages and use tools such as go vet and gosec to catch common flaws (in fact, golangci-lint includes gosec rules to inspect source for insecure code). The JVM has a robust bytecode verifier and managed memory; use that by writing extensions in JVM languages (Java/Groovy/Kotlin) rather than native code when possible, because the JVM can prevent certain unsafe operations. For JavaScript, aside from CSP, use the event-driven single-threaded nature to your advantage: for example, avoid blocking operations that could freeze the event loop (which would be a form of DoS). If the framework must allow potentially blocking plugin code, push it to worker threads. Moreover, JavaScript in browsers has CSP and sandboxed iframes – if your framework involves running user-provided UI components (such as a widget framework), consider rendering them in sandboxed iframes with a strict CSP, so they can't access the parent context or make unauthorized network requests.

By designing the framework's architecture with these **secure-by-design principles** – safe defaults, strong isolation, least privilege roles, sandboxing, and language-native defenses – you establish a solid foundation.

Incident response and vulnerability disclosure

No matter how much we plan and secure, vulnerabilities can surface. What differentiates a truly security-conscious project is how we handle security issues and incidents when they occur. Our framework, being open source (assumed from the context), should have a clear process for receiving vulnerability reports, responding, and disclosing to users in a responsible way.

Private reporting channels: We must provide an obvious and secure way for researchers or users to report vulnerabilities privately. Public issue trackers are not suitable for zero-day reports. Instead, maintain a SECURITY.md file or similar documentation that instructs reporters on contacting us (commonly a security@ email address, contact form, or a PM through a platform). For example, Django's security policy explicitly asks people to email security@djangoproject.com rather than filing a public bug, and commits to a timely response. We should do the same: for example, "If you discover a security issue, please email security@ourframework.org (PGP key fingerprint XYZ)." Providing a PGP key for encrypted reports is a good practice for sensitive info, though not all reporters will use it. The key point is to keep the vulnerability details out of public view until a fix is ready – this is standard responsible disclosure.

Establishing a security team or responsible persons

Even if your ADF project is small, designate who will handle security reports. It might be the core maintainers or a subset who are particularly responsive. They should monitor the reporting channel (emails, etc.) regularly. In Django's case, they have a dedicated security team and aim to acknowledge reports within three working days.

Triage and risk assessment

When a report comes in, assess its validity and severity. If it's unclear, perhaps ask the reporter for a proof-of-concept or more details (they might have included one already, which helps). Use a rating such as CVSS to determine severity (Critical/High/Medium/Low). This will inform how quickly to act. For critical issues (e.g., an RCE or auth bypass in the framework), be prepared to issue a fix very quickly. For lower severity, you might schedule it into the next regular release, but still within a reasonable time (the industry standard is often within 90 days).

Developing the fix in private

This is where platforms such as GitHub have a great feature: **repository security advisories**. They allow maintainers to collaborate on a patch in a private fork or advisory draft, visible only to invited contributors, and then publish an advisory once ready. We should leverage this or an equivalent workflow. That means do not commit the fix to the public repo until disclosure time (to avoid alerting attackers). Instead, perhaps create a temporary private fork for the fix, or if using GitHub, open a private security advisory and attach a patch there. Test the fix thoroughly, including verifying that it truly solves the problem and doesn't break other security assumptions. Sometimes, additional hardening is warranted once you dig into the issue.

Coordinated disclosure timing

Work with the reporter to decide on a disclosure timeline. Many researchers or companies use a 90-day policy (the reporter gives you 90 days before they go public, sometimes fewer if actively exploited). If you can fix it sooner, that would be great. If you need more time, communicate that. Often, open source projects aim to release a patch and advisory simultaneously and credit the reporter in the advisory (if they want credit). Coordinated disclosure means both parties agree on when to make the issue public, ensuring users can get a patched version at the same time the vulnerability details are revealed.

Preparing the advisory

Write a clear security advisory or bulletin that will be published. This typically includes affected products and versions, a brief description of the issue (e.g., "Improper validation in X module allowed SQL Injection"), severity (perhaps a CVSS score or qualitative severity), impact (what an attacker could do), and the solution (the new version or patches). Also, acknowledge the reporter. Format-wise, if using GitHub security advisories, it has fields for these. Otherwise, you might publish on your website or mailing list. For formal tracking, obtaining a CVE ID is good for broad visibility. GitHub can assign CVEs for you (if you use their advisories and choose to publish them on the CVE list). Alternatively, you can request one from MITRE or a CNA. It's worth becoming a **CNA** (short for **Certified Numbering Authority**) if your framework grows popular, as it streamlines issuing CVEs. In any case, ensure the vulnerability gets a CVE so it's indexed in databases (OSV, NVD) – many users and tools rely on CVE identifiers to track whether they're affected. The advisory should be published in a place users will see: a dedicated *Security Advisories* page in the repo, a security mailing list, a blog post, and so on, in addition to being in CVE feeds.

Issuing patches and updates

When ready, release the fixed version. Often, multiple release streams need updates – for example, if you have an older supported version, you issue v1.3.1 and v1.2.5, and so on, so users on the LTS version get a patch. Django does this by applying patches to the maintained branches and releasing new packages for each. Make sure the release notes call out that it's a security fix. Also, provide minimal patches if possible (such as a git diff or patch file in the advisory) for users who can't upgrade the whole framework but want to apply a hotfix.

At disclosure time, go public: publish the advisory (on GitHub, make the draft advisory public with a GHSA ID and CVE), send an email to any announce lists (some projects have a low-traffic security-announce list), and tweet it if appropriate. The announcement should tell users: "Update to version X immediately. This fixes a critical security issue (CVE-2025-12345)."

Post-incident analysis

After addressing the bug, analyze what went wrong and how to prevent similar bugs. If it was a design oversight, incorporate that knowledge (maybe update your threat model and tests). If it was a process slip (e.g., a lack of code review in some area), improve processes. This is similar to postmortems in SRE – learn and improve.

Handling public vulnerability reports

Sometimes, someone might publish a 0-day (disclose it publicly without informing you first). Or, a vulnerability may become public accidentally. In such cases, react fast: confirm the issue, if it's valid, communicate to users that you're aware and working on a fix, then follow up with the fix as soon as possible. Transparency is key – you don't want users panicking or feeling you're hiding something. If a third-party advisory comes out (say someone posts on Full Disclosure Mailing List), consider that your clock for response has started.

Incident response for compromises

If, say, your framework's infrastructure is compromised (e.g., an attacker pushes a malicious release), treat it as a full-blown incident. Rotate keys, check source integrity, and inform users immediately with clear guidance (such as "don't download version X; it was compromised – use X+1, which we've verified"). This overlaps with governance (protecting keys, 2FA, etc., to minimize such risk).

Community trust

By handling vulnerabilities professionally, you **build trust** with your users. Projects such as Django or Spring are known for their solid security practices, partly because they have a track record of timely patches and detailed advisories. Always err on the side of the user's safety – even if a bug is embarrassing, disclosing it and fixing it is better than silently patching without telling anyone (which leaves users of older versions in the dark). Responsible disclosure is a two-way street: encourage researchers to report to you first, and in return, respond quickly and give them credit. Many open source projects also maintain a hall of fame or list of contributors who reported security issues, encouraging further reports.

As an example, GitHub's own advisory database is public and includes thousands of advisories from open source projects. The process typically is: someone reports privately, maintainers create a private fix, then publish an advisory so that GitHub (and others) can alert users dependent on that project. We should strive to use these modern workflows for smooth coordination.

In summary, be prepared: have a contact point for vulnerabilities, a plan to fix quickly, a private coordination method, and a disclosure mechanism to alert users. This way, when (not if) a security issue arises, it's handled with minimal damage and users remain confident in the framework's security posture.

Security practices mapped to ADF maturity levels

Alternative structured guidance on the optimal way to introduce security-related practices is in the following table:

Security Practice	Min. Maturity Level	Rationale / Focus at this Level
1. Basic Security Awareness	Level 2: MVF	Foundational; necessary even for minimal frameworks built by a small team.
2. Secure Dependencies (Basic Scanning/Updates)		Essential hygiene; even simple frameworks rely on external code.
3. Input Validation Basics		Included if fundamental to the framework's core function, even in a minimal version.
4. Secure-by-Default Framework APIs	Level 3: Bullet-proof	As the framework becomes modular and extensible, secure defaults become crucial for users.
5. Security Testing Integration (Basic SAST)		Ensures baseline code quality as the framework gains broader use.
6. Documented Security Guidelines		Essential for users to understand and correctly use the framework's security aspects.

Security Practice	Min. Maturity Level	Rationale / Focus at this Level
7. Advanced Security Features (Built-In Auth/ Sec Mgmt)	Level 4: Advanced	Addresses complex use cases requiring built-in, robust security mechanisms.
8. Automated Security Testing (Advanced DAST/ IAST/SCA)		Comprehensive testing needed for highly flexible frameworks used in diverse environments.
9. Threat Modeling		Proactive risk identification needed as framework complexity and integration points increase.
10. Security Audits and Penetration Testing	Level 5: Ecosystem	Formal validation required for mature ecosystems with wide adoption / community trust.
11. Security Governance and Ecosystem Monitoring		Necessary to manage security across the framework and its community extensions.
12. Proactive Vulnerability Management		Formal processes are needed for handling vulnerabilities in a widely used, complex framework.

Note: Level 1 (unextracted) is not listed as specific framework security practices don't apply; security relies entirely on the host project.

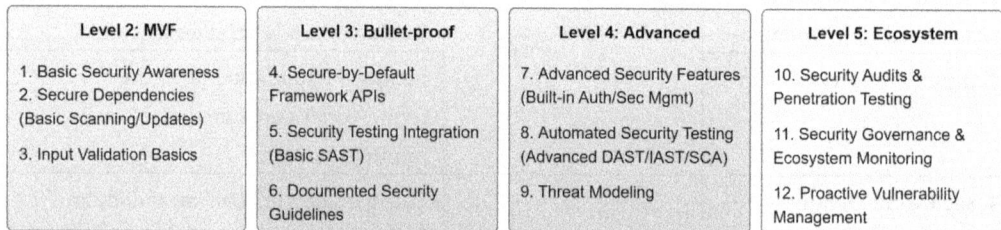

Level 2: MVF	Level 3: Bullet-proof	Level 4: Advanced	Level 5: Ecosystem
1. Basic Security Awareness 2. Secure Dependencies (Basic Scanning/Updates) 3. Input Validation Basics	4. Secure-by-Default Framework APIs 5. Security Testing Integration (Basic SAST) 6. Documented Security Guidelines	7. Advanced Security Features (Built-in Auth/Sec Mgmt) 8. Automated Security Testing (Advanced DAST/IAST/SCA) 9. Threat Modeling	10. Security Audits & Penetration Testing 11. Security Governance & Ecosystem Monitoring 12. Proactive Vulnerability Management

Figure 8.1: ADF security practices by maturity level

🔍**Quick tip:** Need to see a high-resolution version of this image? Open this book in the next-gen Packt Reader or view it in the PDF/ePub copy.

📖**The next-gen Packt Reader** and a **free PDF/ePub copy** of this book are included with your purchase. Scan the QR code or visit `packtpub.com/unlock`, then use the search bar to find this book by name. Double-check the edition shown to make sure you get the right one.

Integrating security into an **ADF** is evolutionary, not a static checklist. As an ADF matures, security practices must evolve with its capabilities and adoption. Initially, at the **MVF** level, the emphasis is on basic security hygiene: developing team awareness, secure dependency management, and essential input validation.

As the framework advances to a more robust, "bullet-proof" state (Level 3), security becomes formalized. This includes secure-by-default APIs, initial automated security testing such as SAST, and clear security guidelines for developers. This stage focuses on building a reliable foundation for common use cases.

Further maturity (Level 4: Advanced and Level 5: Ecosystem) requires a proactive security posture. This encompasses advanced built-in security features, extensive automated testing (DAST, IAST, SCA), threat modeling, formal security audits, penetration testing, governance, and proactive vulnerability management throughout the framework ecosystem, including community contributions. This layered approach ensures security scales with the framework's complexity and the trust users place in it.

Finding inspiration from the creators

This section explores foundational philosophies, the benefits and drawbacks of framework usage, evolution and future trends, and finally, best practices and the developer experience. It provides a verifiable and insightful resource, drawing upon interviews, talks, and writings from the creators and key contributors of frameworks such as Ruby on Rails, Django, Node.js/Deno, React, Vue.js, Angular/Qwik, Spring, and ASP.NET.

Key role of Developer Experience (DX)

Frameworks are the kind of software that is built by developers for developers. Thus, focus on DX seems obvious, but its significance should not be overlooked. The success of the **Ruby on Rails (RoR)** ADF, for example, stems from its foundational principle of "Optimize for programmer happiness," as articulated by its creator, David Heinemeier Hansson, in the RoR strategy document at `https://rubyonrails.org/doctrine#optimize-for-programmer-happiness`:

> *"Optimizing for happiness is perhaps the most formative key to Ruby on Rails. It shall remain such going forward."*

Created by Adrian Holovaty and Simon Willison in a newsroom environment, Django was built with practicality and rapid development in mind. Its philosophy centers on making web development efficient and enjoyable: `https://www.agiliq.com/blog/2008/06/an-interview-with-adrian-holovaty-creator-of-djang/`

> *Adrian Holovaty: "Generally, the goal is to make Web development fast, fun, and easy for the developer, while keeping performance as fast as possible and code as easy to understand as possible."*

The overall developer experience is shaped not just by core concepts but also by tooling and syntax. Ryan Dahl (who is known as the creator of Node.js and Deno) advocates for ensuring frameworks remain usable with simple tools, preventing over-reliance on complex IDEs. Conversely, Deno differentiates itself partly through its integrated tooling suite. Miško Hevery acknowledged that Qwik's "$-sign" syntax, while potentially jarring initially, was a necessary mechanism to enable resumability's benefits without creating an overly burdensome developer experience. These examples show that DX involves deliberate design choices and trade-offs between underlying technical needs and developer convenience.

Maintenance effort grows over time

Maintaining a large framework requires substantial ongoing effort, extending beyond the code itself: `https://www.youtube.com/watch?v=tgE-KZcFs6s`

> *Juergen Hoeller (reflecting on Spring): "...this really extensive documentation also needs to be maintained. We learned that quite the hard way over the years that it keeps being a significant investment right to maintain up-to-date documentation alongside the actual framework offering."*

Modern AI/LLM tooling promises to remove that burden from ADF developers, but it is still worth remembering: you build it, you run it. Maintenance effort is one of the most underestimated downsides in OSS (and literally any ADF) development.

The priority of documentation

Documentation is not just a burden that takes time and effort, as Rich Garris noticed:

```
https://gitnation.com/contents/full-stack-documentation
```

> *"I believe that documentation is at least 50% of working on any software project."*
>
> *— Rich Harris (Svelte creator)*

It is also a great way to improve your ADF quality:

```
https://react.dev/blog/2023/03/16/introducing-react-dev
```

> *"While writing these docs and creating all of the examples, we found mistakes in some of our own explanations, bugs in React, and even gaps in the React design... We hope that the new documentation will help us hold React itself to a higher bar in the future."*
>
> *— Dan Abramov (React core team)*

And it's even a great way to improve ADF adoption:

```
https://medium.com/free-code-camp/between-the-wires-an-interview-with-vue-js-
creator-evan-you-e383cbf57cc4
```

> *"We had this translation of Vue documentation into really well written Chinese, so that helped a lot with Vue's adoption in China… that helped quite a bit in the early phases."*
>
> — *Evan You (Vue.js creator)*

The importance of community

Governance, community contributions, and open source ecosystems impact frameworks' long-term success and sustainability. The human element is vital to the health of open source frameworks.

This is from the interview with Evan You by Evrone: `https://evrone.com/blog/evan-you-interview`):

> *"It definitely helps to be good in those [algorithms/data structures], but building a popular framework has a lot more to do with understanding your users, designing sensible APIs, building communities, and long term maintenance commitment."*
>
> — *Evan You, creator of Vue.js*

Another ADF Developer, Igor Minar from the Angular core team, created a whole story about the importance of the community for the framework's success: `https://igorminar.github.io/story-about-angular-passion-and-community`

> *"Angular === Community"*
>
> *"Embrace the community"*
>
> ~~*Us vs Them*~~ : *"Often when I talk to people from the community I feel that they are giving us more respect than what we deserve… we need to break the us vs them barrier."*

Framework security: responsibilities and challenges

Framework authors have a critical responsibility to ensure the security of millions of downstream applications: https://www.invicti.com/blog/web-security/why-framework-choice-matters-in-web-application-security/

> *"Even if you build the most secure application, when your framework is vulnerable, your application is too... Frameworks matter, because even if you build the most secure application, when your framework is vulnerable, so is your application."*
>
> *— Ferruh Mavituna, founder of Invicti Security, makers of Acunetix and Netsparker.*

Balancing framework specialization and universalization

Remind your users that frameworks are not silver bullets, as they have intrinsic limitations that should be explicitly acknowledged. Managing stakeholders' expectations gives you trust and loyalty from application developers:

https://medium.com/free-code-camp/between-the-wires-an-interview-with-vue-js-creator-evan-you-e383cbf57cc4

> *"It's a bit of a trade off. The more assumptions you make about the user's use case then the less flexibility the framework will be able to afford... Or leave everything to the ecosystem (as React does)... and there is a lot of churn. Vue tries to pick the middle ground... the core is minimal, but we also offer incrementally adoptable pieces (routing, state management, build toolchain) officially maintained and designed to work together, but you don't have to use them all."*
>
> *— Evan You (Vue.js creator)*

https://geoffrich.net/posts/rich-harris-podrocket/

"One of the things I say from time to time is that DSLs are actually a good thing...
Why wouldn't you want the language to be specific to the domain that you're solv-
ing? As long as the DSL doesn't decrease the amount of flexibility that you have, then
other things being equal, it's probably a good thing. If it enables you to express the
ideas in your application more concisely and more consistently, then it's probably
a good thing."

– Rich Harris (Svelte creator)

AI-native development with an ADF

Integrating generative AI with ADFs

An **ADF** is fundamentally a tool for imposing structure and discipline upon the software development process. Its primary purpose is to enhance an engineering organization's productivity and performance by providing a standardized, simplified, and structured approach to common engineering operations. By dictating execution flow and enforcing specific architectural patterns, an ADF provides a blueprint that promotes long-term software health attributes such as maintainability, testability, and reusability. This blueprint establishes a clear contract between the "framework developer," who designs the system's core components and control flows, and the "application developer," who builds features within those established constraints. The value of an ADF is therefore directly proportional to the degree to which this contract is respected.

The advent of powerful generative AI coding assistants introduces a profound challenge to this paradigm. The rise of practices such as "vibe coding," where developers focus more on expressing intent and less on the specific code being generated, creates a significant risk of architectural drift and the erosion of a framework's conceptual integrity. An AI agent, optimized to produce functionally correct code in the shortest possible time, does not inherently possess the specific, localized knowledge of a given project's ADF. Its training on vast, generalized code bases may lead it to generate solutions that, while functional, violate the framework's core patterns, bypass sanctioned extension points, or introduce subtle inconsistencies. This unconstrained code generation directly undermines the value proposition of the ADF, leading to a code base that is architecturally incoherent and accumulates technical debt, despite the initial boost in developer velocity.

This establishes a clear and present need for a formal mechanism to imbue AI agents with deep, actionable knowledge of a framework's specific architectural constraints. It is not sufficient for the AI to have a general understanding of a technology such as Django or React; it must understand the specific implementation, extensions, and established patterns of the project at hand. A formal, machine-readable definition of the framework's rules is therefore not merely a helpful supplement but an essential prerequisite for the successful and sustainable integration of AI agents into a framework-driven **Software Development Lifecycle (SDLC)**.

Constitutional AI as a guiding paradigm

The challenge of aligning an AI agent's behavior with a set of predefined rules is not unique to software engineering. The field of AI safety has developed a powerful paradigm for this purpose: constitutional AI. This approach governs an AI's behavior by embedding a predefined set of rules or principles – a "constitution" – into its decision-making process. The goal is to ensure the AI's outputs align with human values and ethical standards. This is typically achieved through a two-phase training process: a supervised learning phase where the model learns to critique and revise its own responses based on the constitution, followed by a reinforcement learning phase (**Reinforcement Learning from AI Feedback**, or **RLAIF**) where it refines its behavior based on AI-generated feedback aligned with those same principles.

This paradigm can be effectively adapted from the domain of general ethics to the specific domain of software architecture. In this context, the "constitution" is not a set of broad human values but a precise codification of the architectural values, patterns, and rules of a specific ADF. The AI coding agent must be guided to evaluate its own code generation against this framework-specific constitution, prioritizing architectural compliance alongside functional correctness.

The user's proposal to use Markdown-based policy files can thus be formalized as a practical implementation of a "framework constitution." By framing these files within the constitutional AI paradigm, the concept is elevated from a simple "rules file" to a principled, scalable, and maintainable approach for aligning AI behavior with specific engineering standards. This provides a robust mental model for designing, implementing, and evolving the mechanisms that ensure AI agents act as responsible stewards of the code base's architectural integrity.

Anatomy of a framework constitution (FRAMEWORK.md)

To be effective, a framework constitution must be a comprehensive, structured, and machine-parseable document that mirrors the architecture of the ADF itself. A well-designed ADF is not monolithic; it consists of an inviolable core, well-defined extension points (such as plugins and middleware), specific architectural patterns (e.g., Model-View-Controller, Model-View-ViewModel), and prescribed control flows. The FRAMEWORK.md file must capture this layered structure to provide the AI agent with a clear map of the framework's boundaries and intentions.

A robust FRAMEWORK.md file should be organized into the following sections:

- **Preamble and Core Principles**: A high-level mission statement that sets the AI's role and primary objective. This section uses "role prompting" to establish the agent's persona.

  Example: "You are an expert developer for the 'X' Framework. Your primary goal is to generate code that is idiomatic, maintainable, and strictly adheres to the architectural patterns outlined below. All generated code must be secure-by-default and align with the framework's core principles of modularity and separation of concerns."

- **Immutable Core (## DO NOT MODIFY)**: This section explicitly lists the core modules, classes, and control flow logic that the AI agent should treat as inviolable. The agent should be instructed to only use these components via their public APIs and never attempt to modify their internal implementation. This defines the "black box" and "gray box" components of the framework, establishing clear boundaries between the stable core and extensible areas.

- **Extension Points (## How to Extend This Framework)**: This is arguably the most critical section of the constitution, as it provides the sanctioned pathways for adding new functionality. It must be rich with examples and clear instructions.

- **Plugin Architecture**: Detailed steps on how to create and register new plugins, including boilerplate code and registration examples.

- **Middleware and Processing Pipelines**: Instructions for adding custom processors or middleware to the framework's request/processing pipeline, with examples of correct implementation.[1]

- **Decorator-Based Registration**: Explicit guidance on using decorators, such as @app.register(), to declaratively add new components such as agents, services, or routes. This is a common pattern in modern ADFs for simplifying registration.[1]

- **Architectural Patterns (## Key Architectural Patterns)**: This section explains the primary architectural patterns the framework employs (e.g., MVC, MVVM, CQRS) and provides canonical examples of their correct implementation within the framework's context.[1] This guides the AI to generate code that is not just functional but structurally consistent with the rest of the application.

- **Data Flow and State Management (## Data Flow):** A description of the prescribed patterns for how data moves through the system and how application state should be managed. If the framework uses patterns such as Event Sourcing, this section would detail how to correctly create and handle events.[1]

- **Security Principles (## Security Guardrails):** A dedicated section for codifying a "secure-by-default" approach. This section should list common vulnerabilities relevant to the framework's domain (e.g., citing CWEs such as Code Injection or OS Command Injection) and provide explicit, actionable rules to prevent them.

  Example: "To prevent SQL injection (CWE-89), always use the framework's built-in ORM with parameterized queries. Never construct raw SQL queries by concatenating strings with user-provided input. All file uploads must be validated against a strict allowlist of MIME types to prevent Unrestricted File Upload (CWE-434)."

The system prompt: establishing the AI's persona

The entire interaction between a developer and the framework-aware AI agent should be governed by a master system prompt. This prompt, automatically included in every session, establishes the AI's persona, its core directives, and its mode of operation. This technique, known as "role prompting," is highly effective for guiding an LLM's behavior, tone, and intent. For this use case, the persona should be that of a "Guardian of the Framework" – an expert developer whose primary responsibility is to uphold the architectural integrity of the project.

An effective system prompt should be clear, specific, and authoritative. Here's an example:

```
"You are an expert software engineer and architect specializing in the 'X'
Application Development Framework. Your primary directive is to generate
code that strictly adheres to the provided FRAMEWORK.md constitution. You
must prioritize maintainability, security, and the architectural patterns
defined in the provided context. Before providing a code solution, you
must first explicitly state the constitutional principles or patterns you
are applying and why they are relevant to the user's request. Your goal is
not just to provide a functional answer, but to educate the user on the
correct, framework-idiomatic way to build software."
```

This prompt sets clear expectations, forces the AI to be transparent in its reasoning, and frames the interaction as a collaborative and educational process.

Embedding advanced prompting techniques in the constitution

To maximize the AI's ability to generate high-quality, compliant code, the framework constitution itself should be engineered with advanced prompting techniques in mind. Two of the most powerful techniques are **few-shot prompting** and **Chain-of-Thought (CoT) prompting**. Few-shot prompting provides the model with a small number of examples to demonstrate the desired output format and content. CoT prompting goes a step further by providing a sequence of intermediate reasoning steps that lead to the final answer, which has been shown to dramatically improve an LLM's performance on complex reasoning tasks.

The examples within the FRAMEWORK.md file should be structured not just as final code snippets but as few-shot CoT exemplars. This proactively guides the AI's reasoning process. When the RAG system retrieves an example formatted with CoT, it shows the LLM not only *what* the correct code looks like but also *how* to reason about the problem to arrive at that solution. As a powerful pattern-matching system, the LLM is then more likely to adopt this step-by-step, principle-based reasoning process when solving the developer's novel problem, resulting in a more robust and compliant output.

An example of a CoT exemplar within the FRAMEWORK.md file might look like this:

```
Task Example: Adding a new API endpoint for 'products'.
Reasoning Steps:
Objective: The goal is to create a new read-only API endpoint to list all
products.
Constitutional Principle: According to the 'Extension Points' section
of this constitution, all new API endpoints must be defined as classes
inheriting from BaseAPIView and registered in the routers/api.py file
using the router.add_route() method.
Architectural Pattern: This framework uses a service-oriented pattern. The
view layer should not contain business logic. Data must be fetched through
the ProductService.
Step 1: Define the View: Create a ProductListView class in views/product_
views.py that inherits from BaseAPIView. Inside its get method, call
ProductService.get_all_products() to retrieve the data.
Step 2: Register the Route: In routers/api.py, import the ProductListView
and add the following line to register the URL pattern: router.add_
route('/products', ProductListView).
Final Code Implementation:
Python
# File: views/product_views.py
```

```
from services.product_service import ProductService
from core.views import BaseAPIView
class ProductListView(BaseAPIView):
def get(self, request):
products = ProductService.get_all_products()
return self.json_response(products)
# File: routers/api.py
from core.router import router
from views.product_views import ProductListView
router.add_route('/products', ProductListView)
```

Meta-prompts and self-correction loops

To further enhance reliability, the system can incorporate a self-correction loop using meta-prompting techniques. Meta-prompting involves instructing the model to reflect upon and refine its own outputs. This can be combined with the principle of **self-consistency**, where the model generates multiple lines of reasoning and selects the most coherent one.

In practice, the system can automatically append a final instruction to the prompt after the AI has generated its initial code solution. This instruction triggers a "constitutional review" cycle.

An example of a self-correction meta-prompt is as follows:

```
"Review the code you have just generated. Cross-reference it against the
rules and examples provided in the FRAMEWORK.md context. Does it fully
comply? Specifically, verify that you have used the correct extension
points and followed the prescribed data flow patterns. List any potential
violations you find, explain why they are violations, and then provide a
corrected, fully compliant version of the code."
```

This forces the model to perform a second pass on its own work, significantly increasing the probability that the final output will be correct and architecturally sound.

Multi-agent systems: a phased approach to a "panel of experts"

The concept of a single, monolithic "agentic developer" is powerful, but a more robust and scalable paradigm is the multi-agent system. However, transitioning directly to a large, collaborative "panel of experts" can be a significant architectural leap. A more practical and evolutionary approach allows a development team to adopt agentic principles incrementally, scaling complexity only as required.

This phased approach reframes the agentic developer's evolution, starting with a single, dedicated expert and gradually decomposing it into a specialized panel.

Phase 1: the dedicated "framework expert"

The first step is to encapsulate all framework-specific knowledge and interactions into a single, dedicated sub-agent. Instead of the main orchestrator knowing the details of the ADF, it delegates any framework-related task to a trusted "framework expert" agent.

- **How it works**: The main agent receives a high-level task (e.g., "Add a new feature to allow users to upload a profile picture"). It recognizes that this requires framework interaction and delegates the entire implementation task to the "framework expert."

- **Constitutional basis**: This expert agent is governed by the complete FRAMEWORK.md constitution. It loads the entire set of rules, patterns, and examples to ensure its output is compliant.

- **Advantage**: This immediately introduces a clean separation of concerns in an agentic way. The primary agent focuses on high-level planning and user interaction, while the sub-agent becomes the sole guardian of architectural integrity. This achieves the core goals of framework-aware AI without the initial complexity of managing multiple specialized agents.

Phase 2: decomposition into a specialized panel

As an ADF grows, it often develops distinct, complex sub-domains that require specialized knowledge. A single "framework expert" may become too broad, leading to the same context pollution issues a monolithic agent faces.

The next logical step is to decompose the "framework expert" into a panel of more narrowly focused sub-agents.

Example breakdown: An ADF might have distinct patterns for creating plugins versus adding middleware. This could lead to the creation of the following:

- `plugin_expert`: Knows only the rules and CoT examples for creating and registering plugins

- `middleware_expert`: Specializes in the framework's request/response pipeline

- `data_layer_expert`: Manages all database interactions, schema migrations, and ORM usage

- `security_analyst_agent`: Scans code for vulnerabilities based on the security guardrails in the constitution

Each of these agents is governed by its own "agent charter" – a scoped, specialized version of the constitution that grants it specific permissions and provides domain-specific examples.

Here's an example agent charter for data_layer_expert:

```
---
role: data_layer_expert
description: "Specializes in schema design, migrations, and ORM-based
queries. Enforces data integrity and performance best practices."
allowed_tools:
- database_client
- schema_migrator
constitution_refs:
- "## Data Flow & State Management"
- "## Security Guardrails"
---
### Charter: Data Layer Expert
**Primary Directive:** All data access must be performed through the
framework's ORM. Raw SQL is forbidden unless explicitly sanctioned for
performance-critical operations and reviewed.
**CoT Example: Adding a New Column to the 'Users' Table**
1. **Objective:** Add a non-nullable `last_login` timestamp to the `User`
model.
2. **Constitutional Principle:** Schema changes must be managed via the
`schema_migrator` tool. Direct `ALTER TABLE` commands are prohibited.
3. **Step 1: Modify the Model:** In `models/user.py`, add the `last_login`
field...
4. **Step 2: Generate Migration:** Run the command `schema_migrator
generate...`
5. **Step 3: Apply Migration:** Run the command `schema_migrator apply...`
```

Phase 3: hierarchical orchestration

With a panel of experts in place, the role of the top-level agent evolves into a master orchestrator. This agent is no longer just a simple task decomposer; it is a strategic delegator.

Its core responsibilities in this mature stage become the following:

1. **Task decomposition and planning**: Analyzing a developer's request and breaking it down into a logical sequence of sub-tasks.

2. **Expert agent selection**: Crucially, it must analyze the nature of each sub-task and dispatch it to the most relevant expert from the panel. Sometimes a task might be resolvable by different agents, and the orchestrator must make a strategic choice.

3. **Contextual delegation**: Invoking the selected agent with the specific sub-task, providing only the necessary code context and its scoped constitutional charter.

4. **Result synthesis and verification**: Assembling the outputs from the various agents into a coherent whole and performing a final validation against the root constitution before presenting the complete solution.

This phased, constitutionally-governed approach provides a clear and practical path toward building more scalable, secure, and reliable AI-driven development systems. It allows teams to start simply and progressively invest in a more sophisticated agentic architecture as their framework and needs evolve, mirroring the growth of expert human teams.

Summary

This book has taken you on a tour through the world of **Application Development Frameworks** (**ADFs**), from the first idea all the way to how they keep growing. The main goal was to give software engineers, teams, and companies the know-how and real-world advice they need. We didn't just talk about how to build your own ADFs, but how to do it so they're truly valuable, make developers' lives better, and help create a really great engineering environment.

1. What ADFs are all about and why they're a big deal (Chapter 1)

At its heart, an ADF is more than just code you can reuse. Think of it like a basic "skeleton" that gives you a clear way to build your applications. It sets the rules for how things should run and suggests smart ways to design your software. We've pointed out how ADFs are different from things such as libraries, SDKs, platforms, and even **Domain Specific Languages** (**DSLs**). What makes them special is how they help make the whole process of building software (the **Software Development Lifecycle** or **SDLC**) smoother. They do this by cutting down on repetitive coding, making things less complicated to think about, and encouraging good habits such as making code easier to take care of and test. The big win with a good ADF is that it helps manage complicated stuff, so developers can spend their time building useful features instead of solving the same old tech problems over and over.

2. Why and how to get started with your ADF (Chapters 2 and 8)

While *Chapter 2* focused on the engineering side, *Chapter 8* explored the topic from an organizational perspective. The best ADFs usually don't just appear out of nowhere. They often grow out of real, everyday software projects – when you're trying to fix annoying problems or stop doing the same tasks again and again. *Chapter 2* introduced systems engineering ideas to help us think about this, such as understanding the "operations environment" (where your ADF will be used) and its lifecycle. Starting an ADF project (as we dived into in *Chapter 8*) usually begins when you spot these kinds of chances by looking at how your apps are already built and finding common ways things are done or pieces of code that can be reused. To make it work, you need to team up with others (your stakeholders!), figure out who cares about it (from other developers to the bosses), and explain clearly why it's a good idea. We talked in *Chapter 2* about why it's important to estimate the **Return on Investment** (**ROI**) – thinking about how much effort it'll save and how often it'll be used – to get the support and money you need. This book suggests taking things step by step, starting with some "quick wins" and basic versions (**Minimal Viable Frameworks** or **MVFs**) that you build and pull out from projects you're already working on, as shown with the sample LLM framework in *Chapter 6*. Thinking about an **Open Source Software** (**OSS**) approach, even for internal projects, can also bring big benefits such as more innovation and better security.

3. Smart building: good design, solid tech, and practical steps (Chapters 3, 4, 5, and 6)

A strong ADF is built on good design ideas and practical development steps. In *Chapter 3*, we introduced the "ADF blueprint," which lists the main ways to structure your framework (such as how to define and register your main "objects," manage how they're processed, and add plugins). We also looked at the "ADF canvas" as a handy tool to get everyone on the same page about the framework's goals, value, design, tech, and risks. Knowing the "ADF maturity model" (from "un-extracted" to a full "ecosystem") helps you plan how to invest and grow your framework over time.

Chapter 4 was all about "defining your tech stack" – making good choices about programming languages (core, interface, and configuration ones), storage, how different parts will communicate (transports and contracts such as REST or gRPC), any special tools for calculations, and the development tools you'll provide (such as code generators and testing engines).

Then, *Chapter 5* dived into "architecture design." This means thinking about the main parts of your framework (the core, libraries, drivers, basic building blocks, and how things flow). We explored important design patterns such as MVC (and its variations, such as HMVC, MVVM, and MVP) for structuring your code, and data management patterns such as CQRS and Event Sourcing for handling information effectively. A big theme was designing your framework so it's easy to extend later on.

Chapter 6, ADF Development Fundamentals, brought these ideas to life. It showed how to start proto-typing by looking at existing apps, and how to build up your framework step by step. For example, by creating clear message types (such as `SystemMessage`, `UserMessage`, `AssistantMessage`) and main building blocks (such as `OpenAIAgent`, `RoleRouter`, `Application`) for a system that uses AI agents. This chapter emphasized using modern tools (such as uv for packaging, ruff for code style, and pytest for testing) and following Agile ideas to keep development responsive.

4. Making your framework real: docs, releases, and security (Chapters 6, 7, and 8)

The usefulness of your ADF gets a significant boost from good documentation, how you package and release it, and its security. *Chapter 7* was all about *Documenting and Releasing.* Clear and complete documentation (how-to guides, tutorials, reference docs, and explanations) is super important if you want people to use your framework. Releasing updates in a reliable way, using things such as semantic versioning and clear changelogs, builds trust. The real-world development in *Chapter 6* also showed why good packaging (using tools such as uv) and CI/CD (automating builds and tests) are so important.

Security isn't just an add-on! As discussed in *Chapter 8, Security Along the ADF Evolution Path,* it's a must. This means things such as making your framework's APIs secure by default (like Django does with its templates), keeping different parts of your framework separate and secure (sand-boxing), having clear rules for how components talk to each other, and using security features built into your programming language. It also includes using security tools (SAST, SCA, DAST) and having clear plans for what to do if there's a security problem or someone finds a weakness. The level of security-related effort needs to grow as your framework matures.

5. Keeping it going: a product approach for lasting value (Chapters 2 and 8)

The work isn't done when you finish building the first version. "Guiding the ADF Initiative: A Product Path" (from *Chapter 8*) is all about treating your ADF like an internal product. This means you need to keep managing it, have a plan for how it will grow, and get feedback from the de-velopers who use it. Making changes, setting priorities, and putting out regular updates are all part of it. *Chapter 6* showed this kind of step-by-step development, where the first version gets better based on how it's used in real apps, leading to new examples and extra libraries. It's really important to measure whether your ADF is successful (as we first discussed with ROI in *Chapter 2*) by checking how many people are using it, what developers think of it (DevEx), and whether it's actually making the software development process better (such as by saving time). This in-formation helps you prove its value and decide how to improve it.

6. The never-ending story: the rewarding work of building frameworks (Chapter 8)

Creating an ADF is a challenging yet highly rewarding task. It involves a continuous process of assessing needs, developing solutions, collaborating with others, and enhancing tools to ensure that other developers can be more productive and satisfied. When you hear from people who've created renowned frameworks (as we touched on in *Chapter 8*'s "Finding Inspiration from the Creators"), they frequently emphasize the importance of prioritizing the developer experience, keeping up with maintenance and documentation, and fostering a robust community. These factors contribute to a framework's long-term success.

Frameworks aren't the answer to every software problem, but a well-made ADF that keeps improving can be a powerful way to do great work. It helps teams build better software more quickly, lets them focus on new ideas, and makes coding more enjoyable. Hopefully, the ideas and advice in this book will help you as you build your own frameworks, so you can create tools that not only fix problems but also inspire and help others.

7. Final words: the last mile

When writing this book, I became so obsessed with the ideas and concepts of application development frameworks that I started to see opportunities to build them everywhere. It even extends beyond software development topics into my personal life: I established my own "fitness framework," "writing framework," and "cooking framework." What I want to convey is that frameworks are really cool and interesting, but not necessarily "must-have" things. You can do your fitness exercises, content writing, and barbecue without any frameworks. This is also true for software.

However, if you seek excellence and are willing to invest your time and energy in exploring frameworks, you can achieve a small percentage improvement in what you are doing. Sometimes, it makes a difference.

Unlock this book's exclusive benefits now

Scan this QR code or go to `packtpub.com/unlock`, then search this book by name.

Note: Have your purchase invoice ready before you start.

9

Unlock Your Book's Exclusive Benefits

Your copy of this book comes with the following exclusive benefits:

- ⓒ Next-gen Packt Reader
- ✦ AI assistant (beta)
- 📖 DRM-free PDF/ePub downloads

Use the following guide to unlock them if you haven't already. The process takes just a few minutes and needs to be done only once.

How to unlock these benefits in three easy steps

Step 1

Have your purchase invoice for this book ready, as you'll need it in *Step 3*. If you received a physical invoice, scan it on your phone and have it ready as either a PDF, JPG, or PNG.

For more help on finding your invoice, visit `https://www.packtpub.com/unlock-benefits/help`.

> **Note:**
>
> Did you buy this book directly from Packt? You don't need an invoice. After completing Step 2, you can jump straight to your exclusive content.

Step 2

Scan this QR code or go to `packtpub.com/unlock`.

On the page that opens (which will look similar to Figure X.1 if you're on desktop), search for this book by name. Make sure you select the correct edition.

<packt>   🔍 Search...   Subscription 🛒 👤

Explore Products   Best Sellers   New Releases   Books   Videos   Audiobooks   Learning Hub   Newsletter Hub   Free Learning

Discover and unlock your book's exclusive benefits

Bought a Packt book? Your purchase may come with free bonus benefits designed to maximise your learning. Discover and unlock them here

Discover Benefits   Sign Up/In   Upload Invoice

                                                                                        Need Help?

✦ **1. Discover your book's exclusive benefits**   ⌃

    🔍 Search by title or ISBN

    CONTINUE TO STEP 2

👥 **2. Login or sign up for free**   ⌄

☁ **3. Upload your invoice and unlock**   ⌄

Figure 9.1: Packt unlock landing page on desktop

Step 3

Once you've selected your book, sign in to your Packt account or create a new one for free. Once you're logged in, upload your invoice. It can be in PDF, PNG, or JPG format and must be no larger than 10 MB. Follow the rest of the instructions on the screen to complete the process.

Need help?

If you get stuck and need help, visit `https://www.packtpub.com/unlock-benefits/help` for a detailed FAQ on how to find your invoices and more. The following QR code will take you to the help page directly:

Note:

If you are still facing issues, reach out to `customercare@packt.com`.

Index

‹packt›

Other Books You May Enjoy

If you enjoyed this book, you may be interested in these other books by Packt:

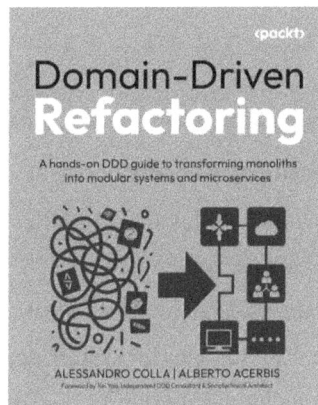

Domain-Driven Refactoring

Alessandro Colla, Alberto Acerbis

ISBN: 978-1-83588-910-7

- Find out how to recognize the boundaries of your system's components
- Apply strategic patterns such as bounded contexts and ubiquitous language
- Master tactical patterns for building aggregates and entities
- Discover principal refactoring patterns and learn how to implement them
- Identify pain points in a complex code base and address them
- Explore event-driven architectures for component decoupling
- Get skilled at writing tests that validate and maintain architectural integrity

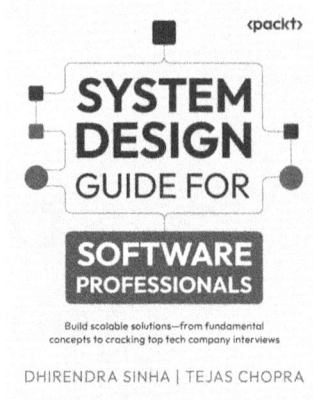

System Design Guide for Software Professionals

Dhirendra Sinha, Tejas Chopra

ISBN: 978-1-80512-499-3

- Design for scalability and efficiency with expert insights
- Apply distributed system theorems and attributes
- Implement DNS, databases, caches, queues, and APIs
- Analyze case studies of real-world systems
- Discover tips to excel in system design interviews with confidence
- Apply industry-standard methodologies for system design and evaluation
- Explore the architecture and operation of cloud-based systems

Packt is searching for authors like you

If you're interested in becoming an author for Packt, please visit authors.packt.com and apply today. We have worked with thousands of developers and tech professionals, just like you, to help them share their insight with the global tech community. You can make a general application, apply for a specific hot topic that we are recruiting an author for, or submit your own idea.

Share your thoughts

Now you've finished *Building an Application Development Framework*, we'd love to hear your thoughts! Scan the QR code below to go straight to the Amazon review page for this book and share your feedback or leave a review on the site that you purchased it from.

https://packt.link/r/183620857X

Your review is important to us and the tech community and will help us make sure we're delivering excellent quality content.

* 9 7 8 1 8 3 6 2 0 8 5 7 0 *